MW00988050

PRAISE FOR *HEALTHY POWER*

A stellar job Craig: a well written, well organized and eminently readable book. I recommend it enthusiastically.

...Wayne Dyer

What began as an exercise in visualization, ended in a 1st Place victory on ABC's Expedition Impossible: Morocco. We can attribute our mental toughness to the Healthy Power developed by Craig's teachings. Through the visualization, team-building, and goal-setting techniques Craig taught us, we were able to come together and function as a single, focused unit. Whenever we began to lose our focus along the way, we were able to call upon Craig's teachings to find our path. Our experience on Expedition Impossible proved the power of these tools, but our biggest reward is having them to use in our everyday lives.

...Eric Bach, Taylor Filasky, & John Leo Post (*The Modern Gypsies*)

As a competitive athlete on the world-level I know first-hand how important it is to stay centered and confident during competition—and even in the training room. There's always a lesson to be learned on the field, in the gym, in the heat of battle. It's not enough to be on top of your game physically. In order to succeed at the highest level you really have to do some tough mental, emotional, psychological and even spiritual training as well. Dr. Piso's guidance has been great for helping me learn the lessons that the seemingly physical sport of CrossFit offers, not only on the field but in the training room as well. The tools and tips he offers for use are simple and effective, but also elegant and profound. Dr. Piso himself is intuitive, compassionate and accessible! This is a great resource for any athlete's support team. Thanks, Dr. Piso!

...Shana Alverson (*CrossFit* World Games competitor:
"One of the 40 Fittest Women on Earth 2009–2012")

Healthy Power

Craig

HEALTHY POWER

Pathways to Success in Work, Love and Life

Craig N. Piso, PhD

BALBOA
PRESS

A DIVISION OF HAY HOUSE

Copyright © 2012 Craig N. Piso, Ph.D.

All rights reserved. No part of this book may be used or reproduced by any means, graphic, electronic, or mechanical, including photocopying, recording, taping or by any information storage retrieval system without the written permission of the publisher except in the case of brief quotations embodied in critical articles and reviews.

Balboa Press books may be ordered through booksellers or by contacting:

Balboa Press
A Division of Hay House
1663 Liberty Drive
Bloomington, IN 47403
www.balboapress.com
1-(877) 407-4847

Because of the dynamic nature of the Internet, any web addresses or links contained in this book may have changed since publication and may no longer be valid. The views expressed in this work are solely those of the author and do not necessarily reflect the views of the publisher, and the publisher hereby disclaims any responsibility for them.

The author of this book does not dispense medical advice or prescribe the use of any technique as a form of treatment for physical, emotional, or medical problems without the advice of a physician, either directly or indirectly. The intent of the author is only to offer information of a general nature to help you in your quest for emotional and spiritual well-being. In the event you use any of the information in this book for yourself, which is your constitutional right, the author and the publisher assume no responsibility for your actions.

Any people depicted in stock imagery provided by Thinkstock are models, and such images are being used for illustrative purposes only.
Certain stock imagery © Thinkstock.

ISBN: 978-1-4525-6382-4 (sc)
ISBN: 978-1-4525-6383-1 (e)
ISBN: 978-1-4525-6384-8 (hc)

Library of Congress Control Number: 2012922975

Printed in the United States of America

Balboa Press rev. date: 12/04/2012

To my parents,
Lorene and Peter-
for teaching me the interplay of light and shadow in each of us

Thus says the Lord: 'Stand by the roads, and look, and ask for the ancient paths, where the good way is; and walk in it, and find rest for your souls.'

Jeremiah 6: 16

Contents

FOREWORD

When an individual puts great effort into a project, such as a career, a work of art, or a relationship, it is commonly stated that they "poured their soul" into it. Nowhere would that phrase be more appropriate than to describe Dr. Craig Piso's book, *Healthy Power*. He has taken loving care to present ideas clearly and in a well-organized fashion with the goal of helping self-examining adults build and maintain their core strengths for the benefit of themselves and others.

The central theme is that all of us can make choices that will draw us away from *Unhealthy Power* and toward *Healthy Power*, which is value-driven and benefits ourselves and others. He has organized his concepts using the acronym POWERFUL (P = *Personal Responsibility*; O = *Optimistic Expectations*; etc.) to describe steps that readers need to take to ensure *Healthy Power*. Each of these positive steps is contrasted with its unhealthy opposite, for example the opposite of *Personal Responsibility* is *Personal Irresponsibility*.

In his opening sentence Dr. Piso states that "I realize that I have been writing this book for my entire life." Indeed, that statement rings true throughout this book. He poured his soul into this work of art by generously sharing his life experiences both from his career as a psychologist as well as his personal relationships, and adding depth with examples from a wide range of areas, such as scientific psychology, religion, or history. Each chapter ends with pearls of wisdom or brief and memorable quotations that supplement the points raised in the text. The *Appendices* section contains useful worksheets. Any self-examining adult, no matter how well educated they are through education or life experiences, is sure to find something of value in these pages.

Samuel Knapp, Ed.D., ABPP, Director of Professional Affairs
Pennsylvania Psychological Association

PREFACE

I dream of fire…those dreams are tied to a horse that will never tire!

Sting

Now recently enjoying my 58th year, I realize that I've been writing this book for my entire life. In many ways, this book has been writing me during most of that time, although I didn't realize it, especially during dark times that seemed not to fit with my otherwise abundant and rich life.

I've always been frightened and intrigued at the same time by people who are eager and capable of inflicting pain and suffering upon others without apparent remorse or guilt, largely because I've never understood such sociopathic behavior. Taken at their extreme, people such as those who commit torture and genocide with impunity cause one to pause and look for explanations for these atrocities, primarily out of a reasonable fear that we might again see a Holocaust like our planet witnessed during World War II. The destruction of human life and retarding of human potential has always been anathema to me, as they are to the majority of our species.

In sharp contrast, I've always been enamored and awestruck by people of greatness, such as Abraham Lincoln, Martin Luther King, Jr., and Mahatma Gandhi—who changed this world for the better through their courage, self-sacrificing commitment, and humility. Such people represent the high-water mark of human potential—heroes for many of us—but they are the elite exceptions among humankind, or so I thought for the longest time.

As a psychologist for more than 30 years now, I've treated many individuals and families who have been perpetrators and/or victims of virtually every form of cruelty and violence, including physical abuse, torture, incest/rape, and murder. My desire to help people has always been guided by a genuine interest in serving as a healer and teacher. However, only in recent years have I come to better understand the dynamics of violence and victimhood. I suspect that my personal journey toward maturity and core strength development has enabled me to become conscious of insights within this dark realm that I previously was ill prepared to bring into consciousness. As some would say, *When the student is ready, the teacher appears!*

In *Man's Search for Meaning* (1959), Viktor Frankl described his experience of the stark reality that the extremes of good and evil co-exist everywhere. As an ember of precious hope, he witnessed empathy and compassionate acts of goodwill toward strangers even amidst the circumstances of concentration camp depravity and depletion, which many would have assumed only to have elicited the dark side of human nature. This simultaneously grim but uplifting message holds the key to understanding not only our capacity for the basest acts of cruelty and atrocity, but also our deepest longing to manifest life and liberty—both for the self and others:

> "From all this we may learn that there are two races of men in this world, but only these two—the 'race' of the decent man and the 'race' of the indecent man. Both are found everywhere; they penetrate into all groups of society. No group consists entirely of decent or indecent people. In this sense, no group is of 'pure race'—and therefore one occasionally found a decent fellow among the camp guards. Life in a concentration camp tore open the human soul and exposed its depths. Is it surprising that in those depths we again found only human qualities which in their very nature were a mixture of good and evil? The rift dividing good from evil, which goes through all human beings, reaches into the lowest depths and becomes apparent even on the bottom of the abyss which is laid open by the concentration camp." (p. 94)

When I began to assimilate the various components of Wellness/Stress Management and Resiliency training that comprised much of my professional activities over the past 20 years, in particular, I became excited when a gestalt picture appeared in my mind's eye: a model and framework for understanding and developing *power* in all of its forms and degrees. It eventually became clear to me how good and evil might be explained as gradients of observable behavior along a continuum, rather than simply ascribing such to heaven and hell as spiritual endowments from outside forces. Further, instead of limiting the discussion to matters of the spirit, it occurred to me that the roots of good and evil could be understood as eight key psychological principles in the model that emerged, and that anyone so inclined could develop in one direction or the other at forks in the road along each of the eight stages toward increasingly healthy or unhealthy behavior.

In order to translate the model into a more useful framework for understanding and developing one's power, I selected the terms *Healthy* and *Unhealthy Power*. Differentiating power into these two categories is for many a paradigm shift of great significance. For example, instead of thinking of oneself as not being interested in gaining power—having interpreted power in a one dimensional manner with negative connotations (e.g., being "power hungry")—the model I am presenting in this book depicts power in its full spectrum and complexity, including its root polar opposite pathways toward light and darkness.

At its foundational bedrock, *Healthy Power* emerges from the development of a person's core strengths and is manifested in effective personal leadership. This, in turn, generates positive, values-driven results through our empowering influence upon others and systems. Accordingly, this book is intended to share a framework for understanding and developing one's *Healthy Power* and its ripple effects, thereby consciously and purposefully choosing not to lead oneself or others with *Unhealthy Power*.

This is not a book intended to convert people to any religious or denominational perspective, although some might become so moved spiritually as a by-product of their personal transformation, psychologically. While I make reference to biblical quotes and Christian teachings throughout this work, they are presented as literary sources of inspiration and wisdom, much as I also include Buddhist and other diverse points of view.

The reader will note from the early portions of this book that I often use the feminine pronouns *her* and *she*, rather than writing in the more traditional masculine or even multiple gender style (e.g., *he/she*). This was a conscious decision in view of the overarching theme of this book: to recognize and empower people universally without regard to such things as gender, nationality, sexual orientation, etc. Moreover, since females across the globe still suffer the disempowering effects of discrimination, oppression, and objectification so that they not only suffer unduly, but also must fight an uphill battle to achieve quality of life and work on a par with their male counterparts, I elected to reveal my biased support of females through this writing style. I also recognize this decision might alienate some male readers, but I hope you'll read the entire work and take to heart the messages regarding *Win-Win Relationships* in Chapter 3, in particular.

You will not view *power* in the same manner after reading this book; rather you'll develop a different view of yourself in the process—the teachings presented here apply universally to people everywhere. It can safely be said that the human journey from womb to tomb is characterized by our innate quest for personal power, for without power there can be no life. On the other hand, the journey down the pathways toward *Unhealthy Power* is destructive to life, both to our self and to others. This book, then, is about making important positive and constructive life-altering choices from an empowered and informed stance. It is a guide book and manual for living in which *power* and its primary features, for better or worse, represent the essential features of both our operating system and environment.

In his closing remarks, Viktor Frankl issued a call for each of us to choose our path toward becoming a *swine* or a *saint* as follows:

> "You may of course ask whether we really need to refer to 'saints.' Wouldn't it suffice just to refer to *decent* people? It is true that they form a minority. More than that, they always will remain a minority. And yet I see therein the very challenge to join the minority. For the world is in a bad state, but everything will become still worse unless each of us does his best. So let us be alert—alert in a two-fold sense: Since Auschwitz we know what man is capable of. And since Hiroshima we know what is at stake." (p. 154)

It is my contention and, therefore, my primary purpose for writing this book, that we can understand and master the psychological tools that enable us to design, build, and maintain our core strength—the essence of *Healthy Power*. I want this book to serve as both an inspiration and guide to those of us who humbly and courageously aspire to become part of the minority of decent people in the world who strive to keep the forces of *Unhealthy Power* at bay. Moreover, it is written in recognition of our dual and conflicting nature—an archetypal struggle between inherent good and evil—and is offered to shed light upon the pathways and means for resolving that struggle in truly productive ways. In this regard, I believe wholeheartedly the assertion of M. Scott Peck in *The Road Less Traveled* (1978):

> "Within each and every one of us there are two selves, one sick and one healthy—the life urge and the death urge, if you will. Each of us represents the whole human race; within each of us is the instinct for godhood and the hope of mankind, and within each of us is the original sin of laziness, the ever present force of entropy pushing us back to childhood, to the womb and to the swamps from which we have evolved." (p. 277)

I feel compelled at this time to share the gifts of knowledge and wisdom that my life and professional work both have brought my way and eventually into my consciousness, including life lessons that when first experienced seemed to be nothing other than tragedies. Upon dispassionate reflection and closer scrutiny, made more possible with the helpful passage of time, I realize that all has been a blessing. Struggle and suffering have worked to edify and strengthen me, for which I am so very grateful. Had I not experienced those tempering fires throughout my life, I would not have developed the inner strength that enabled me to transform hardship into gain, nor would I have experienced the profound fulfillment of assisting others to do likewise.

I believe that you and I are capable of experiencing the joy of tremendous well being and inordinate personal power once we begin to realize our true human potential and blossom into our unique fullness. While it is certainly true that many of us do not progress in our personal growth without first weathering one or more life crises heroically, *Healthy Power* is our birthright, not limited to the rare and notable heroes of history. My dream and commitment for writing this book, therefore, is born out of a fervent wish that you, too, will embrace the technology of *Healthy Power* development described herein in a manner that gives birth to your greatest self—that you become your *own* hero—and that you make important choices fully awakened at every key fork in the road for your life's journey. Thank you for including this little book as part of your journey!

Craig N. Piso, Ph.D.
Wilkes-Barre, Pennsylvania
September 2012

ACKNOWLEDGEMENTS

I had the very good fortune to receive expert input and immense support from professionals, family, and friends throughout this project. While far too many to be all-inclusive, I want to acknowledge the primary contributors to this effort.

After choosing a working title and considering the key messages I wanted to convey in this book, I penciled the cover concept on a napkin then presented it to friend and artist, Linda Shurmaitis, to paint the main graphic for the cover. She became inspired to symbolize the human spirit unleashed and free. When I saw Linda's painting in its vibrant, striking colors—far beyond what had I suggested she do—it captured the positive energy and power I intended to help people discover. There is a profoundly transformative experience when our spirit becomes liberated from the deadening darkness of *Unhealthy Power*, akin to the breaking forth of brilliant light over the horizon at the dawn of a new day, thus I'm so thankful to Linda for bringing her enlightened spirit into the work.

I met Wayne Dyer in Kauai 3 years ago, and he was gracious to have a lengthy conversation about keys to my success. I told him my desire to write a book that would communicate my messages most effectively to the broadest possible audience, adding that I was struggling with how to succeed. He then said, "Just keep talking about what you're doing. It's obviously your future pull—what the world wants you to do—so if you follow it as your dharma, the world will take care of the details." His wise counsel has proven to be accurate, thus I thank Wayne for guiding me onto this path.

My friend and colleague, John Pinto, was the first to provide a thorough critique of the earliest manuscript. His constructive criticisms, initially difficult to acknowledge, proved to be extremely helpful in reworking both the content and writing style, thus I am indebted to him for pushing me continually, rather than allowing me to settle comfortably.

I received marvelous professional editing support from Cynthia Rosso, never having appreciated the value that a skilled editor could bring to my writing style. While many parts of the work are necessarily abstract and complex, Cindy's fine work transformed my words to make them far more readable and understandable, thus her contribution of making the book more reader friendly and useful has been invaluable.

I want to acknowledge Bill O'Hanlon for having provided feedback regarding my voice and tone for an unpublished short story I wrote many years ago. His candid criticism of my storytelling provided keen instruction for my next efforts, having done so generously at no charge. His example of unselfish sharing is consistent with comparable acts of altruism I cite in this book, along with numerous quotes from his voluminous writings. Thank you, Bill, for your coaching and support.

As a graduate student in psychology at the University of Pittsburgh, I had the privilege of taking classes with Ray Naar, Ph.D., a psychologist with an impeccable reputation as a practicing clinician and instructor. I came to know Ray both as his student and as a fellow clinician working for the same community mental health center when I first started my career. About 30 years later when I was making preparations for this book, Ray graciously agreed to interview with me in spite of the fact that he was highly protective of his time—being in his 80's and still engaged in rich personal and professional lives. Not only did he provide me with useful feedback and suggestions for the manuscript, he continued to inspire me to live and work with honor and dignity, like the true gentleman he is.

I'm indebted to the many people with whom I've worked during the course of my career as a therapist, instructor, trainer, coach, and consultant for having entrusted so much of their personhood to me for assistance. Our meaningful connections enabled open communication and sharing, and through that rich exchange I received ongoing education of immeasurable value. This work, then, and any benefit that might be derived from it, is largely the result of people joining with me in their journey of struggle, sharing their knowledge and wisdom with me in the process. Although many have thanked me for my efforts on their behalf, I've received much more than I've given.

My sister, Jill, should be acknowledged not only for her encouragement and support of my book writing, but specifically for her insertion of the idea that each of us should *become our own hero*, rather than just looking outwardly for people with whom to identify. After all, in the end, each of us is so unique that we cannot fully emulate others, nor can they emulate us—our most important hero must emerge from within. Thank you, Jill!

Most importantly, I want to acknowledge the contributions made by my wife, Theresa. She has empowered me more fully and completely than any other person I've ever known, enabling me to learn and grow from her example, and to continue my journey toward personal fulfillment. The ongoing and steadfast demonstration of her pure heart and gentle spirit inspires me to grow likewise. Her life example more than any other is reflected in the soul underlying *Healthy Power*. Thank you for bringing love into my rich, awakened life!

INTRODUCTION

The sword conquered for a while, but the spirit conquers forever!

Sholem Asch

I have a deep abiding faith in our human spirit. I marvel recurrently at its irrepressible zest for life, especially where any one of us is being thwarted from finding our true self. No matter how stuck we seem to be or for how long, each of us burns with an underlying desire for a more fulfilling life—an unquenchable fire that drives each of us toward the expression and realization of our deepest self. In short, since we are born to live life with zeal, as is our shared birthright, we must strive to become ever more powerful in order to live fully and completely. I believe, therefore, that the most valuable gift we can share is to empower transformation: to awaken in another a hopeful dream regarding our deeper potential while liberating our deliberate steps toward its realization.

There is nothing more fundamental to this pursuit of human happiness and functionality than our reservoir of personal power that emerges from core strengths development. In order to function well in relation to ourselves and others, we must develop a mature, healthy, and cohesive sense of self. This requires a stable personality—one that consists of a realistic and healthy identity, feelings of self-worth, basic trust of ourself and others, and a balanced sense of power (choices, self-control) and responsibility (accountability for our choices and their consequences). A mature, healthy personality is also characterized by rational (rather than emotion-based) thinking, the ability to soothe oneself (rather than over-dependency upon others and/or things for comfort), solution-focused (rather than problem-focused) thinking and behavior, empathy (rather than insensitivity or indifference) toward others, and basic life satisfaction (rather than negativity, discontent, and a sense of being a victim). Depending upon the nature and severity of any weaknesses

1

among these areas (i.e., character or personality problems) that we possess or encounter, our quality of living is likely to be compromised.

Developmental psychologists have long understood that stages of emotional growth and maturation are more than mere accompaniments to getting older because, as we readily recognize, many people are emotionally immature for their years. Instead, the process of reaching and exceeding milestones in personality development always involves productive struggle and adjustment, the natural outgrowth of which is emotional advancement toward greater maturity. Accordingly, each of us must endure discomfort in order to grow, especially as we work through periods of regression during transitions that lead to higher-level changes. Of course, people frequently avoid the discomfort of paying the prerequisite tolls essential for their advancement, preferring instead to remain the same and too often fossilizing in the process. As we understand and accept the processes through which personal changes occur, including how tolerance for pain and making the necessary sacrifices enable our growth, we find relevance and value in the popular cliché, *No pain…no gain!*

We also understand, however, that each person adapts uniquely to stressors and other pressures since no cookie cutter fits all. It is clear that people often respond differently to the very same catalyst for change. The truth is that we can exercise relatively little control over those external stimuli that might impinge upon us, although too many people spend inordinate amounts of time and energy being invested in attempting to do so in neurotically defensive behavior.

The undergirding position being presented throughout this book is to live and work with maximum effectiveness from an internal *locus of control* (i.e., origin of power)—to develop our core strengths and personal power to determine our own quality of life. The focus on core strengths development reflects the following premises, which I present based on my observations and understanding of how individuals and systems either grow and change or struggle to do so:

- *Core Strength* development at our center affords openness and flexibility at the surface, enabling adjustment, maturing growth, and adaptive change to take place—a person with a solid core can afford to be open and non-defensive at her surface.

- *Core Weakness* at our center requires a closed, protective shell that manifests as rigidity, resistance to change, failure to make mature adjustments, and developmental arrest—a person with a shaky and vulnerable core must become externally rigid and controlling to protect herself.

This book, then, is intended to provide a framework for understanding *Healthy Power* in effective personal leadership and to delineate the eight psychological principles upon which it is built. It is written especially for self-examining adults at every stage in their lives—those who are striving to understand the keys to core strength development and the means through which to make excellent choices at life's most important forks in the road.

I asserted in the *Preface* that *Healthy Power* emerges from our core strength development and is manifested in effective personal leadership. Further, that *Healthy Power* generates a positive ripple effect by fostering opportunities to influence others. The demonstrated strength and character of those who wield *Healthy Power* spawns development in others so that they, too, are motivated to create positive, values-driven results. People who predominately demonstrate *Healthy Power* first achieve the private victories required for personal leadership, and then they are able to apply their core strengths in ways that naturally influence others to follow their lead, even if they do not possess formal authority. As such, they gain trust and earn respect from others, and it is from such loyally inspired supporters and their committed followership that effective leaders are further empowered to experience public victories. This dynamic interplay of leadership and followership with mutual empowerment—representing the essential features of *Servant Leadership*—accounts largely for its great effectiveness.

Perhaps the best way to understand the contrasting features and dynamics associated with *Healthy* and *Unhealthy Power* is to apply the analogy of a swimming pool and its purification/filtering system. As the water is chemically treated to achieve the right balance of PH, alkalinity, and chlorine, and it is filtered each day to remove foreign materials and contaminants that otherwise cloud and pollute the swimming pool, the water remains clean and sparkling clear, which makes for a high quality swimming experience as well as an attractive sight for nearby observers. Anyone immersed in such a pristine pool at just the right temperature will invariably enjoy a wide array of wonderful aquatic feelings through most of the senses, because it looks, feels, smells, and even tastes inviting.

Now compare the description above to your character and behavior because they, too, generate a vibe that surrounds you, whether it is wholesome and appealing or toxic and repulsive. If you are a person who routinely attracts others for transparently positive reasons—they trust, respect, and lend support to you interdependently—then you are someone who embodies both inner core strength and outward integrity. In a very broad sense, this is the essence of *Healthy Power*.

But, in sharp contrast, using the pool analogy, the system undergoes an increasingly dramatic change of both functionality and aesthetics when the water purification/filtering system either stops or becomes operationally ineffective. When pool maintenance duties are poorly performed and/or neglected, people can enjoy relatively clean water and adequate pool viewing for a short while; however, they soon realize that continued imbalance compromises performance and produces toxic results. As algae grow green on the pool bottom and sides, the water becomes cloudy and murky over time, and the quality of swimming and aesthetics are similarly degraded. Unchanged, the system will inevitably deteriorate into such dysfunction and ugliness that people not only will cease swimming there, they will avoid the sight and smell of it altogether and find a better pool.

The toxicity and eventual deterioration described above are also characteristic of individuals who embody high levels of *Unhealthy Power*. Although not always recognized in the short run, when we become immersed in the systems created by such people, we experience disempowerment, betrayal, and victimization stemming from the core weaknesses and lack of integrity ultimately revealed in those who ascribe to such power. When *Healthy Power* is predominantly absent, the longer term results are predictable. If people survive the toxic tides and violent ripple effects of exposure to such a toxin, they leave in search of a better *pool*, as we've seen in recent years through the overthrow of several Middle Eastern and African dictators and the exodus of countless refugees to other countries to escape the tyranny of oppression and genocide.

In view of these contrasting, abstract depictions of *Healthy* and *Unhealthy*

Power, we need a framework for understanding these dynamic forces in order to apply personal life management strategies so we can develop greater health, well-being, and personal/social effectiveness. Such a framework represents the primary focus of this book and comprises the eight psychological roots of power, both good and evil.

A healthy root system growing deeply downward into fertile soil sustains and nourishes the mighty oak toward mature thriving so that it can branch out, thereby bearing good fruit (acorns) plentifully in its season. By contrast, undeveloped, inadequate roots, or even good roots drawing upon poisonous soil, threaten the tree's very survival and its ability to produce fruit. In this regard, some might relate well to Gary Cooper's portrayal of Alvin York, WWI recipient of the Congressional Medal of Honor in *Sergeant York* (Warner Bros., 1941) in which he expresses confusion about his early life struggles with elder actor, Walter Brennan while plowing a field:

Walter Brennan...

> "Now you see *here*! Take a look at that old oak yonder... looks mighty strong...been standing there since your pa was a boy a-plowing in this same field. Looks like it could go right on standing all by itself, don't it, just a-resting itself and a-feeding on the earth. Well it can't! It can't stand there without there's a lot of deep roots a-holding it up! You can't see the roots, but they're there just the same. It appears to me it's been planned a fella's gotta have his roots in something outside his own self!"

Gary Cooper...

> "I reckon I ain't found no roots that'll hold me up. That's why I'm Hell-bent to fall!"

The framework depicted below shows the continuum for each of the eight *roots* that nourish either form of power, *Healthy* or *Unhealthy*, first within individuals, and then as a systemic ripple effect within their sphere of influence. Accordingly, the more influence we carry within a family or group, the larger and more far-reaching is the ripple effect we generate, positively or negatively. Therefore, this model is an especially important tool for understanding how those at the top of any system's leadership hierarchy influence such intangibles as culture, participant morale, interpersonal relationships, and, ultimately, each affected person's quality of life experience.

Here is the applicable paradigm for understanding POWERFUL individuals and systems:

Healthy Power.............................Unhealthy Power

Personal Responsibility . . . . Personal Irresponsibility

Optimistic Expectations . . . . Orchestrated Suffering

Win-Win Relationships. . . . . Win-Lose Relationships

Energizing Joy. Egocentric Pleasure

Reality-Based Choices . . . . Regressive Choices

Focused Action . . . . Fragmented Activity

Unrelenting Courage. . . . . Unsettling Fear

Lifelong Purpose . . . . Lifelong Grasping

The mechanisms for incorporating this framework into one's lifestyle are presented in the remaining chapters. Each of the eight dimensions of power development is represented by *forks in the road* at which we must make a choice—a choice to follow a path leading to power that is increasingly healthy or unhealthy. In each of the first eight chapters, accordingly, descriptions of the opposing *pathways*—divergent sets of choices—will illuminate the contrasting features of *Healthy* and *Unhealthy Power*. Psychological principles governing human development and interaction will explain the *why* of power formation and *how* such power development impacts both individuals and systems as a person proceeds along either set of opposing pathways. You will find action steps for the development and demonstration of both forms of power. Chapter 9, the *Conclusion*, integrates the eight pathways for developing our maximum *Healthy Power*—each strength working in unison to generate synergies among and between the eight dimensions—an essential feature of this framework.

The pairing of *why* and *how* elements into our power development recognizes that people are most likely to become inspired to change their behavior and then persevere toward goals when two necessary but insufficient conditions are present: 1) They find personal meaning and importance in their desire; and 2) They feel confident about transforming their dream into reality (Miller & Rollnick, 2013). That is, they experience *hope*, the fundamental catalyst that ignites human energy to take action. For with hope we become energized, even to surpass our oftentimes self-imposed limitations. It is my sincere hope that you will become motivated to make informed, responsible, and productive choices in your journey toward self-actualization and personal power by reading this book.

Finally, I want to emphasize the developmental nature of the framework I use to introduce these contrasting features of power. I do not view *good* and *evil* as a variables in a binary equation—as all or none—but as markers of human growth and maturation, or the lack thereof. For example, the self-indulgent and insensitive behavior we normally witness in two-year-olds is certainly primitive and often annoying, but we understand (not condone) it because such immaturity is part of the journey each of us must make in our socialization toward adulthood. Most of us receive sufficient parenting and other guidance/support, including effective discipline, that we are able to make adjustments along the way toward gradual maturity and better self-controls. Such adjustments help us reach developmental milestones that are manifested in better, more functional, and socially acceptable behavior as we make our way gradually toward independent living.

In the cases of those who do not receive adequate parenting during their formative years or who otherwise carry predispositions toward aberrant, anti-social conduct, we witness continued infantile behavior long after such features are tolerable. The delinquent/criminal or otherwise character defective individual is identified eventually as being maladjusted, warranting sanctions and interventions to assist with overdue milestones attainment. I believe it to be a human tragedy that for some, it seems that the immaturity and/or aberration never abates, and they continue self-destructively down the path leading inevitably to failed outcomes, such as misery, drug/alcohol addiction, illness, incarceration, and premature death. Even more tragic for society is the dangerously immature and still primitive person who simply becomes better masked so that the evil lurking beneath the surface can become cloaked in secret, enabling even more insidious offenses—the aberrant political, business, religious, and educational leaders in whom many have placed the most sacred trust.

Rather than simply dismissing dangerously abnormal behavior as being evil and, therefore, unredeemable, I offer this developmental framework so that we can recognize and support any person's behavioral challenges as possible needs for continued maturation, and that such maturation might occur through further development of power in the appropriate direction. When we acknowledge that each of us (without exception) has some degree of room for improvement along one or more of the eight dimensions, then we develop a more hopeful view of growth in our self and/or others as the lens through which we view and understand problems of power and its ripple effects. Accordingly, I hope this perspective empowers you not only to better understand power along its full continuum from heroic to horrific acts, but also to master the psychological principles and technologies for behavioral change that lead to positive growth in each of the eight pathways within this developmental framework.

The *Appendices* section includes eleven items intended to augment the main body with materials, poems, and worksheets to assist you further in understanding and developing *Healthy Power*. Frankly, each piece represents a small step I've taken in my own journey, thus the intent is to provide you with some signposts and travel markers that you, too, might find helpful.

Although the work of full, healthy self-empowerment is usually difficult, and for some of us I dare say impossible, this is a book that will show you the ways toward becoming full-grown in mind, body, and spirit. For those of you who embrace the concepts, muster the courage, and persevere with the self-discipline required to follow the eight pathways, I commend you in advance of finding a remarkable new world—first internally and then externally—as you grow uniquely into your full strength. Welcome to your journey—may you find both personal meaning and confidence in the roadmap to *Healthy Power* that follows!

CHAPTER 1

P...*Personal Responsibility* vs. *Personal Irresponsibility*

I can solve a problem only when I say 'This is my problem and it's up to me to solve it.'

M. Scott Peck

PERSONAL RESPONSIBILITY AND HEALTHY POWER

A number of influential great authors have written about the pivotal role personal responsibility plays in mature power development. Stephen Covey introduced the first of his "7 Habits of Highly Effective People" as learning to be responsibly *proactive*, instead of being emotionally reactive, attributing blame for the latter (i.e., responsibility) to people and/or things outside of oneself. Similarly, Deepak Chopra emphasized in his "7 Spiritual Laws of Success" the critical value of becoming *self-referred* versus *object referred*. He recognized that a sense of personal responsibility sets the stage for self-empowerment, while defining or otherwise allowing ourselves to be driven by outside forces is a pathway toward individual hollowness and eventual failure.

Accordingly, the first root principle in this book's POWERFUL framework stems from the following premise regarding *Personal Responsibility*:

...Power = Responsibility: Power and responsibility develop in direct proportion to each other and are functionally related within healthy individuals and systems...

9

We see a direct relationship between power (control) and responsibility (accountability) since the more power we possess, the more responsibility we bear for how we use it. Further, the relationship between power and responsibility is a functional one since when you increase one side of the equation you get a proportional increase on the other side, and vice versa. The caveat is that we're talking about a reasonably healthy individual operating within a comparably favorable situation. Accordingly, if we are mature, well-developed people working within a predominantly healthy family or societal system, we will become more powerful in healthy ways as we handle our duties more responsibly. Our willingness to take complete ownership of and accountability for our choices propels us down the path to self-empowerment within any healthy system.

Conversely, such a person predictably becomes so much more responsible that she becomes appropriately self-empowered and develops in a supportive environment. It follows, then, that the fundamental way to help someone who has an adequate sense of conscience to become even more responsible in both personal and professional settings is to empower that person (e.g., grant her increased authority; provide instruction/training, supports, and tools), and then hold her reasonably accountable. This is the fundamental nature of good parenting within families, and likewise it is also the essence of good management in work settings, because they share the common goal of promoting successful growth and development that mutually benefit the individual and the system in which she functions.

This process unfolds and becomes clear when we consider how a candidate in training at a police academy responds when first given a loaded handgun for target practice. Suppose you are that candidate. If you are mature, you will recognize immediately that you are holding deadly force in your grasp, increasing dramatically your potential power to destroy lives, including your own, as well as property. Rather than acting carelessly or dangerously, as a scrupulous person, you will adhere closely to safety instructions regarding appropriate weapons discharge and usage, etc., showing your heightened sense of responsibility.

As such a police officer who thinks beyond the training, you will likely be promoted because you demonstrate increasing levels and forms of responsible behavior in the performance of your duties. Within any healthy system, responsible behavior is eventually rewarded with increased authority, since employers generally compensate people for their responsible and valuable performance. People are not usually rewarded or promoted for their authority. Instead, employees gain higher authority and other forms of empowerment to enable them to better meet their responsibilities.

The empowerment lesson here is this:

> *...If you want to become more powerful within any*
> *reasonably healthy system, then act more responsibly...*

Not only does this root principle apply to the fairly commonplace situations of parenting children and managing staff, it also has profoundly important relevance to situations where we are pressed to extremes of hardship by suffering trauma and loss. In his analysis of those men who found inner strength to survive the horrors of concentration camp life versus those who became broken, and often died, Viktor Frankl reported the following account of the relationship between personal accountability and energy for living:

> "The typical reply with which a man rejected all encouraging arguments was, 'I have nothing to expect from life any more.' What sort of answer can one give to that? What was really needed was a fundamental change in our attitude toward life. We had to learn ourselves and, furthermore, we had to teach the despairing men, that *it did not really matter what we expected from life, but rather what life expected from us*. We needed to stop asking about the meaning of life, and instead to think of ourselves as those who were being questioned by life—daily and hourly. Our answer must consist, not in talk and meditation, but in right action and in right conduct."
> (*Man's Search for Meaning*, 1959, p. 85)

Throughout my career, and especially during the past 10 years, understanding the dynamic relationship between power and responsibility has served me as a useful diagnostic formula when evaluating people seeking resolution from their strife. For example, I find it illuminating to ask someone during the interview process about her handling of current and/or previous difficult, challenging situations, personal and/or professional in nature. There is a striking and important distinction between those who report having been able to overcome and solve problems and those who point the finger of blame, make excuses for failures, and present their *victim* role in such responses. Since power and responsibility always travel together in a healthy (i.e., mature, competent) individual, such persons are likely to report a sense of ownership (i.e., responsibility) when having faced earlier problems. Whether or not they solved the problems, they describe their experiences from the perspective of an internal locus of control and, therefore, with a strong sense of accountability for how they handled them.

Among truly great, effective leaders, I've found a consistent relationship between the responsibility they demonstrate and how well they are empowered. This reflects an encouraging interplay of individual behavior and team dynamics, and it has been well described by Jim Collins (*Good to Great*, 2001, Chapter 2): *Level 5* great leaders embody *Humility with Resolve*, demonstrated in part through *The Window and the Mirror*—looking unselfishly through the *Window* to give full credit to staff when things are going well, while looking courageously in the *Mirror* to take responsibility when things are going poorly. It's no surprise that he also found ineffective leaders tended to do the opposite, thereby generating tension and resentment as fallout compromising their effectiveness.

The bottom line is this: *You* hold the trump card of personal power since no one can make you do anything against your will, as long as you are willing be to fully responsible for your choices, including the consequences that your choices could bring upon you. This also means that there is absolutely nothing that you must do in this lifetime. There is a trite phrase that asserts, "The only things you have do in life are to die and pay taxes," a popular but misleading notion since it assumes that you have no choice. While inevitably each of us will one day die, whether by natural causes or tragically, there is absolutely no one who can make you pay taxes. Of course, since there is always a cause-and-effect relationship, failure to pay your taxes is a high-risk decision for which most people do not roll the dice. However, as we all know, there are many people who do withhold payment, proving the point once again that each of us holds the final authority and exercises final control over our actions. Accordingly, each of us is responsible for the choices we make and is rightly held accountable for how we wield our power.

Once you become clear about your personal empowerment in actual and consistent practice, not merely as an exercise in semantics, then and only then will you become totally free. Any prudent person will weigh the probable risks against potential rewards of their choices before committing to taking action. Therefore, for example, most people pay their taxes rather than gamble with adverse consequences (and otherwise to uphold their civic duty). The point emphasized here, however, is that once you perceive yourself as controlled by forces outside of yourself, you not only have someone or something to blame for your actions, you also have abdicated your power in making a shift from an internal to an external locus of control. Remember the principle that power and responsibility go hand in hand, thus we know at least unconsciously that our reduced power equally relieves us of responsibility. This also calls to mind the process through which too many of us subvert our inherent potential power by avoiding or denying responsibility, which brings our discussion about pathways to power eventually to the other side of this same coin.

In the following poignant yet uplifting passage, Viktor Frankl provides us with his account of the universal truth regarding our freedom to make choices at life's most challenging forks in the road, therein reaffirming our responsibility to choose our own path under any circumstances:

> "We who lived in concentration camps can remember the men who walked through the huts comforting others, giving away their last piece of bread. They may have been few in number, but they offer sufficient proof that everything can be taken from a man but one thing: the last of the human freedoms—to choose one's attitude in any given set of circumstances, to choose one's own way...Seen from this point of view, the mental reactions of the inmates of a concentration camp must seem more to us than the mere expression of certain physical and sociological conditions. Even though conditions such as lack of sleep, insufficient food and various mental stresses may suggest that the inmates were bound to react in certain ways, in the final analysis it became clear that the sort of person the prisoner became was the result of an inner decision and not the result of camp influences alone. Fundamentally, therefore, any

man can, even under such circumstances, decide what shall become of him—mentally and spiritually." (*Man's Search for Meaning*, 1959, p. 75)

There are tremendous positive ripple effects interpersonally from growing into *Personal Responsibility* as part of one's character and behavior. First, since we tend to trust individuals who hold themselves accountable as their personal code of conduct, risk-taking naturally increases between people so connected. This, of course, is a critical component of intimacy in all of its forms, for without trust, we tend to keep a safe distance in order to protect against perceived risk. Second, since any leader acquires the power to be effective primarily from those being led, we will enjoy greater empowerment via our people as we win their loyalty and support through consistently responsible use of our authority, as in the *Servant Leadership* description offered earlier. Finally, consistent demonstration of responsible behavior with appropriate accountability inspires others to follow such an example, especially when it is made clear that such is the formula for healthy self-empowerment (i.e., *Power = Responsibility*).

PERSONAL IRRESPONSIBILITY AND UNHEALTHY POWER

Life ultimately means taking the responsibility to find the right answer to its problems and to fulfill the tasks which it constantly sets for each individual.

Viktor Frankl

At the opposing fork in the road is the pathway toward *Personal Irresponsibility*. One obvious way to recognize that we are not leading our life responsibly is when we blame others for the things we are doing. When we go in this direction, whether consciously or otherwise, we progressively deny culpability for our struggles or failings while attributing responsibility to others and/or forces outside of ourselves. The problems we manifest this way often result from clinging tenaciously to our perceived power while shirking and shedding responsibility for bringing painful consequences or otherwise not meeting our own or others' expectations.

Mature people understand that blaming others for our actions is an invalid stance to take since no one ever controls our minds, unless we permit it, and because it is from our own minds that we choose one path or another. Some have argued, "That's wrong because sometimes people make other people do bad things by holding weapons against them, so they are not responsible when they do those bad things!" Although that might sound convincing, the truth remains that the final choice *always* rests with the person with the gun to her head, as long as she is willing to accept the consequences of her decision. Many great heroes from history have chosen torture, imprisonment, and even death rather than be compelled to do something against their inner beliefs and values. They realized unequivocally that they were responsible for their final choice and did not blame others for the choice that they made, no matter how terrible the outcome might have been. They called forth and demonstrated their ultimate freedom to choose...expressing their ultimate power by doing so!

Frankly, the desire to wield power *without* accountability or other negative consequences represents a fundamentally primitive attempt to have the best of both worlds, at least from the standpoint of child-like wishes and fantasies born out of magical thinking. Such a desire, while perhaps initially and superficially attractive, refutes the logic of cause-and-effect relationships. Whenever we make things happen through our choices, we are appropriately responsible for the outcomes we generate through such choices. As Stephen Covey would say of any such universal law governing the human race, this constitutes a "True North Principle."

From a developmental and psychological standpoint, any person's quest for *Unhealthy Power* stems from the normally *egocentric* ("the world revolves around me"), *grandiose* ("I am superior"), and *omnipotent* ("I am all powerful") features that are so recognizable among two-year-old toddlers. Instead of taking responsible ownership for her well-being and better self-control by making adjustments, the egocentric individual at any age is continually in search of external (in lieu of internal) solutions to relieve her from personal distress. Accordingly, she demonstrates little or no intrinsic motivation to change from the inside out. Similarly, her adjustment *muscles* remain under-developed or, if they have already grown, they atrophy through underuse during circumstances in which she is permitted to behave irresponsibly.

Empowering unhealthy expressions of primitive, immature, and rebellious behavior by not setting appropriate limits and enforcing fair, consistent consequences only serves to prolong a person's experiences of omnipotence through undisciplined expansion. Figuratively, it allows the *genie to escape from the bottle* and then to wreak havoc without regard for the feelings or welfare of others. After all, this individual has not been required to adjust her self-image from being the center of the universe to being one of the billions of people who occupy our planet. She clings instinctively to a grandiose sense of self and fails to develop humility, the latter being the cornerstone of reality-based personal-social adjustment, which will be covered more fully in Chapter 5. As described earlier, emotional maturation proceeds only through commensurate adjustment. Therefore, the child or adult who enjoys power without motivation to change via meaningful consequences will predictably remain developmentally arrested. Because enabling such behavior engenders maladjustment, whether in rearing children or in responding to those in authority over us, this aspect of *Unhealthy Power* is usually a prominent feature of relatively unhealthy families and other systems—power without commensurate responsibility.

Of course, it is equally damaging to the psyche of a maturing individual to crush her spirit through overly controlling, domineering, or otherwise abusive treatment, whether within family life for the developing child or for us as adults within the context of our relationship to our supervisor or an oppressive partner at home. Just as it interferes with healthy emotional maturation for someone to enjoy power disproportionate to their accountability—thereby enabling continued physical growth over time without age-appropriate personality advancement—it stifles the maturation process to endure the distress, especially the trauma, of disempowerment born out of toxic exposure to *Unhealthy Power*. Tragically, this too often occurs when someone is held harshly and unfairly responsible by another while not having sufficient power to change or escape the situation.

For example, a woman who is physically and/or emotionally abused within a domestic violence trap she is unable to escape soon learns to identify with her aggressor and internalizes a self-image in which it is safer to believe she deserves her cruel treatment than to oppose her oppressor. In such identification, as a defense against further abuse, she also learns to take responsibility for issues and problems she did not create, such as the misery of her abusive partner and/or the failings of her incompetent and controlling boss.

What often results, especially during early childhood but certainly also well beyond, is a compromised sense of self-esteem, a distorted sense of self and personal identity, and gaping holes in the fulfillment of the emotional needs that, if met, enable her to mature further. Instead, she is compelled to form a hard shell around her vulnerable core, having been damaged so through abuse and disempowerment. Unchanged, this rigid and strong external defense impedes her from moving ahead, year after year. Should she fail to heal her wounds and make gains toward healthier maturity, especially in relation to others, she will predictably avoid intimacy to shield her vulnerable core from further injury and/or unleash her suppressed anger toward others who represent vulnerable safe targets. As a mother, choosing anger often results in child abuse, which perpetuates the generational cycle.

As I said at the outset of this book, *Unhealthy Power* always leaves a destructive wake, even when the suffering lies hidden beneath the surface. Studies of prisoners of war who are tortured and brainwashed, for example, reveal an insidious phenomenon in which initially normal soldiers break down psychologically and become over-identified with their torturers as an unconsciously discovered mechanism for survival. Reportedly, it is common in such cases that the POW will later suffer extreme guilt and depression for having been so broken. However, it is also logical to assume that a large part of such self-loathing is at least partially the product of brainwashing in which the prisoner eventually became convinced that *she* was responsible for the torture she was forced to endure as her just punishment, therein having identified with the aggressor in what is sometimes described as either the *Stockholm* or *Patty Hearst Syndrome.*

As these poignant POW accounts and similar, all too commonplace, reports of child and adult abuses so clearly show, the greater the gap between our power and our responsibility, the more pathological will be the resultant impact that we suffer. Recognize that the operating system of dictators, tyrants, and other dysfunctional individuals is one in which they wield authority while holding others accountable, especially for their problems and/or failure. Thus, *Unhealthy Power* is sought, at least unwittingly, through *Personal Irresponsibility*, and its arising logically manifests in dysfunction. Features of such dysfunctional individuals typically include the following:

- Clinging to power while shirking and/or shifting responsibility for our actions
- Externalizing blame for pain/suffering and/or failures, therein feeling like a victim
- Unwittingly abdicating our power to people and forces outside of ourselves
- Using our framework of perceived suffering, imposed failure, and unfair victimization as leverage points to gain support, sympathy, and attention (i.e., *secondary gain*)
- Failing to adjust and grow because the focus remains fixed externally upon people and/or problems deemed to be needing change (e.g., "I'm not the problem! My pain will stop when Susan changes her behavior and stops annoying me!")
- Striving continually within large systems to be the *tail that wags the dog* in counterproductive fashion, thereby dishonoring and undermining reasonable systems of authority, instead of being self-empowered by learning to change our behavior and/ or adjust

THE PATHWAY TO PERSONAL RESPONSIBILITY

A Metaphor for Self-Direction: *The Wind and the Weather Vane*

Let us consider that a weather vane and the wind that directs it symbolize leadership choices that you might make and the ensuing responsibility. A weather vane typically sits atop a barn and has a horizontal structure with a flat piece of metal shaped like a rooster, an arrow, a horse, etc. This piece has a hole at the bottom used for mounting it on a rod that points vertically toward the sky. A fixed compass also sits at its base to tell us the direction the wind is blowing. As the wind blows against its broad surface, the weather vane spins until it points in the same direction as the wind, where it offers the least amount of resistance. There it will stay until the wind changes direction again, forcing the weather vane to take a new position. In this process, you can see that the weather vane has no control over the direction it points. If it had a mind like ours and was asked, "Which way are you going tomorrow?" it would probably say, "I have no idea—it's not up to me!" If it was asked how it felt during a storm, it would probably say, "I'm spinning out of control, waiting for the wind to stop swirling me around!"

It's likely that you recognize the ideas represented by the weather vane and the wind as personal power and responsibility. First, you cannot enjoy the sense of peace or security that comes from control over your own life when you are a living weather vane, being driven from outside forces and turning at the will of the wind. Second, you must choose to *be* the wind so that you can set your own direction. Remember that the wind is free, not affixed to a rooftop, and because it influences change, it embodies power, energy, and the deliberate generation of movement. Third, it's important to understand that if you are not choosing your own direction, you are following someone else's direction. Once you have chosen your own path, you are acting as a leader, even if it turns out to be the same path you have followed unconsciously until that point. The difference is that once *you* make the choice, you become an active and responsible leader, rather than a passive, disempowered follower.

Now you might ask, "If I'm supposed to be a leader and not a follower, what am I supposed to do when someone in authority, such as my employer or professor, tells me what to do?" The answer in principle is actually quite simple, but not often achieved:

> *...A great leader always takes responsibility for the choices that she makes, whether it is to obey an order/rule/law or to break it...*

The key to this is remembering what was described earlier here about power (control) and responsibility (accountability):

> *...You have ultimate control over the choices that you make, therefore you are free to the extent that you to take responsibility for your decisions and actions...*

Therefore, if you choose to obey an order, you do well to own your decision completely, rather than saying you had no choice in the matter or someone made you do something against your will. This, of course, represents a clear departure from the defense verbalized irresponsibly by many of the Nazi war criminals following the atrocities identified in the Holocaust during the 1945 Nuremburg Trials: "I'm a soldier...I was just taking orders!"

Becoming the *Driver of Your Life*

Here are some helpful ways to take more responsible control of your life, using metaphoric references to driving cars for amplification:

1) The driver of the car takes active control, while the passenger only goes along for the ride.

2) The person who develops good brakes learns how to stop, to slow down, and to avoid accidents along life's highways.

3) The person who learns how to steer discovers many more choices than the person who tends to move straight ahead without turning.

4) A flexible person learns to shift gears in order to move forward more quickly.

5) The ability to travel in reverse is just as important as driving forward, especially when you find out that you've been going down the wrong road.

6) The sooner that you accept that you've made a wrong turn and are lost, the sooner that you'll get back on the right track.

7) The person who gets where she wants to go in life is not the one who thinks she knows all the right directions—it's the one who is humble and respectful enough to stop and to ask for directions.

8) The freedom to drive your life is kept without interruption until you make a bad choice that leads to a fine or loss of license.

9) The person who enjoys the greatest freedom on the road is the one who is most careful to obey the traffic laws because, in the long run, she will still be driving when someone else who breaks the rules is not.

10) Winners show respect and courtesy by sharing the road with others and by thinking of others as winners, too, rather than being a winner by making others lose.

11) Since what you focus upon tends to expand and, *Your car goes where your eyes go!* (Garth Stein, *The Art of Racing in the Rain*, 2008), keep your eyes on the road, rather than letting anything distract you from your destination.

12) Take good and regular care of your car, and it will serve you well daily.

Casting Yourself as the *Director of Your Life Movie*

People usually say that a Hollywood movie based on their favorite book was "not as good as the book," primarily because the visualizations that one creates when reading come from our personal tastes, desires, and fantasies. No director could ever match your best depiction of the characters, action scenes, etc. Similarly, no one else can unilaterally make suggestions for your goals and strategies for change that are personally matched with your unique innermost needs and desires. Therefore, cast yourself as the *Director* to create and implement action steps toward your own life plan, emphasizing your unique ability to create your best possible *movie*.

Action-Oriented Questions for Developing *Personal Responsibility* (from *Do One Thing Different*, Bill O'Hanlon, 1999):

- "What kinds of things would I like to accomplish or have happen in my future?"
- "What dreams did I or do I have for my life?"
- "What kinds of things will I be doing when I have resolved this problem?"
- "What, in my view, stops me from realizing my visions or getting to my goals?"
- "What am I afraid of?"
- "What do I believe must happen before I can realize my visions and goals? Is this really true, or is it just an idea that I or someone else has?"
- "What are the actions that I haven't taken to make my dreams and visions come true?"
- "What are the real barriers that I'll need to deal with to realize my dreams and visions?"
- "What would my role models, mentors, or people I admire do if they were me in order to realize this dream or vision?"

Healthy Power—Prescriptions for Developing *Personal Responsibility* as a Leader in the Workplace:

1) Walk the *Power = Responsibility* talk. Speak frequently about this dynamic when explaining the rationale for your decisions and actions. For example, "Because of the consistent manner in which Jan has made effective choices (exercised her power) to succeed at projects, I recommend her for this promotion with expanded duties (responsibilities)." Conversely, the same principle applies when communicating about negative performance or behavior: "Jane, you are being terminated (being held accountable) as the result of your choice to belittle your supervisor to a vendor after being warned repeatedly and in writing that the next infraction of this sort would result in your loss of employment here."

2) Ask and answer these self-diagnostic questions, including input from trusted staff and peers where feasible:

    a. "Am I an accountable *Servant Leader*, humbly striving to serve a mission greater than myself, or do I impress others as being primarily concerned about my own welfare and prosperity, using my positional authority in self-serving or arrogant ways that could demean, frustrate, or hurt others?"

    b. "Do I demonstrate a democratic leadership style in which others feel empowered, valued/appreciated, and encouraged to find and express their voice, or do I show more of a dictatorial approach (e.g., unilateral decision-making; double standard behavior; controlling others without holding myself equally or more accountable for my actions)?"

    c. "When I become frustrated, anxious, irritable, and tired, do I take responsibility for my reactions to others, graciously trying to become part of the solution, or do I focus upon others and expect them to change or adjust in order for them to improve my moods and feeling states?"

3) Clarify the performance expectations you have for your staff because, in general, all conflicts are the result of two or more people not sharing the same expectations. You will have fewer such conflicts with your staff, and, when necessary, the disciplinary actions through which you hold people accountable will be logically determined by having first empowered them with clear expectations for their performance.

PEARLS OF HEALTHY POWER

Holly Lisle...
Actions have consequences...first rule of life. And the second rule is this: You are the only one responsible for your own actions.

Erica Jong...
Take your life in your own hands and what happens? A terrible thing: no one to blame.

Diane Ackerman...
I don't want to be a passenger in my own life.

Seneca...
We should every night call ourselves to an account: What infirmity have I mastered today? What passions opposed? What temptation resisted? What virtue acquired? Our vices will abort of themselves if they be brought every day to the shrift.

Calls for *Personal Responsibility* from Politicians/Social Reformers

The full extent of *Healthy Power* within the domain of *Personal Responsibility* involves a commitment to being wholly responsible for our own health, safety, happiness and well-being, independent of external circumstances or conditions. This is a tall order, thus to do so would make such a person exceptional—living and working in the 99th percentile— statistically abnormal in the most admirable way.

Echoing the words of former Presidents of the United States from both sides of the aisle during their efforts to rally the citizenry toward positive growth and change, imploring them to do what they deemed to be responsibly right rather than what was merely popular, we recall the following:

> *And so, my fellow Americans: Ask not what your country can do for you—ask what you can do for your country.*

John F. Kennedy's Inaugural Address
January 20, 1961

> *I have asked the Cabinet and my staff a question, and now I put the same question to all of you: If not us, who? And if not now, when?*

Ronald Reagan's Second Inaugural Address
January 21, 1985

And finally, Walt Kelly, in his poster for the first Earth Day in 1972, issued a call to action through his iconic cartoon character, *Pogo*, who stands amidst the trash and debris of a polluted forest scene, holding the populace accountable for the preservation of our environment in declaring:

> *We have met the enemy and he is us!*

CHAPTER 2

O...Optimistic Expectations vs. Orchestrated Suffering

People all say that I've had a bad break. But today, today I consider myself to be the luckiest man on the face of the earth—that I might have been given a bad break—but I've got an awful lot to live for!

Lou Gehrig, July 4, 1939
Farewell Speech

OPTIMISTIC EXPECTATIONS AND HEALTHY POWER

Two mid-twentieth century ground-breaking works set the stage for what has become currently promising research in several technologically accelerated areas of neuroscience: *Psychoneuroimmunology* (i.e., mind-body connection and the immune system); and *Positive Psychology* (i.e., human happiness and emotional well-being). The first work, *The Power of Positive Thinking* (Norman Vincent Peale, 1952), provided an inspirational description of the personal power we can develop from within and then attract toward ourselves through conscious development of faith and optimism, and otherwise by choosing to perceive our world as much as possible through an uplifting lens. The second, *Pygmalion in the Classroom* (Robert Rosenthal & Lenore Jacobson, 1968), provided empirical findings to support the power of expectations to empower or disempower ourselves and/or others via *self-fulfilling prophecy* (i.e., the natural, unconscious tendency to behave in ways that fulfill our predictions, whether positive or negative in nature).

The findings and conclusions of these pioneering authors are directly relevant to this broader discussion about *Healthy Power* in managing our personal lives and overall wellness. Examples from medicine have made us aware and beginning to understand that sometimes when people smile authentically, regain lost hope, feel joyful, and believe that others are praying fervently for them, they predictably experience the positive effects of a strengthened immune system, occasionally and most dramatically in the form of seemingly *miraculous* cures. The power of our beliefs and expectations to influence and even determine our physical and emotional well-being has profound implications for how we think about problems and their possible future course.

Moreover, from an interpersonal standpoint, if we demonstrate authentically positive attitudes and expectations about both people and circumstances, we tend to generate hope and confidence among others, thereby providing psychological energy for a team's goal-directed behavior, including in our families. Since people generally work up or down to the expectations those deemed to be most important in their lives hold about them, these processes in leadership can be a double-edged sword. I will focus in this next section upon the positively self-empowering impact of a person's optimistic expectations when they are embodied in our waking dreams.

The Engine of Self-Empowered Living: *The Hope-Energy Relationship*

The most effective thing that we can do to create emotional energy for living to our fullest potential is to dream—to have goals and plans that originate deep within our soul and, therefore, inspire us to take actions that might fulfill them. Such waking dreams generate hope, and hope produces a natural upwelling of energy to drive us toward turning our dreams into reality, but only when two necessary conditions are met sufficiently: 1) Our dreams are personally meaningful and important to us; and 2) We believe confidently that they are possible and within our reach, at least eventually.

Without such inspiring and uplifting dreams, or when our dreams are shattered somehow, we lose energy and motivation, which is the universal human depression each of us will experience at some point along life's journey. When someone has a difficult loss or other painfully disappointing life experience, there is a normal tendency to shut down—to automatically stop creating dreams, usually for a temporary period—almost as if the mind and heart cannot tolerate another loss or disappointment. This makes sense in light of the relationship between hope and energy: the loss of hope regarding our meaningful dreams diminishes our emotional and even physical energy.

Most of us can relate to the experience of the death of a family pet, frequently resulting in sadness, and even a period of mourning, as if one has lost a beloved family member. Our attachment to such a pet involves an emotional investment that presupposes that she will be there to greet us enthusiastically each time we return home, and this constitutes a waking dream…a fantasy we use to construct our world in a meaningful way and for which we hold some level of confidence that it will continue. However, when she dies or, even worse, is lost and nowhere to be found, we normally become depressed in response to the former and terribly anxious about the latter.

Understand that when we stop dreaming we shut off our supply of life energy, since such energy comes from the hope produced through our dream life. If we dare to dream in deeply personal and meaningful ways, we become vulnerable to possible failure, disappointment, and loss, constituting the huge gamble such risk-taking necessarily requires. On the other hand, our inability or unwillingness to generate such dreams denies us the energy that normally upwells from our hope, and so we live in an emotionally dry dessert that fails to satisfy the spirit. Therefore, to be human in the most fundamental sense is to wrestle with this dilemma at every turn, and how well we wrestle determines the very quality of our lives. As I write this, I vividly recall hearing my father reciting a quote about World War II Naval excursions as they approached potentially hostile enemy waters, "Damn the torpedoes, full speed ahead!"

It is certainly a personal challenge for each of us to embrace our dreams with their inherent risks, and in doing so becoming vulnerable to disappointment and even serious depression. However, it will stultify our energy to the point of lethargy so we will proceed through life on low pilot because we have failed to engage in active dreaming. Since it takes rare *courage* to manage the risks associated with dreaming in the deepest and most meaningful ways (the subject of Chapter 7), we witness all too frequently the tragic reality asserted by Henry David Thoreau: "Most men live lives of quiet desperation."

Adopting the self-empowering alternative, I strongly encourage you to nurture your most meaningful and important dreams—conceived out of your deep, unique personhood—and to pursue their fulfillment with optimism and perseverance, because they represent the source of energy that nourishes our spirit and enables us to live life with engaged commitment. Maintaining a persistently optimistic outlook, especially during the inevitable short-term failures and disappointments, life becomes a mysterious and inviting adventure to be pursued, not merely a problem to be solved.

Therefore, dream courageously today with an optimistic vision of tomorrow, even far into your future, but aware that sometimes we need to create new dreams when our earlier ones do not come to fruition (i.e., "Plan B," etc.). Continually dream great things for you and others that inspire hope, and then go after your dreams with energy, confidence, and *resilience*— the ability to bounce back over and over again through life's setbacks and disappointments (see suggestions for developing *resilience* in Chapter 7). The more we dream in this productive manner, the greater we will fill the reservoir of life energy that sustains us, and there are no limits to how much we can dream in any lifetime except those we place upon ourselves.

Further, make a strong effort to dream even when you are depressed, because the ability to dream and to experience your dreams coming true again is the best way to regain a sense of hope. This is often well prescribed as a directive to *fight through depression*, requiring us to tackle the hard work of following logically helpful ideas rather than allowing a lack of energy and unpleasant feelings to guide our actions, or better said, to retard our activity amidst emotional inertia. It is human nature to engage in this kind of emotion-based reasoning, rather than logical, analytical thought, especially when stressed, which interferes with the ability to see things more objectively. Remember most importantly that *hope* more than anything else keeps us moving forward in life with positive energy.

Lessons about *Healthy* and *Unhealthy Power* from *The Neverending Story*

The Neverending Story (screenplay co-written by Wolfgang Petersen and Herman Weigel, directed by Wolfgang Petersen, 1984, from a novel by Michael Ende, 1979) vividly depicts the unconscious process of recreating in one's external life circumstances the mirror image of one's inner emotional world. Specifically, it presents us with a fantastic but relevant understanding of the power that our dreams hold either to uplift or destroy that inner psychological world at our most vulnerable core. The following is a synopsis from the film version during which a particularly revealing interaction takes place between two mythical characters representing the forces of *good* (i.e., Atreyu) and *evil* (i.e., Gmork), representing the archetypal clash of *Healthy* and *Unhealthy Power*:

- Bastian, age 10, a depressed earthling child whose mother recently died, is reading a fantasy story about a wilderness boy hero, Atreyu, who lives in Fantasia and is the only being in Fantasia that can stop *The Nothing* from destroying it.
- Atreyu comes face-to-face with the Gmork, a huge wolf-like creature who has been seeking to take Atreyu's life so that *The Nothing* and the dark power that drives it can complete the annihilation of Fantasia.
- Atreyu exclaims in desperation that he cannot fight *The Nothing* because he cannot reach the boundaries of Fantasia where he believes a battle could be fought and won, to which the Gmork replies, "Foolish boy! Don't you know anything about Fantasia? It's the world of human fantasy. Every part, every creature of it, is a piece of the dreams and hopes of mankind. Therefore, it *has* no boundaries."
- Atreyu asks, "But why is Fantasia dying then?"
- Gmork replies, "Because people have begun to lose their hopes, and forget their dreams; so *The Nothing* grows stronger."
- Atreyu asks, "What **is** *The Nothing*?"
- Gmork replies, "It's the emptiness that's left—it is like a despair, destroying this world, and I have been trying to help it."
- Atreyu asks, "But **why**?"
- Gmork replies, "Because people who have no hopes are easy to control, and whoever has the control, has the *power!*"
- Atreyu challenges and kills the Gmork in their fight, but *The Nothing* cannot be stopped until the human child Bastian, who

is reading the book about Fantasia (*The Neverending Story*), calls out a new name for his deceased mother.

- Upon reading this unbelievable directive in the book, Bastian courageously cries out a new name for his mother with heartfelt love, thereby enabling him to be transported into Fantasia and meet the Childlike Empress who rules over it as her kingdom.
- When Bastian meets the Childlike Empress she is in a state of almost complete darkness because Fantasia has been obliterated by *The Nothing*, and all that remains is a glimmering speck that the Childlike Empress gently places into Bastian's palm.
- The Childlike Empress implores Bastian, "Fantasia can arise in you—through your dreams and wishes, Bastian. What are you going to wish for?"
- Bastian replies, "I don't know!"
- The Childlike Empress replies tearfully, "Then there will be no Fantasia anymore!"
- Bastian asks her, "How many wishes do I get?"
- The Childlike Empress declares, "As many as you want, and the more wishes you make, the more magnificent Fantasia will become!"
- Bastian smiles gleefully as he recreates the very best of Fantasia through the imagined dreams he had experienced while reading about it earlier in *The Neverending Story*.
- No longer depressed about losing his mother nor afraid of *The Nothing*, Bastian now understands his rich reservoir of inner *Healthy Power* through optimism and, therefore, practices the art of creating his own vivid life through his active, enriching dreams.

Like Bastian, each of us holds the power within to recreate our inner world through fantasies and enriching, waking dreams, once we can boldly *name* them. Daring to dream so, the stage is set to launch steps down pathways that can bring our dreams into tangible reality!

ORCHESTRATED SUFFERING AND UNHEALTHY POWER

> *The voice in the head has a life of its own. Most people are*
> *at the mercy of that voice; they are possessed by thought, by*
> *the mind. And since the mind is conditioned by the past, you*
> *are then forced to reenact the past again and again.*

Eckhart Tolle

Impact of Pessimism upon Self and Others

Let us begin here with an operating premise:

...We cannot generate positive thoughts or feelings from negative ones...

In a common business situation, a new staff member will predictably be buoyed up by a manager who envisions her greater potential, especially if she is treated with compassion and receives favorable support while she is struggling to perform competently early on. Eventually, she is likely to meet or exceed her manager's *Optimistic Expectations* for her success, thereby demonstrating again the positive ripple effect of our *Healthy Power*. Developing and expressing such positive expectations consciously makes the process all the more helpful. Her empowering manager would likely be overheard praising her now accomplished staff member to another manager who had expressed doubts about her chances for success, asserting "I told you so!" with a pleased look of satisfaction.

On the other hand, holding negative expectations through prejudice (i.e., negative self-fulfilling prophecy) can erode that same person's hope, dismantle her confidence, and rob her of motivation to make her best efforts toward success. In sharp contrast to the uplifting experiences of the supported staff member above who received enough encouragement to work through her early struggles to pass the tipping point toward eventual success, another unfortunate new recruit will predictably flounder and quite possibly fail, even though she had brought the raw potential to do her job competently under at least minimally favorable conditions. A disempowering manager would likely be overheard bemoaning her now unaccomplished staff member to another manager who had expressed confidence about her chances of success in saying

"I told you so!" with a self-affirming sneer. Such is one facet of *Unhealthy Power* through pessimism—one of the operating dynamics of *Orchestrated Suffering*—since when we internalize it, our perceptions become our reality and shape our future, accordingly.

If you are familiar with the power of suggestion through hypnosis and with the role of *placebo effects* in medical/surgical outcomes, it will be clear to you that setting genuinely positive expectations with patients with a realistic and prevailing overall sense of confidence toward outcomes is an integral part of any patient-centered, empowering bedside manner. By sharp contrast, much has been written about the power of physicians to exercise undue negative influence upon patient recovery, pain management, and even their mortality by unwittingly predicting an adverse course for a patient's illnesses and/or forecasting when she will be likely to die (*Love, Medicine and Miracles*, Bernie Siegel, MD, 1986). Negativity in the form of pessimism can literally harm and even kill us, especially when we take it to heart.

It has become increasingly clear in recent years that the power of the mind to help or hinder our well-being is a promising and still relatively unexplored area for research, bridging the traditional divide between medicine and psychology. Per Daniel Goleman:

> "In the land of the sick, emotions reign supreme; fear is a thought away. We can be so emotionally fragile while we are ailing because our mental well-being is based in part on the illusion of invulnerability. Sickness—especially a severe illness—bursts that illusion, attacking the premise that our private world is safe and secure. Suddenly we feel weak, helpless, and vulnerable."

Goleman further asserts that sometimes people enact their unconscious will, beliefs, expectations, or fantasies through the body or otherwise through symptoms of distress/dysfunction without knowing it and unable to stop the enactment without skillful help.

> "People who experienced chronic anxiety, long periods of sadness and pessimism, unremitting tension or incessant hostility, relentless cynicism or suspiciousness, were found

to have *double* the risk of disease—including asthma, arthritis, headaches, peptic ulcers, and heart disease (each representative of major, broad categories of disease). This order of magnitude makes distressing emotions as toxic a risk factor as, say, smoking or high cholesterol are for heart disease—in other words, a major threat to health."

While it is certainly fundamental to *Healthy Power* to muster an unwavering sense of optimism through our meaningful dreams, it is also sometimes imperative that we humbly accept the limits of our ability to predict or control the details of our hoped-for outcomes. In the same way that hope has a positive, energizing effect upon an individual's mind and body, *hope dashed against the rocks* can be devastating, as Viktor Frankl observed in the following passage:

"The death rate in the week between Christmas 1944, and New Year's 1945, increased in camp beyond all previous experience. In his (the concentration camp chief doctor's) opinion, the explanation for this increase did not lie in the harder working conditions or the deterioration of our food supplies or a change of weather or new epidemics. It was simply that the majority of the prisoners had lived in the naïve hope that they would be home again by Christmas. As the time drew near and there was no encouraging news, the prisoners lost courage and disappointment overcame them. This had a dangerous influence on their powers of resistance and a great number of them died." (p. 84)

It is worthy to note that this represents an almost exact parallel to the *Stockdale Paradox* reported as part of an interview Jim Collins conducted with Admiral James Stockdale in *Good to Great* (2001). Admiral Stockdale, who was the highest ranking United States military officer within the Hanoi Hilton POW camp during 1965 to 1973 of the Viet Nam War, was reportedly tortured over 20 times during his imprisonment there. Seemingly resilient to the point of being unbreakable, he served as a source of strength and wise counsel for many of the other POWs; however, he was also witness to many severe cases of depression and tragic suicides while there. Based upon such potentially invaluable experience, he was asked by Collins about the secrets of survival amidst those grueling tests of human endurance, "Who didn't make it out?" Admiral Stockdale replied:

> "The optimists. Oh, they were the ones who said, 'We're going to be out by Christmas.' And Christmas would come, and Christmas would go. Then they'd say, 'We're going to be out by Easter.' And Easter would come and Easter would go. And then Thanksgiving, and then it would be Christmas again. And they died of a broken heart...This is a very important lesson. You must never confuse faith that you will prevail in the end—which you can never afford to lose—with the discipline to confront the most brutal facts of your current reality, whatever they might be." (p. 85)

Depression: Choices at the Fork in the Road

Let me begin this segment by recognizing that experiencing depression is not evidence that we lack good character or are otherwise predisposed toward pathology, evil, or *Unhealthy Power*. While it is not uncommon in human experience to become depressed, especially for reasons that are exogenous (i.e., originating outside oneself), such as the loss of a pet, the steps we take to come back from depression determine the timeliness and degree to which we bounce back and return to full strength. Moreover, following helpful steps for a return to our baseline mood and energy, even when the reasons for depression are endogenous (e.g., originating internally from our biology, a medical condition, etc.), can lead us to reconstitute ourselves into more mature and durable people through the challenging processes of bearing up under our suffering and working to make as strong a recovery as possible.

However, there are those of us who, whether consciously or otherwise, derive *secondary gain* from our symptoms of depression, such as malingering to avoid work and other responsibilities, gaining sympathy and attention, and deriving power from others who unwittingly enable or even amplify our symptoms in spite of their good-natured intent to be part of a solution. This is sometimes described as the *power of the symptom bearer*, and such behavior, even when unconscious in its inception and perpetuation, represents a significant form of *Unhealthy Power.*

In this section you will learn about the signs and symptoms of depression in general, the experience of depression, common causes of depression, and helpful means of preventing it. Additionally, you will learn how to cope with depression as it begins in order to avoid its destructive effects, especially the loss of hope that can lead to suicidal thoughts. The role of family/friends and professionals will be covered as important sources of support for fighting against depression. The vitally important role of our waking dreams as the primal source of emotional energy and strategic use of the *Hope-Energy Relationship* for keeping depression under better control were covered earlier and dovetail nicely with these prescriptive suggestions. Finally, you will learn about some key life management skills that help people maintain a positive outlook and healthy levels of energy for living.

With this overview in mind, consider these basic concepts pertaining to depression and suicide:

- Depression is the normal feeling that people have when they experience an important loss, a painful hurt, or a serious disappointment.

- Sometimes depression is the healthy reaction to things that are wrong, providing a person with a *time-out* to reflect, make a change, or to solve a dilemma.

- Depression becomes a problem when it leads a person to make poor choices or otherwise causes unhealthy functioning, such as becoming withdrawn, avoiding contact with people, and losing interest in things that once gave the person good feelings (e.g., eating, sleeping, playing).

- Thoughts of suicide are the normal reaction to feeling hopeless and overwhelmed; however, there are many things that can be done before and/or during suicidal thoughts to prevent a person from acting on the impulse to die.

- There are many helpful ways to manage depression, and practicing them usually leads to better control over it, and even potentially constructive use of it, just like any other skill for living.

Signs and Symptoms of Depression

Most of us are likely to have the following indicators of depression after experiencing a serious loss, disappointment, or other type of overwhelming pain or trauma:

- frequent crying
- difficulty falling asleep or staying asleep (e.g., early morning awakening)
- wanting to sleep too much
- difficulty eating due to loss of appetite
- wanting to eat much more than usual
- loss of energy and enthusiasm
- avoiding contact with others, even friends and family
- loss of interest in things that normally give the person pleasure
- feeling negative, gloomy, even hopeless
- thinking negatively in all-or-none statements, such as "I'll **never** be happy again!," "**No one** will ever love me!," "I can't do **anything** right!," and "**Everybody** else is happy except for me!"
- alcohol/drug abuse to escape feelings of depression
- suicidal thinking and behavior

Some Common and Less Common Causes of Depression

A history of trauma or loss does not, by itself, predict negative effects. Rather, the finding of a lack of resolution is the crucial component in determining the likelihood of negative effects.

Marion F. Solomon, Daniel J. Siegel

Here are some of the most common and less common life events that lead to feelings of depression:

- break-up with a boyfriend or girlfriend
- death of a loved one, friend, or other close attachment, including pets

- severe disappointment, such as discovering an unfaithful spouse or being fired from a job
- being the butt of jokes and bullied, then feeling embarrassed, humiliated, or helpless
- being the victim of abuse and/or neglect, especially with the feeling of not being able to escape from it or change it
- being caught for doing something seriously wrong, with painful guilt, shame, or disgrace, especially if feeling unsupported in the crisis
- serious medical problems, chronic pain, or long-term disability

How to Cope with Depression

There are many helpful things that can empower people to better manage their negative feelings and the impact of depression, including:

- pushing ourselves to do what has always worked well to keep us healthy and happy, even though we don't yet feel like doing those things (e.g., going for a relaxing walk; listening to your favorite music; talking with a close friend)
- eating balanced meals on time, even when we don't feel like eating, we want to eat too much, or we feel like eating junk foods instead
- following the normal sleep schedule and habits, even though we might feel like staying awake or sleeping more than normal
- exercising regularly and sensibly, even though we might feel like simply *vegging out* instead
- staying in close contact with others, especially friends and family, rather than giving in to the feeling of being alone or becoming isolated
- resisting the urge to use alcohol or drugs to escape bad feelings, remembering that alcohol and drug abuse only serve to make the problems progressively worse (note: alcohol is a depressant drug)
- resisting any form of thinking that is negative, especially all-or-none thoughts, replacing them with reasonably positive ones

that give you a sense of confidence and good feelings (e.g., "I **do** have reasons to be happy!", "**Many** people like me!", and "I've been through this kind of struggle before, so **I'll get through it** again!")

- creating new dreams that are both personally important and realistic, such as planning a same-day fun activity that you know you can do

The Roles of Family, Friends, and Professionals

Given that each of us is very dependent upon the love and support we receive from family and friends in staying healthy, it is important that we describe their role in helping to fight depression. Additionally, there are times during which depression becomes so disabling that people need to see a medical doctor, psychiatrist, and/or counselor in order to get the required treatment. Consider the following:

- People who are closest to us can see problems and solutions sometimes better than we can see them ourselves since they are often more objective.
- The love that they give to us has the effect of drawing us back from depression, helping us to regain feelings of self-worth and belonging.
- Activities with friends and family tend to distract us from our depressed feelings, which open us to the possibility that we can feel normal again.
- Professionals are able to treat depression, one of the most common emotional disorders that people face, providing guidance, support, and hope for the depressed person, and medical providers can prescribe medications that frequently reduce or eliminate the feelings and other symptoms of depression.
- Family, friends, and professionals should encourage the depressed person to confront her symptoms, rather than denying or minimizing them, and then offer ongoing support to assist her to regain a sense of emotional stability.
- If you notice a person is suddenly feeling better after being

seriously depressed, ask whether she is thinking about suicide, both because it might mean that she has made a plan to commit suicide and because asking supportively about suicide can have a tension relieving effect.

THE PATHWAY TO OPTIMISTIC EXPECTATIONS

Whether seventy or sixteen, there is in every being's heart a love of wonder; the sweet amazement at the stars, and star-like things and thoughts; the undaunted challenge of events, the unfailing childlike appetite for what comes next, and the joy in the game of life.

Samuel Ullman

The strategy, *Begin with the end in mind*, (*The 7 Habits of Highly Effective People*, Stephen Covey, 1989), is an essential component for making optimism a foundation of our *Healthy Power*. By starting out our journey or goal pathway with a clear visualization of meaningful outcomes as if it they have already been accomplished motivates us to make strong initial and enduring efforts through the kindling and rekindling of hope (i.e.,. the *Hope-Energy Relationship* described above). In order to do so, we do well to form the habit upon awakening each day of creating a positive vision of fresh new perspectives and exciting possibilities, remembering the driving motivation that such dreaming can unleash. It is similarly helpful to remember the integral roles played by our perception of *importance* and *confidence* regarding our goals to produce an upwelling of energy derived from our hope. It is then that we experience a strengthening of our commitment to solve our problems and otherwise clear the pathway to attain our most challenging goals.

Healthy Power—Prescriptions for Developing *Optimistic Expectations* as a Leader in the Workplace:

1) Instill hope in your staff about their goals, their potential, and their long-term success and fulfillment. If you believe genuinely in their unique strengths and untapped potential, they will naturally feel the contagiousness of your positive view of them. For example, when someone says, "I just can't figure this one

out," a helpful reply is, "You will, you just haven't figured it out *yet*."

2) Commit to face-to-face discussion of difficult issues, rather than *splitting* or *triangulating* (i.e., complaining to others while avoiding confrontation and/or conflict), and address issues in a timely manner, rather than allowing them to fester. This courageous commitment to having what some have called *fierce conversations* with everything put on the table in person, ironically, creates a more positive working environment and an atmosphere of increased safety and security because the process increases trust, leaves no stone unturned, and most often results in logical resolution of issues leading to greater stability.

3) Always represent the best interests of the employer and its governance, even when problems are apparent and still unresolved. Just as parents do well to support each other, especially when a complaining child attempts to stir strife at the top of the family pecking order by turning one parent against the other, do not allow anyone to play *divide and conquer* with you and your fellow leaders. Understand and respect the power of words to help or hinder any initiative you oversee. In this regard, never diminish the authority of your staff or supervisors, thereby exposing an *Achilles Heel* at which others will predictably shoot more arrows of negativity.

4) Make deliberate and constructive use of *self-fulfilling prophecy* (i.e., the power of our and others' expectations) by first adopting the most positive possible expectations, and then sharing them with everyone for whom such influence might support them to attainment.

Identify and Rewrite Unhealthy Life *Stories*

In his book, *Do One Thing Different*, Bill O'Hanlon presents a series of helpful insights pertaining to the power of the mind to help or to hinder our life energies as follows:

"People often become so identified with their problems that they begin to think of themselves as the problem. Other people can reinforce this process. Therapists and doctors often use shorthand to refer to their clients or patients: 'I have several depressives in my practice, or I specialize in treating diabetics.' This shorthand can sometimes turn a story into a label that sticks."(p. 120)

Accordingly, he describes four methods for rewriting the negative, problem-focused life scripts that perpetuate *Orchestrated Suffering*. This involves transforming them into more positive, solution-oriented *stories* that produce greater optimism as follows:

1) Acknowledge and describe the facts of your story, situation, history, problem, etc., without judging or evaluating it, thereby helping to gain a more objective, dispassionate view. Accepting, rather than resisting, such facts in a story help most people to realize that painful, difficult life events are not one-sided, thus opening the possibility for reframing them as positive.

2) Find or create counterevidence that refutes any negative or narrow view of yourself relative to your stories. This can include any history of behavior that does not fit your story, or simply learning to behave now in ways that prove that a former story is no longer relevant.

3) Understand and realize that you are not your stories, whether negative or positive, but that we are all much deeper than mere stories. People are better able to see they are capable of changing their behavior once they accept that they are not defined by it, and thus become liberated from all of their stories.

4) View your stories with greater compassion and flexibility. Instead of thinking about what you *should* have done or be doing (thereby creating distress, a sense of failure, etc.), become more self-accepting and forgiving of any perceived fault or problematic behavior. Then create new stories of self-acceptance, patience, and forgiveness.

Generate Hope and Energy

Any behavioral change, including changes in the thoughts and behaviors that influence our moods and energy levels, are most likely to occur when we see the importance—the *why* of making a change–and feel confident about taking successful action—the *how* of making a desired change. We then can become energized by the reasons, value, and possibilities associated with our intentions. Whenever you help yourself or someone else to dream of better lives, seeing the value and opportunity for such, you empower helpful and relevant actions as the likely next steps.

How to do it...

1) Understand and make practical use of *the Hope-Energy Relationship* remembering that energy for action comes from our dreams—those that are personally meaningful and ones we believe to be realistically attainable.
2) The experience of hope for a goal or dream provides us with the motivational energy to take actions that help us to reach our goals and to transform our dreams into reality.
3) In order to assist yourself or someone else as soon as possible when early intervention is typically most effective, remember that the opposite is also true: the loss of hope brings a loss of energy, usually experienced as let-down, burnout, depression, and even suicidal feelings at the extreme.

Instructions from Buddhist Teachings: A Science of the Mind

In Buddhism, master instructors such as Pema Chodron describe how we too often engage in *cinematography* or cognitive/perceptual *movie-making* by affixing psychological lenses through which we perceive our world in a reconstructed manner, rather than being able to discern objective reality in its purer, more objective form via our senses alone. Moreover, it is through such biased perceptions and expectations that human suffering primarily occurs. Similarly, Buddhist instructor and meditation practitioner, Bill Morgan, describes the range of opportunities we all encounter to determine our quality of life through the management of positive and negative ideas and feelings as follows:

The Four Great Endeavors are:

1) *To prevent the arising of unarisen unwholesome states*
2) *To abandon unwholesome states that have already arisen*
3) *To arouse wholesome states that have not yet arisen*
4) *To maintain wholesome states that have already arisen*

PEARLS OF HEALTHY POWER

Ralph Waldo Emerson...

Not he is great who can alter matter, but he who can alter my state of mind.

Oliver Wendell Holmes...

I find the great thing in this world is not so much where we stand, as in what direction we are moving: To reach the port of heaven, we must sail sometimes with the wind and sometimes against it—but we must sail, and not drift, nor lie at anchor.

Franklin D. Roosevelt...

The only limit to our realization of tomorrow will be our doubts of today. Let us move forward with strong and active faith.

Max Ehrmann (excerpt from his poem, *Desiderata*, 1927)...

Nurture strength of spirit to shield you in sudden misfortune. But do not distress yourself with dark imaginings. Many fears are born of fatigue and loneliness.

William James...

A great many people think they are thinking when they are merely rearranging their prejudices.

Walter D. Wintle...

If you think you are beaten, you are. You've got to be sure of yourself before you can ever win a prize.

Maya Angelou...

Self-pity in its early stages is as snug as a feather mattress. Only when it hardens does it become uncomfortable.

Craig N. Piso, PhD

An Invitation to *Optimistic Expectations* through Music–Lyrics from *Smile*, sung by Nat King Cole (1954)

Smile though your heart is aching
Smile even though it's breaking
When there are clouds in the sky, you'll get by
If you smile through your fear and sorrow
Smile and maybe tomorrow
You'll see the sun come shining through for you

Light up your face with gladness
Hide every trace of sadness
Although a tear may be ever so near
That's the time you must keep on trying
Smile, what's the use of crying?
You'll find that life is still worthwhile
If you just smile

CHAPTER 3

W...*Win-Win Relationships* vs. *Win-Lose Relationships*

*Covenantal relationships are open to influence. They fill deep
needs and they enable work to have meaning and to be fulfilling.
Covenantal relationships reflect unity, grace, and poise. They
are an expression of the scared nature of relationships.*

Max DePree

WIN-WIN RELATIONSHIPS AND HEALTHY POWER

I want to set the stage for your further empowerment by beginning this chapter with an operating premise about the vital role played by *power* in all interpersonal relationships, as follows:

*...All great relationships are mutually empowering in healthy ways,
thus you know you're in a great relationship when you and the other
person enjoy increased Healthy Power through your union...*

In any organized system, such as a family or business, it takes a mature, confident, and humble person to contribute toward building a culture in which a *Win-Win* mentality becomes woven into the fabric of the group's interpersonal relationships. This type of culture is characterized largely by its participants showing consistently cooperative and unselfish dedication to each other for the success of the family, business, or society as a whole, even if this means making individual sacrifices at times to support that success. This also runs directly against the grain of many predominantly western values espoused in business, sports, and otherwise where competition and winning are inextricably linked. Vince Lombardi is well remembered for having said, "Winning isn't everything...it's the only thing!"

Whether in family life or in business, productive, healthy teamwork is fostered by parents/leaders who inculcate the group to embrace an *abundance mentality* so that they behave in manners that empower and support each other interdependently. A relationship model then emerges in which there is room for everyone to share in the resources and to become both individually and collectively successful. The investment, therefore, is in creating *winners* across the board, rather than working purposefully to make others lose.

Stephen Covey, an organizational development and leadership icon, argues that what is needed to produce a healthy culture characterized by aligned and empowered team effort is an uncommon perspective: *Think Win-Win or No Deal* (*The 7 Habits of Highly Effective People*, 1989, page 204). While it is certainly helpful in business, and even in family life, to instill a strong sense of competition with outsiders and rise to the highest pinnacle of success that is possible within the larger arena, it is important here to recognize two key reference points for any such efforts: 1) The *locus of control* (i.e., *internal* versus *external*); and 2) The definition of *success* and the related model through which *winning* is achieved. Effective leaders make skillful use of both reference points above in their management efforts.

First, rather than spending time and energy focused upon what the neighbors or the competition might have or be doing (e.g., with envy, fear, distraction, etc.), the group is redirected to pay most careful attention to their own behavior from an *internal locus of control*. Making such a shift is empowering because, as indicated in earlier discussion about *power* and *responsibility*, an internal focus upon one's available choices (*power*) with accompanying ownership for the subsequent outcomes (*responsibility*) leads any mature individual or group to draw more deeply upon core strengths. Borrowing analogous expressions from baseball, they are then able to hit the ball from *within their wheel-house*, thereby generating maximum power to hit more *home runs*. Group members operating from an *internal locus of control* increase their confidence through self-directed, increased competencies and subsequently improved performance.

Second, such a leader will create a *Win-Win* environment in which people become positively other-directed. That is, they become primarily oriented toward their family or group's mission with a service focus, a *Servant Leadership* orientation, altruistic sharing, and the formation of creative synergies to become more productive while, at the same time, living and working more enjoyably. Accordingly, the definition of *success* and the related model through which *winning* is achieved reflect internally focused criteria and no interest in the other party becoming the *loser*. While certainly interested in victory in whatever appropriate form it might take (e.g., winning the game; earning the award; attaining the pinnacle of financial success), mature power in this regard is driven by a primary desire to reach one's greatest potential, rather than simply coming out on top relative to the competition.

While it is clear that Covey initiated this *habit* (i.e., *Think Win-Win*) with many valuable and practical applications to both family and professional group behavior, in this chapter we are focusing primarily on our inner thoughts and feelings as they impinge upon our ability to create such *Win-Win Relationships* with an overview of the key psychological principles that determine the pathway a person is likely to choose within this dimension of personal power.

Attitudes Toward Self and Others

Healthy self-esteem is the cornerstone of our ability to generate the goodwill that accompanies a commitment to building *Win-Win Relationships*. With self-esteem, we experience self-love, not in the sense of primitive, narcissistic self-love, but love that emerges naturally as a person becomes realistically self-aware and self-accepting, *warts* and all. Through this gradual aspect of maturing human development, we become better prepared to engage comfortably in social activities, for example, without becoming self-conscious, guarded, or defensive, depending on how much we've grown in this area of our personhood.

It is also well recognized that healthy self-esteem determines the level of maturity we can demonstrate in forming close attachments to others, especially to love them in mutually rewarding ways. As we develop our sense of separateness with our uniqueness, autonomy, and increasing self-sufficiency, we gain the ability to form intimate attachments without becoming entangled in another's roots. Therefore, we understand that the highest form of intimate attachment humanly possible is that in which there is neither aloof isolation nor overly dependent enmeshment. Instead, there is interdependence—an appreciation that both people are self-sufficient—and then we *choose* closer attachment to our mutual empowerment and increased satisfaction. *Win-Win Relationships*, accordingly, represent the high-water mark of personal intimacy and fulfillment.

People who elevate their intimate attachments toward such a harmonious level playing field necessarily first believe a number of key ideas about themselves and others, and such beliefs become integral to both their value system and their behavior toward others as follows:

- "I am no greater than nor less than any other person on the planet; therefore, I do not judge others, nor do I allow myself to become reactive to others who judge me."
- "I am realistically confident regarding my value as a person and, therefore, comfortable within my own skin, whether I am alone or in social situations."
- "I celebrate the good fortune of others, knowing that I am not lacking."
- "I am independent emotionally, as well as practically self-sufficient."
- "I acknowledge my normal, healthy emotional needs, thus I seek to satisfy them with others in mutually beneficial relationships."
- "I recognize that we are all interconnected as a species; therefore, I relate to others with loving kindness and compassion, rather than acting with any form of violence, behaving in ways that diminish anyone else, or creating unhelpful barriers between others."

WIN-LOSE RELATIONSHIPS AND UNHEALTHY POWER

Hatred—that's my trade. It takes you farther than any other emotion.

Paul Joseph Goebbels, Ph.D.
(Adolph Hitler's Reich Minister of Propaganda)

The now familiar and increasingly prevalent *Win-Lose* paradigm we witness in today's world had its modern era roots in *Social Darwinism*—a socio-economic model that was extrapolated from the early work of Charles Darwin (*On The Origin of Species*, 1859) that made *survival of the fittest* the mantra for empowered business and social competition. Unfortunately, once this work ethic is embraced, it begins to define and permeate all forms of interpersonal relationships so that other people become identified, typecast, and then pigeonholed hierarchically within their place in the pecking order. Such a vertically organized model for the exercise of power allows no level playing field. Followers of this paradigm tend to feel license to play by their own rules because, as some will then claim, "It's a dog-eat-dog world, and this dog won't be eaten!" Further, then, it's not a big leap for many such individuals to live and work under the belief that *the end justifies the means.* Such hoarders of power will all too often leave others floundering in hardship, defeated and swamped under by a one-sided wake of success created through their self-serving efforts to win at any price.

A predominantly *Win-Lose* leadership style in a family, business, or social group tends to propagate cultures that eventually become characterized by systemic mistrust and accompanying in-fighting (e.g., sibling rivalries, *turf wars*; resistance to change; silo behavior). A leader's implicit or explicit attitude and perspective about winning within her group, therefore, becomes a driver at many important forks in the road for others living and working within her sphere of influence. If, for example, the leader operates from a *scarcity mentality*, then the group's culture will become characterized for the most part by behavior also biased toward a *Win-Lose* orientation. Moreover, all relationships, including those existing between family members, teammates, and otherwise peer groups, unfortunately fall prey to becoming pitted against each other (i.e., *kill or be killed*), not simply against outsiders to the group. Since nobody likes to lose or to feel like a *loser*, avoidance of losing becomes a powerful source of negative reinforcement for an individual group member's behavior when a more viable alternative paradigm does not prevail.

In this model, *Unhealthy Power* in its most extreme forms uses and sacrifices all others without regard for healthy competition, sportsmanship, or conscious concern for the greater good. Inherently, because there is no regard for the well-being of others, empathy and compassion toward others are viewed cynically as being irrelevant at best and prohibited at worst. Not only are such people predisposed to defeating others, their efforts are typically undertaken with a disdain for those being subjugated or otherwise diminished. Within this framework and mindset, they believe they are entitled to the spoils of victory, whether in business or in war, just as those being trodden underfoot conversely deserve their awful fate.

One might recognize these phenomena in recent decades of chronically escalating American political in-fighting and non-productive gridlock. These are symptoms of the prevailing leadership model in which the primary agenda is to create *winners* and to avoid becoming *losers* within the narrow context of one's political party and otherwise among a party's loyal followers (e.g., PACs, campaign contributors, and corporate lobbyists). At the same time, a broader focus upon the welfare of the country as a whole, including all its citizens, while universally espoused as the politically correct rhetoric, is frequently used as a smokescreen for the wielding of power strictly along party lines in divisive manners. This ominously represents the emergence of provincial and self-serving *Unhealthy Power* on a national scale at its most tragically flawed state.

This same *Win-Lose* orientation also permeates many for-profit business enterprises across the globe, driven by greed, deception, and depletion of others with comparably toxic side effects. However, in the short-term such systems work with sufficient guile and apparent shared benefit to convince the masses these endeavors are positive, sometimes even noble. In any system in which *Unhealthy Power* predominates, the most vulnerable participants suffer the worst forms of victimization. The tobacco, food, and beverage industries have an ignoble track record of marketing their products to children and adolescents to bolster profits while, at the same time, contributing significantly to the rates of otherwise preventable illnesses and deaths among young people through cancer, obesity, and alcohol abuse. Another more clandestine but nonetheless tragic example worldwide is human trafficking for forced labor and sexual slavery, primarily targeting females as victims, including young children.

When any group of people becomes an object or scapegoat and is then dehumanized, the stage is set for the most horrific human atrocities we could ever witness, by those sufficiently powerful to commit them, including *ethnic cleansing* through mass torture and genocide. Again, this follows from an attitude in which some others are seen as lesser beings, if human at all, and otherwise designated as inferior and blameworthy. Too often, when targeted people are deemed to be *evil*, the related fear and hatred that emerge lead to a determined effort to eradicate the entire group of problematic individuals. Under the Nazi regime, for example, Jews and other groups of targeted people were identified as *vermin* during the Holocaust, thus the *final solution* was to kill millions of them with lethal gas, much as one would eliminate troublesome insects from an otherwise beautiful home.

Racial, ethnic, and cultural prejudices and their all too commonplace accompanying violence and oppression are symptoms of these *Win-Lose Relationships*. Unfortunately, we commonly find these facets of *Unhealthy Power* in humor, such as through jokes and pranks that identify an individual or group as a legitimate, even laughable object of scorn. Since nobody enjoys being labeled a *loser*, many find comfort making scapegoats of others, especially in public with apparent support, even commercial endorsement, as is the case with many stand-up comedians.

Carried to extremes, a person who inwardly fears her own inferiority and wishes to escape from self-loathing and anticipated persecution sometimes finds respite by affiliating with *hate groups*. These groups make it their regular practice to identify those lesser people who then become the deserving target of their persecution in all of its awful forms. Having no other option in view, and lacking the ability to build and maintain *Win-Win Relationships*, they perceive that it's far better to become the perpetrator than to be the victim. Doing so provides the illusion of superiority and temporary relief from her own inadequacies—inadequacies she can ill-afford to acknowledge, even privately. Psychologically speaking, this narcissistic defense mechanism is known as *projective identification*, which is the process of making another person the convenient repository of one's own unacceptable, often repugnant, personal features in order to protect an under-developed and primitive ego that is not yet capable of honest self-appraisal.

Whether we're talking about bullying that so commonly infiltrates school hallways or civil wars in which thousands become amputees, enslaved, and murdered, such dark forces thrive upon notions of superiority and inferiority—driven onward in zealous pursuit of *Unhealthy Power* through *Orchestrated Suffering*—and determined to follow only their own will, rather than submit to any concept of higher authority, morality, or God. As described by M. Scott Peck in *People of the Lie...The Hope for Healing Human Evil* (1983):

> "There are only two states of being: submission to God and goodness or the refusal to submit to anything beyond one's own will—which refusal automatically enslaves one to the forces of evil. (p.83)

Recognize, then, that the *Win-Lose* mentality and associated means of relating to people appeals to the most primitive and developmentally arrested persons of any society. Their quest for power, accordingly, has been driven throughout modern history by an incessant drive to correct what they deem to be wrong with the social order of things. After all, how can the divine will of God be a level playing field of equality when it generates intense suffering among those of a majority culture who are frightened, offended, and ultimately diminished by, for example, drinking from the same water cooler with those of a lesser race comprising a minority? We see a very telling clue about this dynamic even in language pertaining to civil rights when people discuss *tolerance*, as opposed to embracing minorities as equals. In short, the outward expression of *Win-Lose* values and its accompanying mindset is both insidious and destructive to the power base of those so targeted, deemed to be the "naturally" determined underlings of society. As such, it invariably precipitates violent protest and social action toward reform when channels of *Healthy Power* for such changes either fail or are not reliably made available to the populace. People will predictably die fighting for their freedom (e.g., *inalienable rights*), rather than live under oppression, subjugation, or other forms of perpetrating the lie that they are lesser beings.

Violence vs. Peace

Since *Unhealthy Power* is founded in large part upon *Win-Lose Relationships* and inherently built and maintained through violence in its many forms, it is important for us to understand the basic principles of violence and peace in order to recognize how they get started, for better and for worse:

1) Violence erupts when sufficient unhealthy tension is generated in others beyond the tension normally required to keep the peace.

2) It has many forms, including physical, verbal, and nonverbal acts of aggression (e.g., behaviors such as hitting, cursing, and staring).

3) Violence reciprocally creates tension, which causes still more amplified violence amidst an upward spiral of tension.

4) Continued violence almost never produces a lasting solution because revenge most often makes a problem worse.

5) The opposite of violence is peace.

6) Peace is the state of being that one finds during the experience of living without debilitating tension or violence.

7) Respect for self and others are the cornerstones of non-violent, peaceful co-existence.

8) As Covey has asserted, anything other than a *Win-Win Relationship* results long-term in *Lose-Lose*.

Types of Violence

Because there are many forms of violence that exist, it is helpful to attune our *radar screen* to be better able to sense when problems might be starting:

1) Physical aggression
   a. Against a person (hitting, kicking, biting, etc.)
   b. Against property (stealing, breaking, vandalizing, etc.)
2) Verbal aggression
   a. Name-calling
   b. Cursing
   c. Yelling, screaming
   d. Threatening, intimidating

  e. Interrupting

  f. Teasing, taunting

3) Non-Verbal aggression

  a. Staring, making faces, rolling eyes, etc.

  b. Making profane gestures (*giving the finger*, etc.)

4) Sexual aggression

  a. Assault, touching, forcing sexual behavior

  b. Jokes, name-calling, threats, teasing of a sexual nature

Warning Signs of Rage

Once we understand the basics about violence and the many different forms it takes, we also need to know what to look for to prevent a bad situation from getting worse. In order to do that well, we need to be able to recognize these early warning signals that our or another person's tension is building, possibly to the point of rage, and that the chance of violence erupting is increasing:

- ✓ Showing irritation and/or frustration
- ✓ Experiencing bodily tension and discomfort
- ✓ Expressing abusive language—shouting, arguing, and profanity
- ✓ Demonstrating nervousness, restlessness, pacing, and fidgeting
- ✓ Making threats and intimidating others
- ✓ Feeling abused, persecuted, or harassed
- ✓ Making emotional outbursts—crying, embarrassment
- ✓ Becoming preoccupied and overly suspicious
- ✓ Showing withdrawal and isolation
- ✓ Making unreasonable demands
- ✓ Showing hands fisted, jaw clenched, nostrils flared, eyes widened

THE PATHWAY TO WIN-WIN RELATIONSHIPS

The first step in building healthy, rewarding *Win-Win Relationships* is to understand our own strengths and weaknesses. First, we need to gain the skill of honest self-assessment, including our needs, quirks, flaws, etc. We also need to be aware of any *buttons* that others tend to push so we can work to prevent their being pushed during important conversations and sensitive interactions, especially with loved ones. For example, if you have the self-awareness to know you tend to become controlling with others under stress or when feeling anxious, it will be important to do the necessary work to reduce this behavior so friends, family, or co-workers will not experience you as being bossy or trying to put yourself above them somehow. The bottom line is that we do well to look first at ourselves with humility as the primary basis of the relationship that we're trying to build with another person, rather than simply looking at one another's attributes, for better or worse, as the drivers of how it is unfolding between us. Gaining such initial private victories thereby sets the stage for experiencing shared relational victories as much as possible.

Balancing Attachment Risks and Rewards

It is not uncommon for us if we have a painful family history and resultant emotional vulnerabilities to create a kind of thick relationship shell around ourselves in order to avoid further hurt or disappointment. This is especially true for children who have been the victims of physical abuse, emotional neglect, or abandonment by loved ones. It's almost as if the child tells herself, "Since I could be hurt again by trusting or caring for someone else, I better keep my distance and stay away from any kind of close attachment where I might possibly be hurt or disappointed." And so it goes—an emotionally needy person hungering for connection paradoxically keeps her safe distance by avoiding intimacy while paying the toll of continued isolation and loneliness, two key contributing factors of depression described in the previous chapter.

While this *avoidant* style might seem to be a reasonable defense against pain, and even something that many children and adults alike are able to do apparently well for awhile, it goes against our basic human nature to deny our needs for affiliation and closeness. As Abraham Maslow depicted in his *Hierarchy of Needs* pyramid, beyond our most fundamental *Physiological* needs (e.g., air, food, and water), our needs for *Safety* and *Belonging* are prerequisites to growing toward fuller maturation into *Self-Actualization*. We need healthy intimate connections with others to feel safe and secure in this world, no doubt. We are not built to live in isolation, nor as *an island*, cut off from others or lacking close attachments. This is certainly one of the reasons why solitary confinement is recognized worldwide in our collective consciousness as being one of the psychologically harshest of all punishments.

Even if we seem to be content otherwise amidst a busy and rewarding lifestyle, eventually every normal, healthy one of us discovers that we are lonely, or otherwise feel a void of support and happiness that can be satisfied only through deep and meaningful attachments. This pushes us to venture out, knowing on the one hand that it is risky, and on the other hand that it is too painful to live disconnected and apart from others not to muster the courage required to face such risk.

This might help to clarify why people with conflicts about close relationships sometimes feel a strong drive to control the very person with whom they are trying to form an attachment. It's as if they are trying to reduce the risk of losing another person by controlling them, even with aggression and subjugation, such as we often find in extreme situations of domestic violence. However, as I wrote earlier, mature people do not use violence or other means to control others. Instead, while they certainly try to influence others on many levels, as they should, they follow the *Golden Rule: Do unto others as you would have them do unto you.*

The tragedy of trying to prevent loss through domination and/or violence is that such behaviors usually drive the other person away, or at least to avoid getting too close to you. If for any unhealthy reason the person chooses to put up with such abuse or domination, it is predictable that the person who has the upper hand will eventually lose respect for the other, further eroding the opportunity for intimacy and connection.

The most important thing to remember about close relationships, therefore, is to respect one another for our uniqueness, rather than trying to mold each other into someone we are not. This is what Carl Rogers called *unconditional positive regard*—complete acceptance and respect for the other, communicated authentically and from the heart, not simply by words. Attempting to change another person is a way of saying to them that you do not fully accept them as they are, or that you would care for them more if they were different somehow. In either case, it leaves the other person feeling that they have been judged and rejected, at least in part, creating ill feelings, tension, and a growing desire to find another relationship where they might find acceptance for the unique person they actually are. It requires us to be non-judgmental, open, and caring, no matter what. Additionally, such objective, positive mirroring is the best way to enable people to see themselves fully and to take responsibility for their own behavior.

Developing Mutually Empowering Relationships

I made the assertion earlier in this chapter that *All great relationships are mutually empowering in healthy ways* and now will focus on specific skills and strategies that promote interpersonal effectiveness through such mutual empowerment. Since *information is power*, assuming that it is fact-based and accurate, I'll continue to amplify the various ways in which our expressed language can be the central factor in building and maintaining *Win-Win Relationships*.

1) Apply the Power of Words

The words we speak and how we express them, both verbally and non-verbally, are instrumental in forming and maintaining healthy attachments. The positive use of language in this regard should be understood as a source of strengthening the receiver consistently through our communications. We do well, therefore, to choose our words and the means through which we share them with an overarching desire to support and edify our counterpart. We express this most obviously by educating, coaching, encouraging, providing positive feedback, and otherwise uplifting others by sharing information. However, deeper connections necessarily also involve such elements as questioning, challenging, and offering constructive criticism, since often through such seemingly negative exchanges we provide our loved ones, for example, with the catalyst that might lead them toward helpful growth and change. The greater challenge, of course, is first setting the stage for such exchanges by having formed a solid personal connection that can endure potentially rough seas, such as when we are initially misunderstood as attacking the other person, along with mastering the expressive skills of delivery that enable us to calm the waters when necessary.

On the other hand, ironically, there is nothing more commonly abused in close relationships than words—words that are harmful and destructive to the other person in what amounts to verbal violence. This is often the case when people speak in a self-serving manner and otherwise reactively upon impulse out of hurt and anger, rather than taking the time to think more deeply about the other person before they speak. Here the reader might recall the previous material about the role of tension in all forms of violence. Since people frequently use abusive language with words that cause hurt and anger in others, thereby increasing their emotional tension, it is not surprising that verbal violence is almost always the forerunner to physical assaults and even more serious *crimes of passion*, including murder.

2)   Steer the Tongue Like a Rudder

One helpful way to understand the power of words is to liken the tongue to the rudder of a ship—the movable paddle beneath a boat or sailing vessel that determines the direction it will steer, usually guided by the tiller or ship's wheel on deck. By controlling the rudder, which is relatively small, the entire ship is directed to the left or to the right. So also is the case with the choice of words that we speak. A carefully chosen word thoughtfully expressed can soothe or calm others, even when the speaker is feeling upset. Conversely, a poorly chosen word can upset others, even in the midst of a calm situation. Since our words are taken to reflect what is in our hearts and minds, others place great importance upon them, especially in close relationships. Kind and thoughtful words tend to build good emotions in others, helping them to feel safe and accepted, inviting closeness with the person speaking such words. Therefore, taking appropriate time to think before we speak, especially when upset with someone or something, is an effective way to show others that we have good self-control. That is, we reveal one of our fundamental core strengths by showing unpretentious mastery over the words we select and their delivery. Such mastery is one of the keys to building trust with others, who then feel safe enough to take the risk of seeking out and sustaining a closer bond, ideally to our mutual benefit.

3)   Use Your Voice as a Quality Musical Instrument

Applying the metaphor of a finely crafted violin, make use of your voice knowing that the beauty of the sound that you make is a result of the quality of the materials reverberating deep within its construction. A poorly constructed instrument cannot produce world class music, and a sloppy or untrained musician holding a Stradivarius violin will not produce music that reflects its true quality when being poorly played. Our state of mind and spirit, accordingly, create a distinct and perceptible vibe that people can hear and feel, even over the telephone, so always get in *tune* before you begin to speak. This means speaking from our inner beauty with our highest quality and finest precision. While words are only symbols to which we attach meaning so that we can communicate ideas, our most powerful communication is through the melody and resonance of our voice, echoing the truth and beauty of our purest feelings for another person. Such uncensored, heartfelt, and spontaneous expression requires first that we are fully prepared to make externally transparent the thoughts and feelings that comprise us internally— revealing the essential nature of our integrity. You'll learn a great deal about others simply by listening to their instrument, paying close attention to the underlying construction.

4) Make Use of Artistic Expression

Understand the value of expressing our deepest feelings through artistic media, such as writing poetry, drawing and painting, sculpting, dancing, and playing musical instruments. Such outlets for our emotions can be helpful not only in finding greater personal balance, but also as tools to communicate our deeper feelings with close friends and loved ones. If you are a person who sometimes has difficulty finding the right words to express how you feel, then consider the additional choices available to you through art and the unique means through which you can express yourself through various artistic media and forms. Imagine how a loved one will feel the next time a special occasion takes place and you give her an artistically inspired gift that comes from your heart, expressing your deepest emotions in their purest form.

5) Become a Great Listener

Seek first to understand, then to be understood.

Stephen R. Covey

Everyone wants to be heard and understood, and everyone has a normal desire for control over their lives; so it really helps to connect with people by listening well to them. Listen carefully to their words, that is, what they are saying directly. However, we also need to be listening with empathy for what they are saying without words. What is the deeper message to their words? What are they not expressing with words, but perhaps through their tone, rate of speech, breathing pattern, stress level, etc.? We can gain influence with people by listening and truly understanding all they are telling us, and then letting them know that we understand. Also, we help people be more open with us by letting them speak than by attempting to steer or control the conversation. When we offer people the gifts of our attention, time, and patience, it is human nature for most people to reciprocate by directing their interest and attention toward us in return—it's common sense, but not commonly practiced through effective listening. Concentrate on what the other person is saying. We often don't really hear what the person is saying because we are planning what we're going to say in reply. Allow the person to finish the sentence that completes the thought. It is tempting to interrupt before the person is finished—we can rush to conclusions by doing so. Clarify what you heard the person say before you respond (e.g., "What I'm hearing you say is…;" "Did you mean that you want to…").

"True listening, total concentration on the other, is always a manifestation of love. An essential part of true listening is the discipline of bracketing, the temporary giving up or setting aside of one's own prejudices, frames of reference and desires so as to experience as far as possible the speaker's world from the inside, stepping inside his or her shoes. This unification of speaker and listener is actually an extension and enlargement of ourself, and new knowledge is always gained from this. Moreover, since true listening involves bracketing, a setting aside of the self, it also temporarily involves a total acceptance of the other. Sensing this acceptance, the speaker will feel less and less vulnerable and more and more inclined to open up the inner recesses of his or her mind to the listener. As this happens, speaker and listener begin to appreciate each other more and more, and the duet dance of love is again begun. The energy required for the discipline of bracketing and the focusing of total attention is so great that it can be accomplished only through love, by the will to extend oneself for mutual growth." (*The Road Less Traveled*, M. Scott Peck, M.D., 1978, pp. 127-128)

6)   Express Empathy

Put yourself in the other person's state of mind so that you can understand her situation, how she thinks, how she feels, and her perspective about things. Look at things from her point of view (i.e., her values, attitudes, beliefs) so that you truly and deeply understand her perceptions, remembering that for each of us *our perception becomes our reality*. Respect the fact that she thinks and feels the way she does, even if it seems to be wrong or irrational to you.

7)   Communicate Unconditional Acceptance

Express non-possessive warmth—a sense of genuine caring for another person with *no strings attached*. Demonstrate respect for her behavior, thoughts, and feelings, even if you believe she is wrong and you disagree with her, but without enabling or supporting any unhealthy or dangerous behavior. Remember that people are not defined by their behavior, but by their deeper sense of personhood. Therefore, suggest how she might make the choice to change any of her undesired behavior without judging or attacking her—without asking her to change who she is at her deeper core.

8)   Encourage Inclusive Thinking and Speaking

Help the other person put everything on the table by looking at all of her thoughts, feelings, and behaviors, even if they are negative or disturbing. Ask about the good and the not-so-good of her behavior or situation and acknowledge the reality of both. If she becomes irrational and blind to the big picture and its possibilities, encourage her to think and act in rational, more grounded ways, rather than in overly emotional ways. Conversely, if she lets rational thinking devoid of feelings block her view of the big picture and its possibilities, encourage her to connect with her deeper feelings, even if they are unpleasant and stir discomfort.

9)   Make Strategic Use of the *One-Down Position*

Allow yourself to take a subordinate (rather than expert) stance with the other person, thereby showing authentic respect for her ideas, perspectives, and personhood non-judgmentally. Recognize that by becoming open and deferential, rather than closed and controlling, we help people to become more open and less defensive. Understand that taking the one-down position is not being deceptive or manipulative. Rather, it is a genuine stepping down in order to make space for her thoughts, insights, and emotions to be shared and considered transparently with safety. Embrace the paradox that we often gain influence with people by consciously presenting ourselves as non-threatening and subordinate to the other.

10) Support Assertiveness in Others

Encourage the other person to express her own ideas and emotions without hesitation or anxiousness, creating an atmosphere of complete acceptance and safety with you. Be open to disagreement about issues and strategies, conveying your willingness to consider flexibly the opinions that differ from your own without taking any part of the conversation personally. Acknowledge that the other person, more so than you, is the expert regarding her life, thus you respect and value her ideas and decision-making ability. Model assertiveness, not aggressiveness, and then ask her to follow your lead in discussions about helping her to speak confidently, with her own unique voice. Resist the temptation to control or dominate the conversation, as if that is your role or responsibility, or otherwise what experts normally do to help others. Develop a high tolerance for silence, rather than speaking to reduce the tension that occurs during such periods, thereby creating enough space for her to take the lead when she eventually speaks up to break the silence.

11) Manage Your Emotional *Buttons*

Recognize and be mindful of your personal triggers for strong negative emotional reactions to others and the various feelings that you experience, such as anger, frustration, resentment, and anxiety/fear. Acknowledge the barriers to effectiveness that such emotional states have upon your closest relationships, including fatigue and burnout. Remember to act with emotional intelligence, not only recognizing your feelings and their impact upon others, but also being able to manage them better by staying focused upon the topic without personalizing it. Practice relaxation methods before and during difficult conversations in order to become more focused and present, thereby becoming less reactive, emotionally. Here are some key questions to ask yourself, and feedback to seek from your peers and supervisors for keeping track of your progress in managing emotional buttons:

- "How can I catch myself becoming upset and emotional earlier in the process when it's easier to regain my composure, recover, and become objective again?"
- "Is there a pattern of people, situations, and interactions that I should recognize in order to be better prepared for probable triggers that provoke me?"
- "How much more effective will I be with my staff and clients by making progress in this area (i.e., by being more objective, patient, and positively energized)?"
- "Who is a good role model for handling difficult people and situations without getting thrown off center, and how can I learn from her experience?"
- "What related performance improvement goals should I set for myself, and who will serve as a good accountability partner?"

Healthy Power—Prescriptions for Developing *Win-Win Relationships* as a Leader in the Workplace:

1) Enable each and every staff member to feel like a winner by catching her in the act of doing something of extra great value on behalf of the business, and then commemorate that incident with a written memo and/or certificate (suitable for framing) that is kept in her personnel file for reference during the next performance review process. If you cannot do this at least once for each person during the year, then you might have the wrong person in a position (or perhaps you need to adjust your managerial radar in order to notice more of the positives in performance).

2) In addition to developing individual performance goals for the upcoming 12-month review period, develop team-oriented goals for which the team enjoys a shared sense of pride and tangible rewards both for their attainment. Healthy internal competition is also part of this equation, as long as no *loser* is created in the process (i.e., establish tiered rewards for all, rather than a winner-takes-all, all-or-none outcome).

3) If a staff member becomes distracted or derailed by concern over what others are or might be doing, within or outside of the business, redirect her to focus exclusively on the duties of her position. Similarly, assist with making inner comparisons only (e.g., comparing her performance today with that of last month), rather than comparing herself with others.

4) Trust is gained with others when they recognize your competence and perceive your good character (i.e., your trustworthiness). Since trust is the key to making deeper connections with people, we must demonstrate trustworthiness in all that we do, especially when unwatched. Even the smallest things count, so make certain to keep your promises, tell only the truth, and remain vigilant in protecting other's rights and confidentiality. With trust, people take more risks, including opening up and sharing more personal information. Without their trust and deeper sharing, you will stay *in the dark* about the hidden keys to knowing and understanding them and, therefore, miss potential opportunities for building mutually empowering relationships.

5) Respect is earned with others when they experience your strength (e.g., courage, commitment, skills, intelligence, etc.) and understand the benevolent intent (i.e., *Win-Win*) you faithfully wield on their behalf, even when disciplining them. When combined, your strength and benevolent intentions meet the necessary but insufficient conditions alone for earning respect, as well as maintaining self-respect. Without healthy fear—whether from being too hard or too soft—respect from your staff will not be earned, rendering you relatively ineffective as a leader.

6) Recognize that your *Healthy Power* flows upward from your loyal,

committed people and then becomes *quid pro quo* (i.e., "this for that") in a servant leadership paradigm since you and your staff actually share power in alternating roles—at times leading them, at other times following their lead—toward common goals.

PEARLS OF HEALTHY POWER

Martin Luther King, Jr...

Returning violence for violence multiplies violence, adding deeper darkness to a night already devoid of stars. Darkness cannot drive out darkness; only light can do that. Hate cannot drive out hate: only love can do that.

Stephen R. Covey...

The highest forms of synergy focus the four unique human endowments, the motive of Win/Win, and the skills of empathic communication on the toughest challenges we face in life. What results is almost miraculous. We create new alternatives—something that wasn't there before.

Max Ehrmann (excerpts from his poem, *Desiderata*, 1927)...

As far as possible without surrender be on good terms with all persons. Speak your truth quietly and clearly; and listen to others, even to the dull and ignorant; they too have their story...Be yourself. Especially do not feign affection.

Euripides

But this is slavery, not to speak one's thought.

President Woodrow Wilson...

One cool judgment is worth a thousand hasty counsels. The thing to be supplied is light, not heat.

Author unknown...

This kind of intimate knowing doesn't happen by magic. Becoming that attuned to another requires an exquisite sensitivity that knows how to watch, to listen with both ears and heart, to develop trust. It requires a level of familiarity only possible through deep commitment to discovering what someone is all about and embracing what you find. It means responding to the other as he or she is, not as you'd like them to be.

Representative Sam Rayburn...

You'll never get mixed up if you simply tell the truth...You cannot be a leader, and ask other people to follow you, unless you know how to follow, too.

James 3: 4-5...

Look at the ships also; though they are so great and are driven by strong winds, they are guided by a very small rudder wherever the will of the pilot directs. So the tongue is a little member and boasts of great things. How great a forest is set ablaze by a small fire!

Kuan Chung...

When you sow a seed once, you will reap a single harvest. When you teach the people, you will reap a hundred harvests.

CHAPTER 4

E...*Energizing Joy* vs. *Egocentric Pleasure*

Light dawns for the righteous, and joy for the upright in heart.

Psalms 97: 11

ENERGIZING JOY AND HEALTHY POWER

In significant contrast to pleasure, joy always arises as a pure and uplifting emotion that originates from deep within, energizing us and liberating our spirit from an internal center of control. Deeply heartfelt and uniquely personal, it becomes something to develop as an integral means of bringing fulfillment and happiness to our lives through the virtue-laden and values-driven choices we make. Not only can joy become a regular, ongoing life-enhancing set of experiences we can control, it can invigorate our lives without the disempowering effects of external entrapment. Perhaps most importantly, according to Pema Chodron, we can enjoy an endless supply of joy for an entire lifetime, and without suffering any form of *hangover* (*Noble Heart*, Sounds True audio recording, 1998).

Numerous authors who've studied spirituality and fulfillment have reported that almost universally among people and across cultures, joyfulness is spontaneously derived from altruistic, other-directed, mission-focused service for causes greater than oneself that color our life with a deeper sense of meaning (e.g., Deepak Chopra, Wayne Dyer, Thich Nhat Hanh, John Izzo, Bill O'Hanlon, Rick Warren) Let's not confuse this with *Lose-Win*, self-defeating behavior, or martyrdom. Joyful sharing with others, rather, in most situations and settings is reciprocally contagious because it tends to spiral the lives of like-minded individuals upward. Striving to generate joy among those who understand and appreciate our pursuit of shared fulfillment and happiness most often prompts others to connect more deeply as kindred spirits, which perpetuates or at least sets the stage for even more joy by fostering positive personal/social connections.

While you will find further guidance near the end of this chapter, the pathway to joy is not easily found nor readily traversed, even with conscious, well-disciplined effort. But the challenge is certainly worthwhile since joy can be ongoing, even for a lifetime, and you face none of the withdrawal process or other risks to health and safety found in chemical or other forms of over-dependency/addiction. As M. Scott Peck described in *The Road Less Traveled* (1978), the joy producing personal journey toward spiritual development and the loving investment we make to assist others in their journey in a world filled with cynicism, violence, and accompanying misery are key aspects of our *Healthy Power*. I encourage you to study Peck's book to experience firsthand his masterful elaborations. I also strongly recommend his subsequent literary work, *People of the Lie* (1983), to consider the other side of this enigmatic coin, the subject of the next section.

EGOCENTRIC PLEASURE AND UNHEALTHY POWER

All the things I really like to do are either immoral, illegal, or fattening.

Alexander Woollcott

Whenever any of us becomes uncomfortable or unhappy, there is a natural tendency to look outside ourselves initially for increased comfort or at least temporary happiness. Who can argue with the logic of changing the room thermostat, shopping for a new dress when needed, or casually eating a hot fudge sundae...why not after all? However, this is one of the very most important and yet elusive areas for advancement in personal leadership effectiveness, because if we miss the mark in this area, we find ourselves at the fork leading to *Unhealthy Power* in a variety of its insidiously destructive forms.

The richly energizing pursuit of joy remains under-developed in us, if developed at all, largely because many of us neither consider nor comprehend the significant experiential differences between it and our sensual pleasures. Further, and unfortunately for far too many families, businesses, and other organized systems today, leaders who lack this differentiation tend not to develop a leadership style that evokes authentic joy. Moreover, they fail to mobilize the *Healthy Power* that spontaneously arises when people living or working together experience it. To find, for example, a place of employment where the climate among the workforce is truly joyful is the exception rather than the rule these days. Much more commonly, people describe where they work as places of misery, drudgery, and rampant mistrust born out of backbiting by co-workers and undermining by incompetent and/or unscrupulous authority figures. In fact, it has been this way for so long that many have simply come to believe much of the commonly expressed negativity to represent fundamental and indisputable truisms: "Another day in the salt mines;" "Why bother...nobody else cares...nothing ever changes around here;" "Life sucks...and then you die!"

Such toxic sentiments and related perceptions inevitably become embedded into the culture over water cooler gossip, during poorly led, endless meetings, and while commiserating over *Happy Hour*. Moreover, in the typical dynamic spawned in the workplace, some employees pursue predominantly self-serving forms of pleasure while also avoiding discomfort. Once a disgruntled worker is no longer aligned with the corporate mission, for example, she will often turn instinctively toward her own mission to enable her personal survival, even when it places her at odds with her employer and co-workers. This turn of events demonstrates the type of *Win-Lose Relationship* discussed in the previous chapter. Consequently, when she equates her job duties toward the larger mission for which she is employed with personal suffering, she sometimes begins to resent and resist her work, making for very long and tedious hours on the job if, in fact, she even shows up for work on any given day.

There is currently a widespread epidemic of people who are burned out and dispirited about both life and work. While the majority are not clinically depressed and will likely report feeling at least statistically *normal*, many indicate a kind of chronic malaise or dysphoria—a low-grade, general sense of negativity and overall discomfort—without either a clear explanation of their symptom etiology (origin or cause) or a pathway they believe will predictably lead them to meaningful or lasting symptom improvement. Not surprisingly, then, significant numbers of people attempt to right what is wrong in their lives through seriously counterproductive means. Such failures at self-empowerment now account for a large percentage of our spiraling health care costs stemming from poorly managed stress, health-endangering lifestyle habits in unsuccessful efforts to avoid or escape their distress (e.g., overeating; drug and alcohol abuse), and physical symptoms that directly or indirectly result from prolonged emotional distress (i.e., psychosomatic illnesses, such as high blood pressure, severe headaches, and peptic ulcers).

I believe it is a national tragedy that the potential economic engine that could spawn so much of our nation's recovery and its return to global prominence through increased productivity and financial solvency has too frequently become restless, bored, and under-stimulated in a compromised quality of life and work. Presenteeism and unresolved workplace stress-related illnesses have become commonplace, including in educational institutions and many of the traditionally noble non-profit organizations that once flourished because of their historic esprit de corps spawned by volunteerism. While certainly disappointing to witness, it should be no surprise to find many people across these and so many other settings foraging at every opportunity for external stimulation in all of its forms: surfing the Internet; engaging in juicy, inappropriate storytelling; abusing caffeine, nicotine, and junk foods; and, in more extreme instances, participating in one type or another of sexual harassment or white collar crime.

When the pursuit of pleasure in the workplace is overdone or misguided, and otherwise overshadows opportunities to generate joy, the workplace and its people become entrapped in ongoing, unsuccessful attempts to enjoy the *Unhealthy Power* they've found. Like with any addiction, these pursuits are ultimately disempowering because they redirect primary energies toward the self, looking for and acquiring doses of pleasure and/or pain avoidance at every opportunity, and yet never being satisfied more than briefly. The accompanying roller coaster of such emotional ups and downs usually creates a cadre of co-workers who share their unhappiness, and since *misery loves company*, they feel victimized, the latter stemming directly from the law of *Power = Responsibility* described in Chapter One. Externalizing *Responsibility* by looking outside ourselves for pleasure and pain relief naturally leads to an externalization of our *Power*, and when we are unhappy in this scenario, we will feel like a victim: suffering, unable to change things substantively, and not responsible for the sense of helplessness we find inescapable.

In view of these potentially unhealthy, even life threatening dynamics both in our work and personal life, let us examine the inherent differences between *pleasure* and *joy* and the lessons we can learn about developing truly great, empowered self-leadership and personal freedom, including the key implications for leading others in a manner that likewise empowers them.

Addictions vs. Freedom

At the third cup, wine drinks the man.

Hokekyo Sho

First, it is important to understand that the primordial nature of all living things, including human beings, is to be propelled by our own pursuit of pleasure and avoidance of pain in what is known as *hedonism*—the primitive instinct to follow our most basic appetitive and avoidant drives without regard for others or showing consideration beyond ourselves. Second, while pain can either originate from outside sources (e.g., when we're burned) or from inside our organs (e.g., when we are injured or ill), pleasure is most commonly triggered by outside stimuli. Impulses originating from people and things outside ourselves are perceived through the senses and then act as forces that switch on the brain's pleasure center. Healthy pleasures are certainly part of human experiences that season our lives and make them more worth living, such as the taste of a delicious home-cooked meal, the awe-inspiring vista of a Rocky Mountain landscape, the inviting sound of a babbling brook, or the uniquely special fragrance and romantic touch of our beloved partner.

However, this same basic process can also foster our dependency on any externally triggered pleasure. In doing so time after time, when we unwittingly shift our natural, internally based power toward an external locus of control, it can lead us progressively into dependency or even addiction, whether chemical or behavioral. Like so many things in life, we enjoy relatively good control within certain limits and boundaries, but we begin to sacrifice control the more those limits and boundaries are crossed.

Over-dependency and addiction are most often perpetuated through the defense mechanism of *denial*—the self-deception of believing what we need or want to believe in lieu of facts. It keeps us convinced that nothing else matters, that dangers are not real, that values and morals are irrelevant, even foolish, and should be changed or forgotten, and that negative, even fatal consequences will not happen. Ongoing denial of the risks and dangers associated with overly dependent or addictive behavior inclines us to fall prey to what Andrew Olendzki describes as the *hedonic treadmill* (*Unlimiting Mind*, 2010, page 6). Such behavior is most clearly evident when we strive relentlessly for *Egocentric Pleasure* while sacrificing people and things that were earlier priorities, including our own family, safety and health. When we ignore warning signs and the deterrents to continued dysfunctional behavior, it disempowers us because any form of deception, especially self-deception, erodes our *Healthy Power*. Individuals who unwittingly sacrifice real power for the illusion of control in an unending cycle of craving and compulsion get only temporary relief from their discomfort while inviting even more serious problems, because they have ignored or otherwise been unable to recognize the truths about misdirected or excessive pleasure-seeking behavior.

I'm reminded while writing this section of psychological studies that were conducted with rats in the 1970s to better understand how direct, self-induced stimulation of the pleasure center of the brain might affect behavior, making the assumption that any lessons learned from rats might be generalized to human behavior. I was an undergraduate Psychology student taking my first class in *Physiological Psychology*. The professor showed us photographs of laboratory rats in Skinner Boxes (after one of the key early founders of *Behaviorism*, B.F. Skinner). Early in the study, the seemingly healthy rats had discovered their own ability to produce micro-volts of electronic stimulation to the pleasure center by pressing a bar that would then send stimulating current through fine wires that had been surgically implanted into their brains. The tragic course of events was repeated time after time with these rats. In the beginning, the rats seemed to become enlivened with increased energy and activity, including their normal routines of feeding, drinking, and exercising, in addition to the deliberate pursuit of self-stimulating behavior. However, the study showed consistent changes in behavior in which the rats would spend progressively more time pressing the bar to induce apparent pleasure while spending proportionately less and less time in the other activities. This compromised their health as they became physically emaciated, sleep deprived, and lethargic. I especially remember the photographs at the final stages of this research process in which each rat had become solely focused upon pressing the bar for still another jolt of pleasure, lying almost dead upon the wire mesh floor of the box, trying desperately to reach the bar in weakness and exhaustion, usually as its last act of will before finally dying. This disturbing experience as a young student sufficiently frightened me to refrain completely from such comparable activities as snorting cocaine or smoking crack, which are similar examples of direct, self-induced stimulation of the brain's pleasure center, often with comparably devastating results. At the behavioral level, you might also recognize how sexual addiction, compulsive gambling, and workaholism take hold of people with promises of controlled pleasure as the smokescreen for the reality of disempowered living amidst great risks and dangers.

Lying to ourselves and others and similar deceptions are commonly prominent features of serious alcoholism, chemical dependencies, and behavioral (i.e., non-chemical) addictions (e.g., gambling; sex). Willingness to commit crimes with casual dispassion, including armed robbery and embezzlement, forgery and other fraud, prostitution, and illegal drug manufacturing/dealing (when doing so pre-addiction would have been unthinkable) showcases how *Unhealthy Power* can render our conscience ineffective. What transpires can be likened to a *Dr. Jekyll and Mr. Hyde* transformation and character regression in which anything goes in order to satisfy cravings for drugs, etc., or the money required expediently to support the addiction. A crack addict mother, for example, who would never have been a prostitute before becoming chemically dependent, might very well become a prostitute or even sell her young daughter to have sex with a pedophile once her reality is distorted enough to take hold and her body craves still more crack. Once her unselfish human values and morals are exchanged or forgotten in the compellingly animalistic drive toward *Egocentric Pleasure*, any concerns about her or her daughter's health and safety are seemingly ignored, squelched, or overruled—if she is even conscious of them at all—to pursue what she feels desperately compelled to do again, and again. It can be thought of as worshipping a sadistic god that requires everything, including human sacrifice, and no one, including the addict herself, will be spared. It is also analogous to the phenomenon of a black hole in space in that its gravitational pull is so great that not even light returns—relentlessly all-consuming but giving back nothing—cloaked invisibly in a shroud of indistinguishable darkness. In the world of alcoholism and drug abuse, this is commonly known as *a hole in the soul* in which addicts experience a seemingly endless pouring of the object of their hunger to fill it, but they never achieve a lasting sense of satisfaction or contentment.

This phenomenon is intricately linked to the worship of God or another higher power, as many of us in substantial recovery from addiction will often attest. Where once we might have revered God and made healthy spirituality central to our life, humbly surrendering our will to what we believed to be a divine will, God instead becomes supplanted through tunnel-vision and preoccupation with drugs, alcohol, or another addiction. After all, as an addict with denial fully engaged and the belief that we exercise complete free will and powerful self-control, why take the risk of trusting any higher power when we believe ourselves all knowing and all powerful? The tragic deception of the whole process is that the addict thinks and behaves in ways that show the awful truth: the addiction is in control, it has made its victim physically and/or psychologically dependent, and it has transformed the mind to believe the lies that keep an addict enslaved to it. Moreover, it is one of the most powerful forms of psychological entrapment a person can experience, robbing one of real power and freedom, mostly because the truth is so successfully masked.

Typically, some terrible but survivable crisis helps to break down an addict's denial so that the obscured truth can be unveiled and understood. This is where the addict hits bottom and has the best chance of breaking the pattern of addictive behaviors, because in manageable crisis, an addict is better able to see the truth of what has happened. Such a breakdown can serve as the breakthrough event permitting the addict, usually with help from others, to mobilize actual power to effect needed changes toward lasting recovery. Otherwise, if the addict simply uses more cocaine, for example, to escape suffering, the cycle of progressive addiction and disempowerment goes on, and another crisis will certainly follow, including undue risk of premature death.

Demonstrating a tragic case of hopelessness when denial no longer works, revealing unbearable truths, consider this newspaper clipping that was reportedly found with the body of a young woman who had committed suicide in North Carolina, and was then reprinted in the *North Carolina News Herald* on May 12, 1971:

> "King Heroin is my shepherd, I shall always want. He maketh me to lie down in the gutters. He leadeth me beside the troubled waters. He destroyeth my soul. He leadeth me in the paths of wickedness for the effort's sake. Yea, I shall walk through the valley of poverty and will fear all evil for thou, Heroin, art with me. Thy Needle and capsule try to comfort me. Thou strippest the table of groceries in the presence of my family. Thou robbest my head of reason. My cup of sorrow runneth over. Surely heroin addiction shall stalk me all the days of my life and I will dwell in the House of the Damned forever." (Author unknown, "The Psalm of the Addict,"*Congressional Record*, July 31, 1971, vol. 117, p. 28511)

Entrapment: *The Monkey and the Gourd*

A method used apparently for centuries by African tribesmen was to catch monkeys using a gourd as a lure and trap. A vegetable that grows like a squash, only larger, a gourd can be hollowed out to make bowls, drums, and traps. For this purpose, the hunters cut the gourd at its neck and then hollow it, leaving a hole just wide enough for a monkey to squeeze its extended and narrow hand down into the gourd. They then drop delicious food (according to monkey tastes) at the bottom of a host of gourd and place them at the base of a tree where the monkeys congregate in large numbers and nest at night. Of course, the monkeys scatter up the tree to escape capture while the traps are being laid beneath them.

Later, after the hunters are far removed from the tree, the curious monkeys descend to ground once more to explore the strange vessels and scavenge for the enticing food that apparently was left somewhere behind. Smelling the food that is close by, albeit still out of sight, they begin to get excited, searching faster to find the delectable morsels in the gourds, certainly not wanting to miss the upcoming feeding frenzy since the slow or meek among the group get no food! When one of the monkeys discovers its favorite food sitting irresistibly at the bottom of the gourd, it forces its eager hand into the opening until it can grasp it. However, it soon finds that it cannot take its hand back out of the gourd. When making a fist to retrieve the food, its clenched hand will not pass back through the neck. As long as it clings stubbornly to the food in its broad fist it is forced to carry the gourd everywhere it goes. When the hunters return, they easily spot the monkeys wearing gourds on one and sometimes both arms because they cannot climb the tree to safety. Also, with only one or neither hand free, they're more easily captured without being able to fight the hunters, who subsequently steal away with their prize. (As an aside, I've wondered since first hearing this story if a monkey making the rare decision to let go of the food or otherwise breaking free is the origin the expression we hear when people seem to be disturbingly out of control: "He's out of his gourd!")

This story about entrapping animals symbolizes some vitally important life lessons for us all as well:

1) To realize that very often we must let go of something we deem to be important in order to gain something even more important, just as the hungry monkey had to release its prized food in order to gain its freedom and to save its very life. In the same way, we must recognize the things to which we might be clinging willfully that keep us from being free to reach for something better, or to get back something that we have lost in the process of reaching for something new.

2) To remember that *cooler heads prevail* in a crisis. That is, the monkey became so nervous about being caught and/or losing its prize once in-hand that it couldn't see the solution at its very fingertips. Otherwise, it might have been willing to let go of the food in order to avoid capture. That panic, combined with a stubborn will and denial regarding consequences, likely resulted in either becoming dinner that night or being sold to spend its life within a zoo. An effective person makes good

decisions, especially when facing a crisis, because she does not let her feelings sabotage the logical reasoning that empowers her problem-solving skills.

3) To recognize that there are traps in our world everywhere. People who want to take control over others lay them carefully in order to acquire another's possessions, or even to take another's life. They mask such traps as benign and innocent, or even benevolent, much like the delicious food in the seemingly harmless gourds. *Hunters* across our globe (e.g., drug dealers; pimps; pedophiles) attempt to lure others by promising things will give pleasure, control, money, etc. However, after being entrapped in some manner, we quickly discover the painful truth that we have been tricked and deceived. Such facts of life occur in nature frequently without mercy. For example, the Venus Fly Trap lures any unsuspecting insect with its fragrant beauty and false promises of wholesome nectar awaiting it inside. But instead, once it has a hold upon its eager visitor, it envelops its prey and casts it downward where it finds only darkness, slow digestion, and death.

THE PATHWAY TO ENERGIZING JOY

Love and Joy

Love plays an instrumental role in the experience of joy, both the love of self and others. This, I suspect, will be confirmed at last by neuroscientific research when conclusive evidence indicates that joy emanates from the heart, along with supporting ideation and perceptions originating in the mind. Conversely, we experience pleasure through the mind's processing of external sensory signals (e.g., visual input) and/or stimulation from the mind itself (e.g., fantasies). In sharp contrast to the pathways followed in hedonism—the pursuit of pleasure and avoidance of pain while framing the self as the primary or even exclusive focus of attention—the experience of healthy self-love enables us to extend our benevolent intentions and good wishes toward others and for causes that take us beyond the confines of our personal boundaries. It represents an expansion of the focus of our life mission beyond the limits of our self, but also inclusive of the self, in the *Win-Win* relational fashion discussed in Chapter 3. And, it is only through a commitment to becoming loving and living with love externally directed that we become energized and liberated in ways that open the doors to joy. Examples would be: witnessing life renewed as a miracle at our newborn's safe delivery; sharing her wide-eyed glee when as a toddler she stands unassisted for first time; celebrating her high school graduation with anticipation as she begins the next chapter of her life's adventure; and taking keepsake photographs tearfully as she weds in blissful hope of her future dreams being fulfilled in lasting unity.

In this context, it might be helpful to conceive this overarching love as analogous to the *operating system* or platform that makes helpful *software* programs run. Specifically, let's consider the three primary drivers for human motivation and behavior identified by Daniel Pink in his book *Drive, The Surprising Truth About What Motivates Us* (2009) as the functional enactment of healthy self-love and its expression. Moreover, it is useful to recognize the author's assertion that we require a new operating system, *Motivation 3.0*, in order to understand what motivates people above and beyond the basic *carrots and sticks* (rewards and punishments) orientation and, thus, to experience joy in living and working:

> "Human beings have an innate inner drive to be autonomous, self-determined, and connected to one another. And when that drive is liberated, people achieve more and richer lives."
> (p. 73)

Let's begin this review of motivation in the context of what produces or expresses joy with *Autonomy*—living and working with freedom and self-direction. The work involved in true self-liberation first requires self-love. It can be likened to Covey's description of being *proactive* (as opposed to *reactive*) and to Chopra's description of being *self-referred* (as opposed to *object-referred*). Demonstrating healthy self-love in this regard moves us beyond mere hedonism where arrested or fixed development offers only the promise of the addictive pleasures described earlier. Again, we find the essence of *Healthy Power*, in this case *Energizing Joy*, emanating from an internal locus of control. Rather than becoming entrapped under the delusion that *more is better*, a person with authentic self-esteem commits to personal development and higher levels of maturation. To experience freedom, not just freedom of movement but the freeing of one's mind and spirit, is a tremendous source of joy. Moreover, healthy self-regard and the joy of attaining increasing liberation set the stage for the extension of our love toward others, which opens infinite possibilities for joy through the expression of such other-directed energy.

The second driver Pink identifies, *Mastery*—enjoying our own competence and control—can express still another facet of healthy self-love because it involves a commitment to the growth and development of our personal skills, without which mastery would not be possible. Not only does mastery produce joy as an intrinsic value once experienced, it further produces joy when we extend support and service to others. As such, we do not pursue mastery to inflate our ego or to showcase our greatness for others to see or evaluate, even though being paid to perform masterfully before a crowd can certainly be a viable career alternative. We understand it more aptly at higher levels of maturity as the blissful experience of free play into *flow* as Mihaly Csikszentmihalyi described based on his research in his book *Flow: The Psychology of Optimal Experience* (1990). Similarly, a person naturally experiences joy when spontaneously engaged in *Self 2* activities without self-consciousness or self-criticism, as described in the foreword to *The Inner Game of Tennis, Revised Edition*, by W. Timothy Gallwey (1997): "Self 2 is like an acorn that, when first discovered, seems quite small yet turns out to have the uncanny ability not only to become a magnificent tree but, if it has the right conditions, can generate an entire forest." However, we're all familiar with world-class entertainers and athletes, for example, who while famous and wealthy, do not experience joy when publicly performing or exhibiting their skills and often become entrenched in lifestyles limited to pleasurable self-indulgences (i.e., *living like a rock star*). Because the development of mastery when driven by love of self and others produces joy, it is highly motivating. But when the quest for mastery is driven by neurotic defensiveness (e.g., perfectionism), self-indulgent, grandiose wishes, or other efforts to bolster the ego it produces merely temporal pleasure and not joy. We again realize that joy is produced through masterful giving and sharing, which has the effect of empowering others and supporting missions beyond our self.

And that brings us to the third driver, *Purpose*—striving toward meaningful and fulfilling results for purpose(s) greater than our self. While this represents the final part of the acronym POWERFUL (i.e., *Lifelong Purpose* vs. *Lifelong Grasping*) and is explored more fully in a later chapter, I'll touch upon it briefly here in the context of the relationship between love and joy. It is well recognized from numerous studies that a commitment to the welfare of others with unconditional giving and sharing is almost universally a joy-producing experience. Finding and following the compelling urge to pursue our higher calling or *dharma* is one of Chopra's instructions for the fulfillment of our dreams in *The Seven Spiritual Laws of Success* (1994), and Wayne Dyer also prescribes that we attract and manifest our *future pull* in his 2009 movie, *The Shift*. Doing the right things for the right reasons with no strings attached, rather than the mutual back-scratching that typifies so much giving behavior, turns out to be its own reward and much greater than mere tangible rewards so commonly pursued. The love of self is the prerequisite for loving others, and it is a wholesome love in that it does not judge nor discriminate in its benevolent urgings. While not in the habit of making sacrifices toward depletion of self or otherwise acting in self-defeating ways, the altruistic person looks for opportunity to pay it forward with random acts of kindness, spontaneous giving and supporting, and otherwise strategic use of her resources and abilities that have the effect of creating a beautiful footprint and leaving an inspiring legacy.

Joy and Sorrow

Just as pain is the counterpart to pleasure, sorrow is the counterpart to joy. Similarly, just as pleasure and pain are two sides of hedonism, both joy and sorrow are two sides of love. Heartfelt sorrow regarding the self or others is based upon love that has been disappointed or thwarted. And while sorrow is unpleasant, it can be thought of as cutting a trough for future joy, and the deeper that trough is cut through sorrow, the deeper will be our capacity to hold and express love. Returning then to the idea held by many that all addictions can be traced to some form of trauma, abuse, or neglect that rips *a hole in the soul*, it is more aptly described as a tear in the heart and, therein, an assault on our ability to receive and express love. Accordingly, if we believe that love can mend the wounds and tears of the heart—rather than endlessly pursuing any object of addiction as if we have a hole waiting to be filled—then we arrive at this key question: "If love is the basis for all healing and joy, especially the healthy self-love that is the prerequisite for loving others altruistically, then how can we grow in our healthy self-love?" While this book is not dedicated primarily to that topic, since a partial answer to the question is certainly germane, we will cover it in the next section. Also see Appendix D: *Moral Code for Youth* (Collier's, *The National Weekly*, 1925) for a sample of the virtues once taught as a mainstay in American public education to help steer our youth along paths toward joy instead of sorrow.

Self-Love via Stillness: *The Roulette Wheel*

This is a metaphor for understanding activity versus stillness as it relates to finding restorative peace and rest. Picture in your mind how a roulette wheel is constructed. It usually looks like a large, fairly flat wooden bowl that has smooth inner surfaces, except for the notches cut out with accompanying numbers to identify winning and losing gamblers. The wheel spins on a central axis much like a lazy Susan holding condiments at mealtime rotates atop a kitchen table. At the start, a little ball is pitched along the top edge as the wheel is spun in an opposite direction. The centrifugal force on the ball while both it and the wheel are moving fast tends to keep it high on the wheel. Gradually, the ball begins its slow descent on the wheel as their shared speed and centrifugal force lessen. If it were not for the notches cut along the walls of the roulette wheel, bringing each spin to an exciting end, gravity would certainly continue to pull the ball downward until it would become completely still at the wheel's center, its deepest point, when movement ceases.

It's not a big leap to understand how this parallels our normal pursuit of peace and rest by slowing down or stopping all activity, such as when we take a break, relax mindlessly in front of the television, or take a beach vacation with minimal exertion. However, there is a catch. At the same time that we find potential escape and respite when making the journey inward, even connecting with our soul during meaningful periods of reflection, in that same space our problems, deeply seated issues, and unfinished business also reside. Some would say that we then have the opportunity to come face-to-face with and battle our *demons*, both old and new, and the victor has the opportunity to realize well earned serenity, and even joy. If, however, we have previously lost the battle or avoided it altogether out of fear or sometimes even terror, it seems only natural to resume our frenetic pace in order to stay one step ahead of what lies beneath.

This is known as encountering a *double-bind*—while there is no easy solution with either choice, still a choice must be made and each requires us to pay a toll. However, one choice is much more common than the other because, frankly, it's easier and seems for awhile to be adequately effective. Rather than doing the invariably challenging and arduous work of facing our innermost demons and resolving issues satisfactorily so we can find an inner place of sanctuary to achieve peace and rest (often requiring professional assistance and strenuous self-discipline), many people simply busy themselves on a treadmill of activities, day and night; they stay safely *high on the wheel*, just like the ball that is prevented from coming toward the wheel's center by centrifugal force. While it can be highly effective as defense mechanisms go, in the long run it is exhausting, poses a threat to both emotional and physical well-being, and frequently becomes an impediment to forming and maintaining intimate relationships.

Practically speaking, engaging in this type of defensive over-activity, such as workaholism and other compulsively driven behavior, also creates a serious barrier to good sleep hygiene, an important contributor to positive energies and overall wellness. Consider first that entering into healthy stages of sleep is only made possible when we lower our defensive shields, slowing both physical and mental activities, and then turning inward toward the depths of our unconscious mind. But this journey toward hoped-for pleasant dreams also brings us into to the same chamber where nightmares take place. Our otherwise restful, dreamy sleep is preempted by a deeper haunting that arises when we begin to feel unguarded and relaxed, often in the form of ruminating thoughts, fears, and imaginings that emerge eerily from deep within our psyche. And so begins the merciless torture of endless thinking and physical restlessness that prohibits us from falling and/or staying asleep. The age-old truth remains that we can run but cannot hide forever from the underlying unpleasant realities affecting our lives.

Chronic insomnia has become a widespread problem in American culture. I believe that a strong, significant contributing factor is an overreliance on activity—*spinning* incessantly through physical and cognitive over-activity—

as the preferred substitute for wrestling with our demons and achieving some form of resolution to our deeper problems. While the ideal answer, of course, would be to make peace with underlying issues and otherwise resolve seemingly insurmountable problems as much as possible, many people simply numb themselves with sleeping pills, prescription painkillers, illegal drugs, and alcohol in order to induce a kind of unconsciousness that mimics normal, restful sleep. Discovering that these are not, in fact, safe or effective solutions to sleep struggles, we ultimately, find revitalizing peace and rest only when we achieve harmony with our spirit and connect with it joyfully in repose within its sanctuary, the deepest part of our psyche. Since spinning expansively and finding peace inwardly are antithetical activities, it becomes clear that each of us must do this work as much and as often as necessary so that serenity and joy amidst stillness and peace can become our normal ways of living, rather than the exceptional states of the fortunate few.

Pleasure and Joy

Up to this point you may have gotten the mistaken impression that pleasure is somehow unwholesome and contrary to the enactment of *Healthy Power*, but that is certainly not what I wish to convey here. Instead, I believe that *Healthy Power* within this dimension ideally consists of a harmonious blend of pleasure and joy, and the key to achieving this harmony, as described throughout this chapter, is underpinned by love in all that we do. Rather than eagerly following the path toward *Egocentric Pleasure* in purely hedonistic fashion, we strive to attain the pinnacle of *Energizing Joy*. Nowhere is this more abundantly the case than when partners share romantic love, both emotionally and physically, as the embodiment of boundless intimacy. While it is commonly described as *making love*, it is more accurate to think of sexual intimacy as expressing love through shared physical pleasure and emotional connectedness. However, to go through the motions of sexual intimacy without a heartfelt connection of love becomes a mere pleasure seeking experience rather than one that produces joy. Remembering again that joy always emanates from love, both of self and others, we come to understand that the mutual sharing of pleasure through sexuality and its inherent intimacy characterize the zenith of our deepest loving relationships. If this were not the case, one could simply engage the services of a prostitute for sexual interaction in pursuit of joyful living, but this is certainly not normally the reported experience. Instead, purchasing services within the sex trade or otherwise seeking sex through one-night stands and the like involve what Russell Crowe depicting John Nash in the movie *A Beautiful Mind* (2001) asserted was simply the *exchange of bodily fluids*—an erotically pleasant but joyless event. Therefore, we give and receive pleasure in truly intimate connections not only for the mutual enjoyment of bodily sensations, but also to experience the joy of giving and receiving heartfelt love.

Healthy Sexual Behavior

While it would certainly be appropriate to offer suggestions for habits of moderation (rather than over-dependency or addiction) in numerous areas of pleasurable activity, I've limited the discussion here to sexual behavior both because of its power as a central driver among human beings and because of the immense potential it holds for producing joy between beloved partners. Therefore, these descriptions are intended to suggest what it means to develop the thoughts, feelings, and actions of healthy sexual behavior:

- *Monogamy*—This is the practice of remaining exclusive and faithful to our sexual, romantic partner. Sometimes referred to as *pair bonding* in the animal world, scientists have known for quite some time that people generally function better and lead more healthy and productive lives by forming harmonious, long-term monogamous relationships. It means that the couple lives as one unit without another person being permitted to violate the special bond that they have made to each other, including the sexual intimacy that defines that special bond between them. Note that polygamy is the practice of having multiple wives, which is illegal throughout most of the United States largely because the practice is not based on principles that support healthy closeness through equality of status.
- *Sensuality*—This is having the ability to accept and to enjoy our sexuality in every sense of the word, including bodily sensations, emotional longings and feelings, and shared romantic intimacy with another person. In order to find joy in these positive sensual

experiences, we must first appreciate our body, sexual identity, and feelings without shame, nervousness, or guilt. We are best able to do these things, and thus become free in the expression of our sexuality, once we have balanced our inner longings with the expectations, morals, and laws that govern society and culture. If we have desires/fantasies that represent unhealthy and/or illegal behavior (e.g., those experienced by pedophiles), the best solution is to accept that such feelings/desires exist, but commit to refraining from acting upon those impulses. By recognizing and including such unhealthy feelings/desires, rather than denying they exist, we gain better control over actual behavior and are more likely to enjoy the healthy fulfillment of our sensuality through other, more appropriate behavior.

- *Judgment and delayed gratification*—This is the practice of knowing the difference between what is appropriate and safe versus what is inappropriate and/or dangerous sexual behavior. People who exercise better controls over their impulses are those who understand and pay close attention to their sexual arousal via that which excites them. Since is it normal as human beings to lose sight of good judgment when highly sexually aroused, it is very important that we learn how to limit and to control the stimulation to which we are exposed through effective planning and limit-setting, also known as *stimulus control*. This is because people often make impulsive decisions during the heat of the moment (e.g., having unprotected sex, rather than waiting until a better, safer time). *Delayed gratification* refers to the process that we learn when we stop ourselves from acting on impulses, so that we exercise self-discipline and restraint, permitting our cooler head to prevail (i.e., logical thinking takes over instead of emotionality alone).

- *Freedom from compulsion*—This is the state of sexuality in which we both enjoy sexual behavior and maintain good controls over our actions at all times. It is the condition of allowing the free expression of sexuality within the boundaries of what we understand to be personally/socially appropriate and safe, including resolution in relation to any contrary opinions held by those within our family, culture, and society. It is a helpful strategy to understand and manage our relapse triggers—the people, places, and things associated with any problematic sexual impulses. It is also helpful for us to develop a state of mind in which we recognize the importance of moderation, judgment, and control, rather than overdependence and addiction. As such, any form of compulsive sexual acting out behavior is a sign that we have not yet achieved healthy sexual freedom. Once achieved, we become free to enjoy the entire physical, emotional, and spiritual fulfillment that healthy sexual relationships afford to each of us.

Healthy Power—Prescriptions for Developing *Energizing Joy* as a Leader in the Workplace:

1) Seek joy through inner transformation, relaxed self-mastery, and autonomous freedom. Minimize cravings for external pleasures and any accompanying self-deception, over-dependency, and addiction.

2) Practice being non-defensive with all others by developing realistic self-confidence and self-acceptance in order not to take things personally. Act as your own final judge, holding yourself wholly accountable for your choices with authenticity and public transparency. Model these traits with humility and grace, and coach others to do likewise to create a more joyful atmosphere.

3) Count your blessings with daily appreciation and a joyful focus, comparing yourself and your professional life situation with no one else. Failure to appreciate our blessings is the root of discontent, a sense of want, and painful envy. Instead, as much as possible, inspire others to focus upon and appreciate every aspect of each moment by being mindfully present at work with a positive, *glass half-full* outlook.

4) Dare to dream regarding your developing leadership role with zest and passion, a sense of adventure, and excitement

about embracing appropriate professional risks. Faith in your meaningful dreams generates hope contagiously throughout the enterprise, and hope provides you and your team with energy for striving more productively and with greater fulfillment during the journey toward goal attainment.

PEARLS OF HEALTHY POWER

Martin Luther King, Jr...

Occasionally in life there are those moments of unutterable fulfillment which cannot be completely explained by those symbols called words. Their meanings can only be articulated by the inaudible language of the heart.

Dianne Keaton as Annie Hall in the 1977 movie *Annie Hall*...

Sex without love is an empty experience! (Note Woody Allen's reply portraying her boyfriend, Alvy Singer: *Yes, but as far as empty experiences go, it's one of the best!*)

Jack Haley as The Tin Man in the 1939 movie *The Wizard of Oz*...

Oh joy, rapture...upon receiving his new heart, no longer hollow or empty, and no longer frozen in place developmentally... *Now I know I've got a heart, 'cause it's breaking*...the capacity for love opens the door also to the experience of sorrow.

Judy Garland as Dorothy Gale in the 1939 movie *The Wizard of Oz*...

There's no place like home...there's no place like home...through the heartfelt experience of appreciation and by taking personal responsibility she recognizes the power she had all along to fulfill her wish to return safely to her home and family.

Psalms 46: 10...

Be still and know that I am God.

Psalms 51: 10-12...

Create in me a clean heart, O God, and put a new and right spirit within me. Cast me not away from thy presence, and take not thy holy spirit from me. Restore to me the joy of thy salvation, and uphold me with a willing spirit.

Seneca…

Most powerful is he who has himself in his own power.

Benjamin Franklin…

Search others for their virtues, thyself for thy vices.

CHAPTER 5

R...*Reality-Based Choices* vs. *Regressive Choices*

*If you have built castles in the air, your work need not be lost; that
is where they should be. Now put the foundations under them.*

Henry David Thoreau

REALITY-BASED CHOICES AND HEALTHY POWER

Like all living creatures, we human beings at our most primitive depend upon
basic sensory input in order to know and navigate through our world. Visual
input, for example, provides data within our field of vision to recognize a
neutral object, a familiar friend, or on-coming traffic approaching from the
opposite lane, thus it guides us to make choices that support our survival.
Moreover, humans are capable of applying sophisticated cognitive mechanisms
for interpreting data, evaluating situations, and generating expectations for
the future, features that clearly set us apart from most if not all other sentient
creatures on our planet. For the most part, this ability to process sensory input
is highly adaptive, such as when one deduces after multiple episodes of the
same occurrence that an important pattern exists which may save one's life.
Accordingly, from an early age, we learn how to process sensory information
with an overlay of interpretations, evaluations, and perceptions that color our
world both functionally and aesthetically. In essence, through the advanced
workings of the human mind to interpret and create abstractions from raw
data, our perceptions eventually become our reality. And while some of

these mechanisms operate to our benefit through our conscious actions (e.g., stopping at a red light), the majority of them take place and serve our needs well at an unconscious level (e.g., subconsciously following one's intuition to slow down when driving through a patch of fog).

On the other hand, the way we add something to the raw input of our senses through these same cognitive workings of the mind can misinform us. Like Pavlov's dogs, which learned through classical conditioning to associate the ringing of a bell with the presentation of meat powder and then began to salivate simply when a bell rang as if meat powder were on the way, even the most intelligent of human beings is prone to making errors based upon conditioned biases, expectations, and other cognitive distortions. This chapter, then, considers *Healthy Power* associated with accurate discernment of reality and the choices that follow from more valid information, versus *Unhealthy Power*—choice making that stems from regressive, immature, and defensive mechanisms for filtering and processing the data input of one's life experience. *Healthy Power* within this dimension emerges primarily in recognition of the premise that *information is power*. Of course, the caveat for power to be healthy is that the information received and processed is objectively clear and accurate. That is, any processing and interpretation of data through the senses strengthens rather than distorts the information. A highly skillful person within this realm of power development makes decisions based upon unfiltered and unbiased discernment of facts, data, and perceptions of reality—an intact sense of *reality testing ability*. These cognitive skills, therefore, are not simply a natural byproduct of keen intelligence, at least not of intelligence in its traditional understanding. Instead, the powerful person making *Reality-Based Choices* has learned not only to limit the cognitive distortions that occur through emotionality, but also how and when to trust her intuitive judgment in addition to logical thinking in decision-making. This melding of logical reasoning with accurate discernment through the emotions to generate higher level reasoning, problem-solving ability, and interpersonal effectiveness has been amply described in works by Daniel Goleman, most especially his book, *Emotional Intelligence* (1995).

A more recent work by Daniel Kahneman, *Thinking, Fast and Slow* (2011), provides a comprehensive analysis of heuristics—the perceptual sets and modes of interpreting input from our senses that empower our thinking and decision-making, except for the times when they contribute to cognitive distortions, errors in judgment, and other forms of disempowered thought processes. We can conclude from his studies throughout a lengthy and successful career—including a Nobel Prize in Economics and being credited for launching the field of *Behavioral Economics*—that we do well to understand how our thought processes, biases, expectations, interpretations, and emotionality can lead us toward empowered or disempowered decisions and actions. This point becomes even more imperative when we consider that most of these processes occur unconsciously and operate beyond our conscious control. One such example is what he describes as "a bias of confidence over doubt" in which we lean toward reaching premature closure with faith in our thinking and conclusions, especially in ambiguously gray situations and where we perceive urgency about answering a question or solving a problem. And it is this bias toward arriving at conclusions prematurely that leads many of us to make important decisions confidently but erroneously.

Kahneman further asserts that melding a degree of motivated effort with restraint in our decision-making is a hallmark of people best suited to understanding information accurately and, thus, making more valid decisions in life and work:

> "Those who avoid the sin of intellectual sloth could be called 'engaged.' They are more alert, more intellectually active, less willing to be satisfied with superficially attractive answers, more skeptical about their intuitions." (p. 46)

A striking example of such an *engaged* individual was portrayed by Henry Fonda as the courageously lone dissenting juror in the film, *12 Angry Men* (1957, Metro-Goldwyn-Mayer and United Artists). The other 11 jurors were initially ready to deliver a *guilty* sentence without reservation or doubt for a teenage Puerto Rican boy on trial for the alleged stabbing death of his father, based on the evidence presented during the trial. However, Henry Fonda asserted that he could not reach the same conclusion beyond the shadow of a doubt, not because he necessarily believed in the accused boy's innocence, but because his understanding of the evidence presented was unclear and less than conclusive in his mind. And during the course of their heated emotional deliberations, he methodically exposed each of his fellow jurors' biases, prejudices, and tendency to jump to conclusions inappropriately with undue urgency and confidence. By the close of the film, each of the jurors had relented and reversed his vote so that all 12 of them agreed upon a *not guilty* verdict. Such is the power, the *Healthy Power*, of effective leadership and decision making based on dispassionate reasoning, fuller discernment of objective reality, and sound emotional self-regulation, including the ability to resist the tensions of ambiguity that tempt us to reach premature closure. Not only did Henry Fonda embody *Reality-Based Choices* individually, his steadfast commitment to doing the right thing, especially when it was initially so unpopular, had a transformational and positive ripple effect among his peers. As we know, speaking the truth when it is unpopular or even dangerous is one of the primary means that has changed the course of human history for the better, usually at a high cost. While commonly associated with the dynamics of addictions within families and systems, it also holds true more broadly that *what we do not confront we enable*. This kind of exceptional action to transform people and circumstances through appropriate and effective confrontation certainly requires both discernment and courage. Such action will be the primary focus of a later chapter: *Unrelenting Courage* versus *Unsettling Fear*.

The most salient feature of *Healthy Power* within this dimension, therefore, is our ability to perceive and understand *truth*. With accurate, uncensored, unfiltered, and unbiased discernment of sensory data, especially when paradoxical or contradictory, we experience undistorted perception of such input to best represent reality. Through the accurate discernment, understanding, and acceptance of any truth, even the most unpleasant of truths, we are liberated to make more confident, fact-based decisions grounded in reality and therefore more valid, empowering our decisions and choices to act.

Many modern day Buddhist scholars and teachers encourage recognition of the normal tendency to use the mind for *movie-making*—the *cinematography* of looking through psychologically colored and/or filtered lenses in ways that follow from our *Director* role rather than our role as receiver of objective reality through the senses alone. Once we call a tree a *tree*, for example, we trigger a cascade of thoughts and associations at deep levels that add something to the mere visual input signal we receive through the cornea. Remember that we first see the tree as a light image that is cast upon our retina, much like a camera receives light images upon film. The image is then converted automatically and transferred along the optic nerve to the occipital region of the brain, which receives and further processes it. This is where we develop our film, so to speak, and this is where the power of the mind to make sense of and possibly distort images also occurs. No longer a tree in the purest, preverbal sense within the mind's eye, it will be cast by the mind to play an expected role within our schema of the world and its associations to trees from our history.

Generally, this is a helpful process for making cognitive leaps that add to our powers of discernment; but sometimes we make judgments in error, basing them largely on our emotional states and how we're primed to experience biases in our perceptions (recall the power of *self-fulfilling prophecy* from Chapter 2). If we spy the tree at dusk with ambiguous images from afar— much like viewing an amorphous inkblot during a psychological test—and we're not certain what species of tree it might be, our hopes and fears can influence how we perceive the signal, especially if our feelings about the tree are intense for any reason. Accordingly, we'll be prone to seeing it as a cherry tree adorned with lovely pink blossoms if we're in a happy mood or feeling sensually romantic, and we're likely to add some red ripening cherries if we're hungry as well. If, however, we're feeling vulnerable and thus anxious, we'll be likely to perceive the very same tree as one that is perched to topple over and possibly destroy us, our loved ones, our property, etc., if we get too close, eliciting a very different set of emotional responses. If we're depressed, we'll be especially attuned to noticing dead branches where gypsy moths have created ominous webs we believe are killing the tree, thereby achieving a harmony between how we're feeling and how the world appears. Our feelings tend to influence our perceptions and vice versa: our perceptions tend to reinforce and validate how we feel, making the process of change often difficult until we become unstuck somehow. You can see in this example how our emotional states and biases even about things seemingly as innocuous as trees can affect both the sensorial input to our mind and how our mind processes that signal. More importantly, it is the same with the images we hold of people showing up along life's journey!

REGRESSIVE CHOICES AND UNHEALTHY POWER

> *For the great enemy of the truth is very often not the lie—deliberate,*
> *contrived, and dishonest—but the myth—persistent, persuasive, and unrealistic.*

President John F. Kennedy

Why should we care about such things as these machinations of the mind, and how do they affect one's personal power, well being, and intimate relationships with any significance? The answer: because our predominantly unconscious reliance upon movies of the mind to solve problems and otherwise improve our quality of life experiences and relationships inevitably results in suffering, sometimes with far-reaching devastation and despair.

Consider the experience of well-meaning religious leaders and missionaries throughout human history and the horrific acts of cruelty they enacted against the indigenous peoples of foreign lands once they determined that targeted populations needed to be saved spiritually because they were *savages*, *barbarians*, *witches*, or some other form of *sinner*. At least sometimes with zeal and even loving concern by the perpetrators many thousands of innocent people were tortured, drowned and burned at the stake during the Spanish Inquisition, intended to purge the lands of impurity and save souls rather than allow them to perish into damnation and everlasting hell. Acts of evil were promulgated as acts of benevolence, even holy and beyond reproach, because those with supreme power endorsed the ghastly script and its gruesome plot in quest of an imagined greater good. It is also probable that those who, in fact, were driven by evil hid their real motives under the guise of this same seemingly wholesome story line, much as wolves in sheep's clothing, and they enjoyed the fruits of *Unhealthy Power* (e.g., avarice and lust), accordingly. Whether by conscious design to enact evil or as the tragic by-product of misguided intentions based upon errant perceptions, the world has witnessed the destructive power of *Regressive Choices* throughout history.

More recently, but no less tragic in its scope of devastation, Native American Indians suffered oppression and genocide under the widely held belief in *Manifest Destiny*—the conviction that the United States of America was ordained by God to reach the shores of the Pacific as a holy and blessed nation, no matter who or what obstacle blocked that path—and that Native Americans were unsaved heathens destined to roam the Earth as people from ancient times, abandoned by God for their rebellion and sinfulness. Although early missionaries tried to convert and save them from their plight, large masses of them died when Europeans brought diseases for which the natives had no immunity. When it became too costly to wage conventional war against these peoples, the American government endorsed the mass slaughter of buffalo, not only to deny the Native Americans a primary source of food and materials for their sustenance, but also to eradicate their culture and way of life. Starved and demoralized people give up hope more quickly and thus are more easily subjugated, as history has repeatedly revealed. Relegated thereafter to a diminished status in life on government-established reservations, many did, in fact, give up hope. The wake of such dogmatic ideas, beliefs, and perceptions continues to overwhelm many descendants of that national movement, as evidenced by inordinate percentages of alcohol/drug abuse, domestic violence, and suicides among Native Americans today, long after the Indian Wars of the 18th and 19th centuries.

Another historical tragedy that persisted for many centuries—and its disempowering ripple effects endure in American society today—involved the capture and enslavement of millions of African natives to support European and later American commercial interests. The rampant commercialization of human beings and the widespread denigration of their personhood were fueled not only by greed and lust for control over other beings, but also by the widespread belief that they were subhuman and no more worthy of freedom and dignity than the beasts of burden that worked alongside them in the toils of unrewarded plantation labor. In sharp debate against the American abolitionists during the 19th century, sparked initially by Quakers in particular, pro-slavery politicians in the years leading up to the Civil War asserted that slaves were happier and enjoyed a standard of living far superior to that of their countrymen in Africa, referring to slavery as a *positive good*:

> "But let me not be understood as admitting, even by implication, that the existing relations between the two races in the slaveholding States is an evil—far otherwise; I hold it to be a good, as it has thus far proved itself to be to both, and will continue to prove so if not disturbed by the fell spirit of abolition. I appeal to facts. Never before has the black race of

Central Africa, from the dawn of history to the present day, attained a condition so civilized and so improved, not only physically, but morally and intellectually...But I take higher ground. I hold that in the present state of civilization, where two races of different origin, and distinguished by color, and other physical differences, as well as intellectual, are brought together, the relation now existing in the slaveholding States between the two, is, instead of an evil, a good—a positive good."

John C. Calhoun, February 6, 1837

While no one to my knowledge has ever provided a shred of scientific evidence to support the claims that enabled these movements of human suffering—although Social Darwinists certainly influenced many corroborating beliefs for a portion of these events—those wielding the tools of oppression and genocide acted none-the-less with righteous conviction and confident execution of power in performing their assigned duties. Such is the risk of empowered action by leaders when it is based upon errant perceptions and beliefs, especially when their authority is far-reaching and enduring. Much like their Native American counterparts, many African Americans since the era of slavery have continued to identify with the aggressor, at least unconsciously, and thus have internalized second class standing and self-loathing, not infrequently to their self-destruction. Is it surprising then to find the disproportionately high representation of black males within the American prison system today when we consider the enduring toxic ripple effect of *Unhealthy Power*, in this case racial prejudice, as a multi-generational projection process?

In your own life, perhaps you've *directed a movie* with a frightening story line when a loved one did not arrive home as scheduled. Before she finally came home safely, you had imagined her terrible capture, unfortunate imprisonment, untimely death or other fantasy that was painted on the canvas of ambiguity by your worst fears for her. Upon seeing her safely on your doorstep once more, you probably realized how profoundly you had invented the drama based solely on your fears and fantasies, and that you had suffered needlessly (at which point you felt compelled to scold her for putting you through the agony, of course). It serves us well to learn the methods of recognizing and curtailing any such movie-making since it provides premature closure without solid grounding and thereby stirs strife among those cast to play their part in the script (e.g., your accused wife replies indignantly, "How could you possibly have thought that I would betray you by spending time with my ex-husband?").

Let us also recognize that *Unhealthy Power* via *Regressive Choices* always seeks to perpetuate itself through deception and misuse of information with others. We empower people to make changes when facts replace distortions of truth and myths. However, any form of falsehood—lies, distortions, propaganda—is the currency through which immature and/or aberrant persons often acquire and expand their base of power by influencing decisions through misinformation, so they can manipulate, ensnare, and control others for personal gain.

Per Mark Weber: "Although German historian Helmut Heiber paints a highly critical and generally unflattering portrait in his biography, *Goebbels* (New York: Hawthorn, 1972), at the same time, he acknowledges Goebbels' talents and strengths. He notes:

> "(Goebbels) was able, until the very last minute, to encourage and exploit a blind trust in Hitler and his genius. It is indeed one of the macabre phenomena of the Third Reich that even in their country's agony the mass of the German people remained docile and faithful to Hitler's banner...In spite of everything they had experienced, they kept the faith." (p. 133)

I would be remiss, however, if I omitted discussion of circular causality in the enactment of *Unhealthy Power* in this context. It is too easy to identify ourselves as victims of those who orchestrate conscious evil and to take no responsibility for the adverse consequences we suffer in the process. It is relatively easy to combat the forces of evil when their destructive actions are recognized in the clear light of day: we are awakened to the problem, and people of integrity and courage always answer the call to fight against obvious wrongdoing, such as the oppression and persecution of others. However, the most insidious evil throughout history has recurrently succeeded by cloaking itself under veils of benevolence and goodwill, thereby engendering popular trust and support, sometimes taking advantage of naiveté even on a national scale. Evil masquerading as good preys upon the human tendency to judge books by their cover, especially when they evoke positive identification with seemingly admirable people doing great things—often our heroes for a time. Once we commit to our perceptions of people and their activities and become comfortably wedded to them, we risk developing blind spots. It is in our periods of relative blindness that we inadvertently give license to individuals and systems to wreak havoc upon others and our environment. Whether we consider the aberrant behavior of priests and decades of enabling by the Roman Catholic Church or the predatory behavior of a football coach who was revered by a nationwide throng of diehard fans until the truth of child sexual abuse and its cover-up emerged in scandal, loyal followers of such institutions continue their support for a time while being covertly deceived. Frequently described as being *surreal* (i.e., dreamlike and unreal, as in a nightmare) when the truth of well hidden misdeeds finally comes to light, we can appreciate how unthinkable and thus unreasonable the obscured truth had remained to so many onlookers until they could no longer deny it. And while we should fault these institutions and their leadership for orchestrating such evil and/ or its cover-up, I contend that each of us is responsible for maintaining healthy vigilance over our beliefs and loyalties. Criminals usually thrive on opportunity, drawn toward areas of darkness in order to act with impunity in the greatest secrecy, but without such opportunities, their goals would be denied or minimized. Later in this chapter, we'll consider the primary means each of us can use to develop healthy vigilance by making more accurate perceptions and forming more valid beliefs that lead to well-grounded loyalties for truly *Healthy Power*. I will present information there about three keys on the pathway toward making *Reality-Based Choices*: Humility, Mindfulness, and Emotion Management—Anger.

Developmental Considerations

We tend to have great difficulty *keeping the jury out*, in general, and especially during times of intense emotional upheaval. Whether we're fearful or excited, we tend to fill in the blanks with expectations, and then react to our expectations as if they represent future reality, including feelings that suit the impending scenario. This certainly accounts for the shock and displeasure we witness or experience ourselves when things don't happen the way they *should*. Moreover, the greater we rely upon such movie-making to manage stress, the more likely we are to suffer when actual events do not fit our expectations. While flexibility is a key feature of *Healthy Power* in terms of making predictions—humbly allowing for the prospect of being wrong in our expectations and making adjustments accordingly when needed—problems emerge to the degree that we become rigidly fixed in our design of things to come. We make a kind of ego investment in our commitment to the future and are both surprised and frustrated when the world behaves differently. This involves in many ways a degree of *magical thinking*—the child-like and regressive tendency to believe what we need or want to believe, selectively ignoring facts or other information that would contradict our thought process. This form of thinking is frequently accompanied by hubris, especially arrogance about our power to predict and control life events, and the more we demonstrate such hubris, the more god-like we seem to ourselves. When we engage in magical thinking, we are not only prone to inevitable suffering when life throws us a curve ball against our expectations, but also those who sense a degree of gullibility and feed our errant expectations with exactly what we hope to hear disempower us, akin to *The Emperor's New Clothes*. One of the most notable examples from history is the shock and dismay Adolf Hitler expressed when during the 1936 Olympic Games in Berlin black American Jesse Owens won four gold medals, eroding support for his theory of Aryan supremacy. Not able to adjust his belief systems, even in the face of overwhelming evidence to the contrary, Hitler went on to build the Third Reich on a global scale based on faulty ideas regarding superiority/inferiority among races and cultures. The ripple effect of his misguided but popular belief systems enabled the Nazi party to orchestrate the Holocaust and the eventual destruction of Germany itself.

At a more conventional level, people who tend to make choices based upon incomplete and/or inaccurate data suffer the painful, energy wasting consequences of rework and repair after lesser quality decisions have been made. Relatively ineffective people too frequently deny and/or avoid the truth out of fear, insecurity, or simply a lack of resilience—the ability to rebound from a setback after finding that a mistake has been made—which, ironically, contributes to making more mistakes.

A reasonable question then is this: "How is it that even the most intelligent of people sometimes make bad, even fatal decisions through their inability to perceive reality and truth accurately?" In the majority of cases, we do not find the answer by attributing psychiatric disorders or mental challenges to such individuals. Instead, their disempowerment can best be understood as being the byproduct of developmental immaturity and/or regressive ways of navigating through their life experiences. But what is the origin of such developmental arrest and/or regression when gross errors of judgment and aberrant behavior occur throughout adulthood?

The answer lies in early childhood and the development of a cohesive and realistic sense of self. No child receives perfect parenting. A minority of children receives great parenting, most receive good enough parenting, and far too many receive parenting that involves some tragic combination of abuse and/or neglect. The vulnerable child is fairly fragile, and she must learn to defend her ego in order to feel secure in her world as a good-enough self. Accordingly, she will develop one or more forms of defense mechanism (e.g., denial; avoidance; minimization) when such is required to protect her immature, vulnerable core. By continuing to use defense mechanisms, while they may help her adapt to a world filled with threats to her emotional well-being, requires her to pay a very heavy price. The toll she pays for defending against reality through comforting distortions of truth is the disempowerment that follows from not being fully connected with reality, including especially what is realistically true about her strengths and weaknesses.

Another aspect of *Unhealthy Power* through *Regressive Choices* is the tendency to amplify and perpetuate weaknesses in others, compelling them to feel vulnerable and become defensive. We disempower others to the degree that we provoke their need to make use of their ego defenses. Any time that we are being shielded from reality and truth, we have substituted comfort for actual power, amounting to a *house of cards* at the mercy of the wind. Consider *grandiosity* as a defense mechanism in which the person develops an inflated sense of self with exaggerated ideas about her strengths and capabilities in order to protect her from an underlying sense of inadequacy and vulnerability, which have been instilled through repeated psychological and/or physical abuse. While we can have compassion and readily understand her need for such grandiose defenses in order to protect her from the lies inherent in her mistreatment, we should also have compassion for her disempowerment to the degree that her defensive strategy is also built on false information and lies. And we are well grounded in our concern that her interpersonal relationships will be fraught with difficulty if she interacts in a manner that hides what she believes is the underlying truth about her inadequacies—such as when she behaves with her loved one as if she is superior and in control of the other. Of course, she is blind to the fact that her defenses skew the truth and that she is, in reality, disempowered in the process. She cannot afford to recognize that she does, in fact, live in a house of cards, although unconsciously this truth haunts and frightens her. The tragedy of *Unhealthy Power* in this respect is that distortions of truth perpetuated in public most often distort the truth for the person as well—our blind spots keep us in the dark where *ignorance is bliss.*

THE PATHWAY TO REALITY-BASED CHOICES

> *Men and women are not prisoners of fate, but*
> *only prisoners of their own minds.*
>
> Franklin D. Roosevelt

Now I will present three components of *Healthy Power* that help us find and follow the pathway that strengthens our ability to make *Reality-Based Choices*: Humility, Mindfulness, and Emotion Management, the latter with a particular focus on managing anger.

Humility

> *Humility is the blossom of which death to self is the perfect fruit.*
>
> Andrew Murray

Throughout my career, I've often heard the following types of questions: "What is the essential foundation of mental health and wellness?" "How is it that some people are better than others at being resilient with the ability to bounce back from tragedy?" "Why is it that I struggle so hard to make changes in my life?" While these certainly are complex questions with a wide array of possible answers, there is one element that rises far above the others as an overarching theme: the *Healthy Power* that is inherent in *Humility.*

Humility is the quality of being modest and unassuming, which first requires that we become conscious of our defects, short-comings, and weaknesses. However, it also requires us to become attuned to the truths about our most prominent strengths. Moreover, it means being objective and realistic when assessing these things, neither under- nor over-estimating them. While it is relatively easy to be clear internally about our qualities, it is hard not to exaggerate them in order to bolster our self-esteem and/or to aggrandize ourselves in the eyes of others, often not even recognizing the arrogance into which we've slipped. Because it is even more difficult for us to recognize our flaws and vulnerabilities, we tend to overlook or minimize their presence in our thoughts and actions. At other times, if we overstate them in our mind, we create unhelpful barriers to success that are not only self-imposed, but also self-reinforcing each time we live down to our own deflated expectations. Therefore, it is a hallmark of emotional maturity to develop humility since it requires sufficient core strength to be able to accept any unflattering or disturbing self truths that apply while also appreciating our reservoir of actual strengths accurately so we can fully and skillfully recognize them. We remain deceived, thus immature and disempowered, to the extent that we are not accurately attuned to the truths of our very nature, for better or worse. Therefore, *know thyself* and *to thine own self be true* are not merely trite phrases but wise instruction on the pathway toward humility.

As stated earlier, understanding and acceptance of any truth empowers us with objective data we can use to set goals, form strategies, and otherwise to make our best choices. Humility, therefore, enables us to become more empowered as we mature to greater awareness of truths about ourselves and our life circumstances. As we become more self-aware, we become more humble. That is, we know ourselves inside out, so that there is progressively less self-deception. Just as *truth* nourishes the root of self-empowerment, *deception* lies at the root of our disempowerment.

One of the most important lessons we have learned from people who have struggled with drug/alcohol and other addictions is that treatment often does not work, or work for very long, unless the person is totally committed to making a lasting recovery. The most successful programs, including the *Twelve Step* programs and *Alcoholics Anonymous*, have relied heavily upon the spiritual aspect of the first step: to admit that their drug/alcohol or other behavior of abuse has become progressively beyond their control, and to recognize that their faith in a *Higher Power* is the key to making a successful recovery, *one day at a time.*

It is clear that people across the globe benefit in many ways by developing a personal faith in someone or something greater than themselves. When we make a meaningful connection somehow with our Higher Power, we frequently discover that we can function in a healthier manner, find peace, and have a reliable way of satisfying our emotional dependency needs. It also has become clear that humility—the realistic acceptance of one's strengths and weaknesses without arrogance or bitterness—is the cornerstone for developing a close bond with one's Higher Power. Otherwise, the person prone to addictions runs the very great risk of choosing unhealthy behaviors and forming habits that only mask those dependency needs, causing the habit to grow into addiction, loss of control, and eventual destruction or death. When we can accept our normal human needs without shame or pride getting in the way, then we can ask for help. When our acceptance frees us to let go of the need to over-control things, we can direct our attention and efforts toward those things we can control and, therefore, become more successful. This maturing, spiritual process reduces the risk that we will come to depend on anything unhealthy in our pursuit of security and joy.

The Serenity Prayer has been a mainstay credo for participants in *Alcoholics Anonymous* because it represents the role of humility in retaking control of life amidst the cruel deception and entrapment of addiction; but it is equally applicable to us all:

> *God grant me the serenity to accept the things I cannot change; courage to change the things I can; and wisdom to know the difference.*

> Reinhold Niebuhr

Serenity is the quality of living with tranquility, peace, and security. The above prayer contains the prescription for serenity through truthful recognition of what we can and cannot change, which comes with wisdom over time and maturing life experience. The humble person knows realistically both her limitations and potential for success, including the likely result of any choice that is made. Such a person is more prone, therefore, to choose wisely, whether it pertains to diet, exercise, risk-taking, or any other facet of lifestyle.

Informed, wise choices promote quality of life through health promotion in mind, body, and spirit. The humble person learns to trust herself in this world and to thrive, not because the world is always predictable or safe, but because she knows how to make choices that are based upon truths about how to best navigate within the world.

When we are inflated, humility has the paradoxical feature of first making us feel small, as if shrinking in power and strength; but it enables us to grow authentic, core strength from more accurate self-awareness and the empowerment that truth affords us. A helpful metaphor in this regard is what I call the *Balloon and the BB*. At a glance, an inflated balloon appears to have substantial mass and even significance; however, the more it is inflated the more vulnerable it becomes, such as when it is dropped on a cactus. Then we quickly discover in its explosive deflation that it was hollow, lacking real substance, and frail, in spite of its appearance. By contrast, consider the small brass BB cradled in the palm of your hand which from afar might seem like nothing at all. And yet, it remains whole and intact when dropped on the same cactus since it has concentrated mass and durability. Such is the nature of authentic humility: we become strong and durable based upon core substance and resilience, without primary concern for appearances. Self-esteem melded with humility fosters reality-based self-confidence. Let us humbly seek such wisdom and truth about ourselves in pursuit of serenity, resilience, and the well-being that follows from authenticity.

Mindfulness: A Doorway to Reality

We don't see things as they are, we see them as we are.

Anais Nin

By way of introduction, here are selected quotes from the chapter entitled *Mindfulness: What Is It? Where Does It Come From?* by Ronald D. Siegel, Psy.D., Christopher K. Germer, Ph.D., and Andrew Olendzki in *Clinical Handbook of Mindfulness* (2008):

> "Mindfulness is ultimately part of a project designed to uproot entrenched habits of mind that cause unhappiness, such as the afflictive emotions of anger, envy, or greed, or

behaviors that harm ourselves and others…Mindfulness involves being present to our lives…Because we practice noticing the contents of the mind, we come to notice our emotions more fully and vividly. Our ability to recognize how we feel increases as we relinquish normal defenses, such as distracting ourselves from discomfort with entertainment or eating…Regardless of the chosen object of attention, we practice being aware of our present experience with acceptance." (pp. 4-10)

Fundamentally, mindfulness involves developing present-minded awareness and concentration, attunement to sensory input, and expanded recognition of our mental activities, all of which are refined through a variety of meditation practices available to any lay person. While there is certainly a place for remembering and enjoying past experiences, and dreaming of future plans with positive expectancy, the premise of mindfulness is that we attain our highest quality of living when we maximize our time spent in present moment awareness. Too many of us escape the present moment or otherwise rob ourselves of richer life experience when we dedicate our cognitive *bandwidth* to past and/or future contemplations. This constitutes a kind of tumbling forward through life as if the present were expendable in pursuit of a preferred or dreaded future, or otherwise looking backward to fond or unpleasant memories to reminisce or obsess about past events. In either case, the immediate life experience becomes diluted with our shift in temporal focus, and it is this mental distractibility (i.e., mindlessness) that lessens the fullness with which we live our lives and connect with people and things. Moreover, the assertion is made that with increased mindfulness we function more optimally and powerfully with freedom from distraction in each present moment. Hearkening back to the premise that information is power, we can see that the practices of mindfulness maximize the information available to us from external sources at any given moment, which makes it a source of psychological empowerment. Our focus on any such information can be either purposely narrow or quite broad, the latter known as *open field awareness*, depending upon the goal and method of mindfulness meditation we use. While this certainly contradicts popular contemporary notions that encourage multi-tasking, the truth remains that the mind is maximally effective and efficient when it maintains a singular focus, although it is capable of handling multiple simple tasks in combination. For a rich examination of these concepts and their application for daily living, I strongly recommend reading *The Power of Now: A Guide to Spiritual Enlightenment* (2004) by Eckhart Tolle.

The burgeoning interest in mindfulness today represents a convergence of Western psychological principles and ancient Buddhist concepts from approximately 2,500 years ago. One of the most compelling of these concepts is the differentiation between pain and suffering. When you stub your toe, for example, a signal from the injury site goes to the area of the brain that triggers the subjective experience of pain; and Buddhists describe this event metaphorically as being *shot with the first arrow*. It's what we do following this primary pain signal that determines whether or not or how much we suffer, such as generating thoughts like: "Oh my God, I broke my toe, this is awful, who left their toy on the floor where I walk, and how could she/I be so stupid!?" While pain in life is certainly inevitable, suffering is largely optional since our self-talk and resistance to the initial event comprise the *second arrow* with which we also shoot ourselves. In fact, studies of people engaged in mindfulness meditation who are subjected to a painful stimulus— mild electric shock—report that while they are more attuned to the pain signal (i.e., the first arrow), they endure little or no suffering—the second arrow—to the degree that they accept the pain and offer no resistance to the event. By sharp contrast, those who received the same electric shock without any mindfulness training reacted with conventional resistance to the event and suffered significantly more than the first group. Another underlying premise that comes into play here is that *what we resist persists*. Therefore, it is paradoxically true that our acceptance of external negative stimuli enables us to maintain a stronger internal locus of control and, thus, maximum personal power in the face of adversity. By contrast, when we react instinctively to pain, difficulty, setback, etc., we give our power to the person or situation that originated it, thereby missing the opportunity to generate core strength for growth and change. Therefore, embrace any situation, not evaluating and labeling events as *good* or *bad*, with the same general sense of acceptance that enables more clear-headed responses and rational next steps. Buddhists refer to this as developing *equanimity*: the process of open-minded and open-hearted awareness that leads to the dispassionate acceptance of life's events as they appear at our doorstep. Practicing mindfulness with equanimity maximizes our power to accept, change, or otherwise manage even the most challenging life situations through the process of making *Reality-Based Choices*.

Another key Buddhist concept for this discussion is the myth of *permanence*—our longing for good things to come and stay and our fear that bad things will come and never leave—representing another primary source of human suffering since it denies the underlying truth of universal *impermanence*. Our ability to treat all people and things with equanimity is one of the keys to emotional well-being and the prevention of suffering. We suffer when we attempt to cling to positive life experiences when, in fact, all things are in a constant state of flux and eventually pass away, including each living thing. Similarly, we suffer when we resist those life experiences we've judged to be unpleasant, unfair, or otherwise unwanted. This is not to suggest that we should expect to feel good about illness, death, or loss, but instead that we do our best to accept rather than resist these pain-inducing experiences, thereby escaping—or at least reducing—the second arrow of suffering.

Finally, the practice of mindfulness is not intended simply to be a timeout from life during which we sit on a cushion with our eyes closed or gaze placidly while poised solemnly like a Buddha. Instead, there are multiple practices and forms of meditation that enable virtually any person to incorporate mindfulness into daily life meaningfully, such as while walking, driving, bathing, and cooking. Moreover, it is insufficient to describe these practices simply as methods through which a person might become more present-minded, focused, and aware because there is a qualitative aspect to these aspirations: that we live our lives interdependently with tenderhearted compassion, benevolent intention, and skillful actions that support all living things and our planet. Not to be misunderstood as a moralistic or evangelical pursuit, mindfulness practices are intended to improve the quality of life for each living thing residing within our interdependent world. Accordingly, each practice is undergirded by an aspiration that we all experience rich and full lives free of suffering and through meaningful immersion in *Win-Win Relationships*.

Rather than viewing each person as a separate self, inevitably propelling individuals to defend their ego in what amounts to win-lose behavior...

ultimately wars, Buddhist contemplatives over the past 2,500 years continue to teach us that our individual identities—complex schemata that support conventional functioning—are merely constructions of our mind based upon the evolutionary need to protect ourselves within a harsh and perilous world. When we enjoy the luxuries of safety and security enough to lower our defensive shields (as in mindfulness meditation) and realize that the boundaries that maintain our sense of separateness are also constructions of the mind to further substantiate and protect the ego, then we awaken to this mind-boggling reality. In truth, we are as interconnected with everything in our world, including every animate and inanimate thing, as electrons and protons with differing charges interconnect to comprise each atom, which is further connected with every other atom, and so on. In spite of our well conditioned ideas and experiences that suggest otherwise, the truth remains that we are all connected in this world in vast fields of energy—as well as to everything extending beyond our planet in the cosmos—as modern-day physicists are concluding. We do well, therefore, to develop virtues of patience, compassion, and benevolence with skillfulness in serving as each other's keeper since it is the most basic way we experience joy and prevent suffering. To do otherwise is to fall prey to the primordial regressive leanings of the ego that drive us to protect and perpetuate our DNA in competition with others, both literally and figuratively—a return to the *survival of the fittest* paradigm discussed in Chapter 3. We find the overarching value of mindfulness, therefore, through practices that reveal these fundamental truths and wisdom regarding life and death, pain and suffering, permanence versus impermanence, present-mindedness versus distraction and depletion, equanimity versus clinging and rejecting, and compassionate interdependence versus ego-driven isolation, competition, and violence.

Emotion Management: Anger

No one can make you feel inferior without your consent.

Eleanor Roosevelt

Reality-Based Choices are more likely to be recognized and implemented when we manage our emotions well, as suggested earlier. However, intense feelings, both positive and negative, can overwhelm good judgment and logical reasoning, thereby spawning what Daniel Goleman calls an *emotional hijacking.* Therefore, developing the skills of effective emotion management is essential to keeping us connected with reality and, therefore, empowered to be more rational and sensible.

In *Emotional Intelligence* (page 43) he describes:

1) Emotional self-awareness—*Knowing one's emotions*
2) Emotional self-regulation—*Managing emotions*
3) Emotional self-control—*Motivating oneself*
4) Empathy—*Recognizing emotions in others*
5) Managing emotions in others—*Handling relationships*

An exhaustive review of management strategies for a range of negative emotions, such as anxiety, self-doubt, and guilt, and would be beyond the scope of this book, and since anger tends to be so pervasively debilitating to our perceptual and reasoning skills, I have included it to illustrate a concept.

Now, I invite you to consider valuable ways to look at anger and how to manage it. Viewing anger as a source of fuel you can harness, you should understand anger not only as a problem when poorly controlled, but also as a resource when well managed. With this in mind, please consider the following concepts as the foundation for the rest of this section:

- Anger is the normal feeling that people experience when they are frustrated, hurt, or disappointed.
- Sometimes anger is the healthy reaction to things that are wrong, providing a person with energy to make a change or to solve a problem.
- Like many things, anger becomes a problem when it leads a person to make poor choices, such as becoming violent, seeking unhealthy revenge, and acting before thinking about consequences.
- Anger usually is a reaction to tension, which often drives people to misbehave when they try to reduce their tension in the wrong manner, such as by hitting someone who has upset them.
- There are many helpful ways to manage anger, and practicing those usually leads to the development of better control over it, even its constructive usage, just like any other skill for living.

The *Fight or Flight Response*

Human beings are built to react to danger and other stressful situations with one of two basic instincts: fight or flight. These actions are normal urges we feel when frustrated, scared, hurt, or angry. It means that we are first driven by impulses that tell us to attack the source of our problem (fight) or to escape from it (flight); however, we also have other choices. For example, we do not have to fight, even when under attack, although it is very hard to resist our basic instincts. Also, we do not have to flee, even when we are scared, although it is very hard to face things that frighten us. To summarize: the *fight or flight* instinct is a natural but primitive pull toward an external focus amidst distress or perceived threat, whereas the state of *flow* is a higher order self-management process in which we retain maximum power from the inside out by remaining poised.

The main points here are: 1) We have basic instincts that tend to cause us to react in certain ways when we are threatened or otherwise become upset—to fight or flee; 2) although it takes more effort and practice, we can learn additional ways of responding to stressful situations, rather than simply reacting to them as if programmed like a computer; and 3) most important here is to recognize the difference between reacting (instinct) and responding (making a choice), so that we demonstrate the best possible control over our impulses during difficult times. In this regard, Andrew Olendzki asserts:

> "Freedom means being able to choose how we respond to things. When wisdom is not well developed, it can be easily circumvented by the provocations of others. In such cases we might as well be animals or robots. If there is no space between an insulting stimulus and its immediate conditioned response—anger—then we are in fact under the control of others. Mindfulness opens up such a space, and when wisdom is there to fill it one is capable of responding with forbearance. It's not that anger is repressed; anger never arises in the first place." (p. 101)

Sources of Anger

It's important to understand and recognize some of the most common experiences that lead people to feel angry so we can avoid those experiences whenever possible and practice good emotional self-regulation when we cannot. Consider also how each precursor to anger can be linked to failures in the mature development of *humility*:

- *Frustration*—not having our way by being blocked and stalled from doing what we intend to do
- *Irritation*—feeling provoked by a person or situation that is prompting us to become agitated
- *Disappointment*—not having our desired and expected outcome, especially after we've had hope about it
- *Pain and/or suffering*—experiencing pain resulting from injury or illness (the *first arrow*) and the subjective experience of suffering (the *second arrow*), the latter leading to anger, which serves to cover our painful feelings temporarily, but interferes with the actual healing process
- *Loss*—losing someone or something personally important, leading to anger to cover the actual pain and hurt that lies beneath it (i.e., anger anesthetizes emotional hurt but never heals it)
- *Attack or threat to self*—experiencing physical or emotional assault—being threatened in some important way—provoking us to defend ourselves and/or to make a counter-attack
- *Control*—feeling that we've lost self-control or control over another person or thing, especially when we believe that the person or thing should fall under our control

Skills for Managing Anger

The following coping skills can help us become more effective in preventing anger or bringing it under more effective control—even to become an asset—when it does arise. Consider also how each of these strategies can be traced back to the discussion regarding *mindfulness*:

- *Avoiding*

    This is the skill of avoiding those people or situations that tend to upset us, rather than enduring provocation or returning to the trap of becoming upset still again. Not to be confused with cowardice or dereliction of one's duty, this involves restraint and prudent judgment to find right actions.

- *Diffusing*

    Counting to 10, taking a few deep breaths, or walking away to collect our thoughts in the context of the much larger picture when getting angry are a few examples of diffusing anger instead of blowing up. It's akin to adding fresh water to soup when too much salt is ruining the taste, or removing logs from a fire in order to extinguish it.

- *Reframing*

    Like putting a new frame around a painting to make it look better, this involves viewing a person or situation we find to be upsetting in another light. Still the same person or situation, but she or it looks more positive within a new *frame*—from a new perspective (e.g., a misfortune becomes recognized as a *blessing in disguise*).

- *Tension Reducing*

    Calming others when they are angry, rather than joining them, can also reduce our tension and anger. On the other hand, maintaining just the right amount of tension, including our own, sometimes is necessary to support peace among people—another *Goldilocks* phenomenon—per Ray Naar, Ph.D.

- *Channeling*

    When we find that something is wrong or unfair, we do well to channel and direct our anger into problem solving or other efforts to make changes—harnessing our feelings and empowering our actions but not losing control irresponsibly because of them.

- *Expressing*

    It is tension-reducing to *let off steam* by talking with others or by venting negative thoughts and feelings through writing, drawing, and other expressive art forms, rather than allowing toxic material to fester and produce inward and/or outward damage.

- *Empathic Understanding*

  Taking the time to get all of the facts and working to best understand another person with whom we are angry is far better than *flying off the handle* through misunderstanding, so we aspire to look at things fully from the other person's point of view with empathy.

- *Foreseeing*

  Thinking about probable consequences, not merely the need to reduce immediate tension—recall *hedonism*—helps to determine our better choices when upset because too often we can lose sight of tomorrow when thinking only about today's emotionality.

- *Forbearing*

  This is the skill of patiently tolerating and enduring, rather than resisting, some form of hardship, such as illness, time delays, and other life challenges, including death—recall the *Serenity Prayer*.

- *Forgiving*

  The most precious skill in this area is the virtue of forgiving ourselves and others when something has gone wrong, rather than bemoaning mistakes made, staying angry, holding a grudge, or seeking revenge. Limitless compassion for self and others is a hallmark of enlightenment and, therefore, a key to personal power.

Healthy Power—Prescriptions for Developing *Reality-Based Choices* as a Leader in the Workplace:

1) Study and develop your *Emotional Intelligence* (Daniel Goleman, 1995) in order to reduce or eliminate any emotional hijacking that triggers you to become blind to what is factual and real. Recognize your leadership buttons that when pushed tend to render you less discerning and poised, and then practice the skills that will disable those buttons (e.g., refrain from making impulsive decisions; ask for help from trusted peers; embrace all truths as dispassionately as possible).

2) Keep the jury out when you hear reports of interpersonal strife and conflict in the office. That is, give the benefit of the doubt regarding any negative report you hear about a person, including

peers, administration, customers, vendors, competitors, etc. Reserve judgment until all of the required facts are understood, thereby restraining the urge to reach closure prematurely, especially under the strain of intense feelings, such as anger/frustration, eagerness, and worry.

3) Allow your more rational thinking and behavior under pressure to flow into edifying calm and personal poise. Show others how to let cooler heads prevail amidst the chaos through your silence and dispassionate reflection whenever necessary.

4) Let your word be your bond. Always mean what you say and say what you mean. Without exception, demonstrate an unwavering commitment to truthfulness through your honesty, transparency, and authenticity, thereby prompting people to listen to what you say with validated trust and confidence. Your impeccable honesty engenders trust, and trust produces followership and loyalty—basic sources of power for any leader. Maintain confidences, keep your promises, take responsibility when appropriate, and apologize when you're mistaken. Follow these prescriptions faithfully and your staff will more reliably make *Reality-Based Choices*, too.

PEARLS OF HEALTHY POWER

Stephen Covey…

If the only vision we have of ourselves comes from the social mirror—from the current social paradigm and from the opinions, perceptions, and paradigms of the people around us—our view of ourselves is like the reflection in the crazy mirror room at the carnival.

Demosthenes…

Nothing is easier than self-deceit. For what each man wishes, that he also believes to be true.

Bill O'Hanlon…

This is different from positive thinking, in that it acknowledges problems and barriers to change at the same time as it acknowledges possibilities for change. If you don't do both, you risk getting stuck in negative, bitter thinking or getting caught unawares when unrealistic, pie-in-the-sky plans go wrong.

Job 28: 28...

And he said to man, 'Behold, the fear of the Lord, that is wisdom; and to depart from evil is understanding.

Polonius (in Shakespeare's *Hamlet*, inspired by Socrates)...

This above all: to thine own self be true, and it must follow, as the night the day, thou canst not then be false to any man.

Tao Te Ching...

Knowing others is intelligence; knowing yourself is true wisdom. Mastering others is strength; mastering yourself is true power.

Eckhart Tolle...

When you are seemingly diminished in some way and remain in absolute nonreaction, not just externally but also internally, you realize that nothing real has been diminished, that through becoming 'less,' you become more.

Carl Jung...

Everything that irritates us about others can lead us to an understanding of ourselves.

Shunryu Suzuki...

In the beginner's mind there are many possibilities; in the expert's mind there are few.

Ronald Siegel...

Mindfulness is not a path to perfection, but a path to wholeness.

CHAPTER 6

F...*Focused Action* vs. *Fragmented Activity*

The greatest need we have in this whitewater world, this permanent whitewater world, is something that does not change...a changeless core.

Stephen Covey

FOCUSED ACTION AND HEALTHY POWER

Hindsight being 20/20, I became painfully aware as an adult that I had been an academic underachiever throughout my early schooling, not because I was lazy, but because I struggled to sustain enough focus and attention. This compromised my educational achievement particularly in reading since I found it extremely difficult to maintain steady focus without becoming either anxious or bored. In fact, these limitations of mine at that time not only made it difficult to excel at a level that would be commensurate with my intelligence, it came to represent a plaguing source of self-criticism, which further interfered with my school performance.

At the same time that I struggled academically and could not understand why I was underachieving—especially knowing that I was highly motivated and putting forth what I thought were my best efforts—I sat in awe of my fellow students who seemed to be able to apply their keen intelligence almost effortlessly toward superior achievement, making it look not only easy, but also fun. And since then, I continue to envy individuals who demonstrate career and life management skills seemingly effortlessly while bearing good fruits. Although I've made great strides in this regard—for instance, enabling me to achieve the focus and sustained attention required to write this book—I recognize my own upside potential to become more powerfully effective through *Focused Action*.

Friend and colleague John Pinto shared some brilliant pearls in a conversation this past year, likening the power generated through *Focused Action* to pressing the sharp point of an awl or ice pick into a plasterboard wall, making a deep, penetrating impact quite effectively. By contrast, he described the relatively futile effort to make a hole in the wall by pressing the palm of the hand onto the same spot. The laws of physics tell us that when we concentrate the point of the awl with maximized pressure into a narrower, precise focal area—in contrast to the broader surface being pressed by the hand—we generate increased force that breaks through the wall. He drew a parallel to what is required to become most successful in any pursuit: making a penetrating impact toward breakthrough. Thus, this chapter will focus on personal and organizational leadership behavior that drives positive growth and change through strategically focused, concentrated effort by individuals and/or teams—*Focused Action*.

It was an inspiring act of powerfully focused leadership heroism when Chesley Burnett "Sully" Sullenberger, III saved the lives of all 155 people on board US Airways Flight 1549 on January 15, 2009 by successfully ditching the aircraft in the Hudson River off Manhattan, New York City. The entire nation seemed to find it inconceivable that a pilot in that emergent situation, facing such incredibly poor odds while bearing almost unimaginable responsibility, could have maintained such focus and poise that he could achieve the impossible. Speaking afterward with news anchor Katie Couric about how he prepared over many years for such an event and his exceptional performance, Sullenberger said:

> "One way of looking at this might be that for 42 years, I've been making small, regular deposits in this bank of experience: education and training. And on January 15 the balance was sufficient so that I could make a very large withdrawal." (Newcott, Bill, May–June 2009, "Wisdom of the Elders", *AARP Magazine*: 52)

So, what are the primary characteristics and skills of those of us who demonstrate inordinate feats and accomplishments through *Focused Action*?

The following represents a short list of these key features (you'll find details for their enactment later in this chapter):

- Determining our own priorities with autonomy and confidence
- Visualizing desired outcomes and results at the onset of goal-setting
- Translating broad, abstract goals into short-term practical steps and tactics that support the accomplishment of long-term goals
- Managing our self—rather than our time—with strong self-discipline and ongoing motivation in the face of competing priorities and unplanned events
- Attaining laser-like focus with freedom from distraction, derailment, or discouragement—avoiding *Fragmented Activity*
- Sustaining concentrated attention in support of prioritized goals with perseverance leading ultimately to successful goal attainment

Focus: Viewing the World from Three Facets

In order to understand how focus contributes to *Healthy Power*—and later in this chapter how fragmentation contributes to *Unhealthy Power*—we must first recognize the three key components that comprise focus: *Selection*; *Concentration*, and *Perspective*. Because each is a facet through which we can view the larger jewel, we will describe them briefly.

Selection refers to those people/things toward which we direct our attention. Moreover, it describes what we focus on internally (including thoughts, visualizations, and feelings), as well as externally. Selecting the object(s) of our focus is at best a conscious act of intention while keeping in mind all available options. It is widely recognized that because *what we focus on tends to expand*, careful and positive selection tends to empower our thoughts, feelings, and actions. Maintaining a clear sense of responsibility for making wise choices under our own power is inherent in the process, as opposed to being scattered and without focus, or otherwise allowing our attention to be redirected by other people and/or external forces.

Concentration can be best understood as maintaining an intentional and refined focus free of distraction—like a LASER, in contrast to diffuse light.

This is certainly integral to coaching children to "keep your eye on the ball." Choosing the ball to focus on in the first place is, in this case, the object of *Selection*. The coach instructs the child further to sustain that focus by completing the task—the bat making solid contact with the ball through good *Concentration*. People who can sustain good attention while engaged in healthy pursuits enjoy the power associated with pure and efficient effort over time—hitting streaks in baseball, and, more importantly, in their lives. And this is especially relevant for those tasks and emotional challenges that require perseverance of high-quality effort, such as earning a college degree, building quality relationships with one's children, and enjoying a successful, harmonious marriage.

Perspective as a component of focus involves the lenses and filters through which we view things. In this regard, focus refers not so much to the object of attention or the ability to sustain attention to it, but to the attitudes and perspectives that affect our subjective experience of what is in view. Hearkening back to the discussion of mindfulness in the last chapter, recall *moviemaking* as an overlay to the raw sensory data processed within the mind. *Healthy Power* in this regard involves a minimum of unhelpful cinematography. Although this certainly overlaps with the coverage in Chapter 2 of optimism, self-fulfilling prophecy, and pessimism, I've reintroduced it here to help understand focus more fully as it relates to taking empowered, effective action. The following section, on the other hand, addresses the role of *Perspective* in *Fragmented Activity*—which undermines our effectiveness.

FRAGMENTED ACTIVITY AND UNHEALTHY POWER

And then one day you find ten years have got behind you.
No one told you when to run, you missed the starting gun.

Pink Floyd

At the other fork in the road within this dimension of personal power are the disturbances of focus that cause *Fragmented Activity*. In this regard, such fragmentation disempowers us whether it is the result of our own missteps and failings or as the adverse consequence of our actions—or inaction—upon others.

In sharp contrast to *Focused Action*, *Fragmented Activity* is characterized by the following deficiencies, lack of skills, and poor choices:

- Failing to identify our priorities, and then allowing others or circumstances to define them, resulting in a lack of committed effort
- Failing to visualize desired outcomes and results at the onset of goal-setting, or visualizing them either with unfounded confidence or with pessimism and doubt
- Failing to identify the short-term practical steps and tactics that will support progress toward broader long-term goals
- Failing to manage ourselves with strong self-discipline and ongoing motivation in the face of competing priorities and unplanned events
- Failure to maintain laser-like focus with freedom from distraction, derailment, or discouragement—falling prey to *Fragmented Activity* by being scattered, inefficient, and ineffective (e.g., procrastinating)
- Failure to sustain attention in support of prioritized goals with the perseverance required for eventual goal attainment

How, then, does a person become so fragmented and thereby disempowered? There is a wide variety of contributing factors, but only one fundamental answer: the failure to develop and utilize an internal locus of control. When we operate predominantly from an internal center of control, we follow naturally helpful processes in *Selection*, *Concentration*, and *Perspective* regarding our focus. That is, we focus primarily on the top priorities we've identified, we sustain our good attention on them, and we view them through helpful lenses that inspire our action steps and energize our perseverance, the combination of which supports our goal attainment.

However, how much we become fragmented depends on whether we operate from an external locus of control regarding our focus. In their book, *First Things First* (1994), Stephen Covey, A. Roger Merrill, and Rebecca R. Merrill differentiate self-management from time management, using a time management quadrant to identify behaviors associated with personal effectiveness. They distinguish *urgent* tasks against those that are *important*.

An urgent task cries out for attention, often driving people to shift their focus, even drop what they're doing, feeling compelled to act. In contrast, they define important tasks as those high leverage activities for which there is a strong probability of return on investment—achieving goals related to our primary mission. And while it is often the case that urgent tasks calling for our attention and action are also important—often described in the workplace as *putting out fires*—the challenge is to apply judgment and self-discipline to resist "urgencies" that are of lesser importance and frequently not important whatsoever (e.g., opening the mail; answering the phone; accommodating the request from a co-worker, "Do you have a minute?").

When we operate from an internal locus of control to manage our focus and related action steps, we apply positive tunnel vision and remain steadfastly undeterred and uninterrupted. However, many people suffer from what the authors describe as an inability to resist the pull of compelling but relatively unimportant forces: "Urgency addiction is a self-destructive behavior that temporarily fills the void created by unmet needs." (p. 35) Not surprisingly, a person who falls prey to this phenomenon will stay busy, often working very hard, only to express frustration and dismay at the end of the day exclaiming, "I was really busy today, but I got nothing done!" Such expressions reveal a lack of personal power through *Fragmented Activity*, and the most common of these failings that undermines productivity and blocks success is procrastination.

Procrastination: *The Monster in the Closet*

Each of us can probably relate well to this phenomenon: we have a major project of great importance that needs to be accomplished in the midst of a busy life and a schedule filled with routine activities and short-term demands. Sometimes described as a *gorilla project*, we recognize that it will require substantial attention over time, usually requiring focused and sustained effort to meet the challenges of completing it. We surmise, then, that it will be difficult not only because of the task itself, but also because we just can't seem to find the time to embrace it and get started. After all, we're already busy taking care of daily necessities that seemingly cannot wait. I describe such a gorilla project as the *Monster in the Closet* because it takes on a life of its own and evokes fear that needs to be contained.

Given the opportunity to delay getting started, we find it stress-relieving to corral the monster into a closet and then lock the door, so to speak, where *out of sight is out of mind.* Avoidance and denial become successful defense mechanisms, enabling us to go about our business under the illusion we're exercising good control over our to-do list. However, there is a catch—a governing principle—to this metaphoric story: *the monster feeds on our inattention,* thus the longer it remains tucked away and neglected in the closet, the larger and more powerful it becomes.

Initially haunted by this at an unconscious level, we're able to avoid and deny the monster for a while. But in our moments of reckoning, such as while daydreaming or attempting to fall asleep at night, we hear the monster scratching at the door, craving our attention, and becoming larger and more frightening with each passing day. As the deadline to complete the project looms near, or otherwise we will face serious consequences, we realize we must face the monster in spite of our now habitual pattern to avoid and delay action. The prescription I routinely recommend in such cases where a fully fed monster has been created and is haunting my client is this: *muster the courage to open the closet door and hug your monster,* remembering that it fed on inattention and that by paying it attention it begins to shrink in size. How many of us has had this experience of finally accepting the reality that *Focused Action* toward our task must begin—albeit with dread—only to discover that it wasn't so bad after all once we made a commitment to tackle it? We do, in fact, make *mountains out of molehills* that generate self-induced stress and compromise our performance. Given that courage is a critical feature of applying this strategy, without which people never open the door, it deserves more thorough examination, which you'll find in the next chapter.

Blind Spots: Too Little or Too Much Focus

So far in this discussion, we've made the point that an intensification of focus is positively self-empowering, and that a scattered or fragmented approach to viewing tasks leads to poor execution. And while both points are generally valid, more needs to be said about adjusting our focus to meet the demands of variable tasks.

One of the common problems people face when they become too intently focused is that their field of vision becomes obscured to additional information on the periphery, when sometimes that peripheral information holds the key to solving problems and completing tasks successfully. Daniel Kahneman asserts, "Intense focusing on a task can make people effectively blind, even to stimuli that normally attract attention." (p. 23)

On the other hand, sometimes we demonstrate the opposite problem: we remain so globally focused on the big picture that we fail to refine our focus on details and tasks that support better problem-solving and goal attainment. Similarly, in discussing the power of focus upon our thoughts to bias how we see personal life events in an amplified manner, either positively or negatively, Kahneman asserts:

> "Any aspect of life to which attention is directed will loom large in a global evaluation. This is the essence of the *focusing illusion*, which can be described in a single sentence: nothing in life is as important as you think it is when you are thinking about it." (p. 402)

Whether it's not seeing the forest for the trees or not seeing the trees for the forest, the blind spots we experience through either too narrow or too broad of a focus impede our personal power and effectiveness. Therefore, flexibility and skill in focus management are keys to self-empowerment... more to follow.

External Manipulation of Our Focus

It's not paranoia but a mere fact of life that there are those of us who make it our business to influence and attempt to control others, usually for commercial or political gain, by manipulating one or more facets of our focus. To illustrate this, I'll discuss some of the strategies and tactics that gambling casinos use—legally legitimate business enterprises—to amplify these points. However, I invite you to consider much broader applications of these insights beyond the gaming industries.

In the area of *Selection*, casino patrons immediately become immersed in carefully staged environmental stimuli once they enter the building in a cacophony of sights and sounds that are all intended to define your focus, hold your attention, and draw you ever closer to behaviors leading you to gamble your money. For example, the architectural design and decor omit key aspects of reality. No clocks exist, nor are there any windows revealing natural light, making it more difficult to remain oriented to the reality of your normal routine and lifestyle. Amid such information deprivation and sensory overstimulation, a fragmented focus makes it easier to behave mindlessly, such as when gamblers remain engaged in risk-taking activities much longer than they had intended. Similarly, our focus on reality is diluted through the mechanisms of payoff in the slot machines. Instead of hard coin as payment—like the silver dollars that once clinked as they dropped noticeably into the receiving tray—the gambler receives numeric *credits* while flashing lights go off and a sound effect suggests that coins are actually dropping into an invisible trough. The machine reports a *win* when, in fact, the credits awarded are often less than the wager. There's something very different about printing out a bland ticket with a number of credits compared to holding cash in our hand. This *Monopoly money* phenomenon contributes to us viewing our activity as something less serious than actually gambling with personal funds (e.g., "I'm playing with the house's money!"). Even more subliminally, it enables us to enjoy the illusory experience of wielding power without incurring responsibility, playing to the child-like desires, magical thinking, and *Regressive Choices* described in previous chapters.

Consider also the strategic effort applied by casinos to disperse the gambler's attention knowing that a gambler who maintains a strong, reality-based focus through the lens of objective truth will use better judgment and restraint than one who is essentially gullible. And they capitalize on such gullibility with practices like deploying young, scantily dressed cocktail servers to encourage you to further disperse your focus by consuming alcohol—which further weakens your self-discipline and usual restraint. Because *Concentration* normally favors the gambler, a debilitating tactic casinos use is to make it as difficult as possible to concentrate. Regarding *Selection*, casino operators want you to focus with tunnel vision on their gambling activities, but with as little conscious awareness and concentrated reasoning as possible. Since increasing profits is the primary objective—and rightly so—it's better for business when visitors become disarmed and more cooperative.

Regarding *Perspective*, the gambler is subtly invited to see everything through the lens of highly energized and positive activity: optimism is bred, winners are highly rewarded, hedonistic pleasures abound, alcohol and avarice are publicly promoted (while covertly amplifying their disempowering effects), and seriously negative consequences never happen—after all, *what happens in Vegas stays in Vegas!* The dynamics that foster addiction operate in full swing, including a *variable ratio schedule of reinforcement*—randomized numbers of slot machine "pulls" or button presses between pay-outs—well recognized as a potent means to drive repeated behavior in spite of lapses and losses of money in the interim. The gambler is led unwittingly down a path of unreality which fosters defense mechanisms of denial and false optimism that tend to replace rational judgment and sound decision-making.

Lastly, there are cognitive phenomena described by Daniel Kahneman operating primarily at an unconscious level that further deepen the entrapment being orchestrated. These include illusions of control, overconfidence in predictive abilities, and emergence of the *sunk-cost fallacy*. The sunk-cost fallacy is still another driver contributing to compulsive gambling. It occurs when we experience a losing streak and recognize logically that it's time to go home; but our logic is over-ruled by our compelling emotional drive to recover our losses—it's just unacceptable to do otherwise. Fully engaged in denial, overly confident, and committed to our own fabricated story of redemption—at least to break even—we pour even more money into these high risk activities knowing full well that the statistical probability of making profit through gambling always favors the house, especially the longer we play.

You might say, therefore, that a prudent, discerning person will exercise countermeasures when entering the casino, even if choosing to gamble at all, and you would be right. Any of us with an active and disciplined mind will approach gambling with our eyes wide open to the potential manipulations we face upon entering the casino door and consciously exercise self-control by following strategies that can mitigate potential losses: determining ahead of time our spending budget for this activity; framing our outing as entertainment rather than an income earning activity; paying faithful attention to the time; bringing along one or more mature friends as accountability partners; refraining from drinking alcohol; and determining a precise exit strategy regarding our funds in play—the upper and lower limits at which we will cash out—no matter what.

Borrowing some hard lessons from our discussion of the dynamics of gambling casinos and their attempts to manipulate the focus of their patrons that are simply part of the game, we all do well to give up the naïve notion that such forces are not also in operation while watching television commercials, hearing political speeches, and considering the counsel of "expert" financial advisors. Many enjoy the *voluntary suspension of disbelief* that we experience while watching feats of magic and shows involving illusion that hold us spellbound, but in the real world people are using comparable smoke and mirrors, distractions, and storytelling to attempt to take advantage of us through the *Fragmented Activity* they strive to produce in their target audiences.

THE PATHWAY TO FOCUSED ACTION

When you change the way you look at things, the things you look at change.

Wayne Dyer

Continuing now with Covey's recommendations from *First Things First*, personal effectiveness follows from an active, ongoing process of judgment and decision-making regarding the relative importance and urgency of tasks. It is a high leverage activity that supports our effectiveness to say "No" to those tasks that are either urgent but not important, or neither urgent nor important. Moreover, the most successful people are not only effective in handling urgent tasks of truly great importance—putting out fires adroitly— they invest the time and energy required to prevent fires in the first place. This translates into carving out time for strategic analysis and creative problem-solving—important but not urgent activities—in order to strengthen our core as an individual and/or system.

Applied to our livelihood, especially as an organizational leader, consistently demonstrating self-mastery of focus is contagious: its ripple effect supports positive alignment of effort among others and stimulates their results-oriented behavior. High-performance teamwork follows from leadership that consistently drives intensely concentrated, focused behavior toward a prescribed set of clearly defined priorities. In doing so, the leader differentiates tasks that are most important, both urgently so and otherwise, from those that should receive little or no attention. Since, per Covey, it is a *True North Principle* that what we focus upon tends to expand, it becomes critical in all forms of leadership that we select and maintain the most appropriate and important focus day to day, both individually and collectively. What, then, will expand is the developing nucleus of effort needed to make the penetrating impact required for goal attainment and breakthrough success—working more like an *awl* than the *palm of the hand*.

Jim Collins in *Good to Great* (2001) has written about the research based paradigm he uncovered for building and maintaining business greatness through the identification of one's empowering strategic focus: *The Hedgehog Concept*—borrowing terminology from Isaiah Berlin's essay on Tolstoy, *The Hedgehog and the Fox*—which he described as follows:

> "More precisely, a Hedgehog Concept is a simple, crystalline concept that flows from deep understanding about the intersection of the following three circles: 1) What you can be the best in the world at (and, equally important, what you cannot be the best in the world at); 2) What drives your economic engine; and 3) What you are deeply passionate about." (pp. 95-96)

He contends that people and businesses tend to lose their greatness and sometimes fail when they act *foxy*, allowing themselves to become distracted and derailed by drifting away from the primary focus that produced their initial success. Moreover, he asserts that each of us becomes self-empowered when we consider the same three circles and their intersection in mapping out our strategic life focus and long-term vision for personal greatness. It is noteworthy that Covey described a comparable model that he labeled the *Center of Focus*, representing the area into which our concentrated effort also produces maximum results relative to the larger mission. (p. 150)

This model could be misused, however, if I failed to include cautionary ideas presented by Daniel Kahneman regarding the relative ineffectiveness of acting like a hedgehog, especially when doing so can be considered an overdone strength. While he acknowledges that concentrated effort with sustained focus applied in the right directions produces more consistently robust results, he cautions that errors of hubris are more likely when we hold a narrow and overly confident view regarding what are, in fact, complex and unpredictable issues. Thus he contends,

> "Foxes, by contrast, are complex thinkers. They don't believe that one big thing drives the march of history...Instead the foxes recognize that reality emerges from the interactions of many different agents and forces, including blind luck, often producing large and unpredictable outcomes." (p. 220)

It appears, therefore, that healthy personal power within this dimension is enhanced when we demonstrate skills in achieving focus with flexibility in our thinking and behavior by remaining devoid of ego investment about being right. We are thereby better able to temper our convictions and intuitions with healthy skepticism and helpful restraint through self-doubt. Moreover, applying humility in self-monitoring our perspectives and beliefs supports the practice of making *Reality-Based Choices* more reliably.

Bill O'Hanlon offers a variety of enriching ideas regarding the constructive use of focus in therapy and otherwise for coping with and solving general life challenges in his book, *Do One Thing Different* (1999):

> "Our culture is steeped in problem-orientation. We have an idea that when problems happen, they are caused or determined by the past and that things are just the way they are, set in concrete. If you simply do or think something different, however, many things can change. If you change your focus from problems to solutions, things can change even more quickly." (p. 78)

Since focus is within the realm of things we can consciously manage and learn to control (and thus is our responsibility), learning to shift our focus through one or more of its three facets becomes a pathway to self-empowerment.

An Example of Shifting Perspective: *The Printer*

Many years ago when I was working as a program director in a small business and was responsible for the management of existing customer relationships and new business contracts, I was working on a Friday afternoon to meet a deadline for a promised proposal to a prospective new client, and failure to deliver on time would bring serious consequences. I had been proactive all week in planning to meet this deadline, even allowing for a cushion of time toward the end should I be thrown a curveball. Just as I was attempting to print the final document in preparation for faxing it to the customer (documents were not transferred via e-mail at the time), a message appeared on my printer that I had run out of ink—my curveball had arrived. I immediately thought of alternative solutions: using another printer within the offices, finding a replacement ink cartridge in the supply closet, and racing to the nearest office-supply store to purchase an ink cartridge as the last resort. After quickly ruling out the first two options, I considered making the trek to purchase a replacement ink cartridge. I hesitated because this option was highly undesirable since it involved making a sprint to my car parked a long distance from the office, racing against Friday afternoon traffic to make my purchase and return, leaving only a few moments to spare if, and only if, everything went smoothly. I sat in my chair nervously pondering what to do, and it occurred to me to practice what I had been teaching about creative problem-solving: to change the angle of viewing the problem and make the assumption that the solution can almost always be discovered right in front of us if only we can see past the problem to find it.

The clock was ticking as I sat frozen—yet sweating—in my ambivalence, wondering whether to begin the sprint to the office supply store or to put my messages to the test, the latter being quite frightening should I invalidate my own teachings. Unwilling to consider the possibility that I was a hypocrite, at least in this instance, I shifted my chair to a new position so that I could stare at my printer from a different angle, and then I began to meditate with as much relaxed calm and open-mindedness as I could muster. While I didn't glance at my watch, I quietly asked myself how long it would take for my epiphany to occur, assuming that an answer was eventually forthcoming. After approximately 20 seconds of this meditative state in which I put myself and my beliefs to the test, staring intently at my inanimate and inactive printer awaiting its next command, the answer emerged from somewhere within my consciousness: although I was out of black ink, the color cartridge was available to print using Navy blue, and it would appear to be black when transmitted to the customer via fax! Instead of running the risk of a heart attack or a speeding ticket while trying to be heroic in solving the problem, I had solved the mystery in less than a minute with virtually no stress, much to my amusement and joy—what a relief! That lesson has stayed with me subsequently during numerous similar instances when I've been reminded that a change of focus—in this instance *Perspective*—both externally and internally—is a powerful strategy for evoking creative solutions in support of peak performance. It was also a reminder of a teaching from my Tai Chi studies long ago: when facing challenging circumstances, *the slowest is the fastest*—another paradoxical truth.

Focus in Sports Psychology

Focused Action is essentially synonymous with peak performance, and this is most clearly evident when we witness or experience athletic performance that is fluidly strong and emotionally unencumbered—playing *in the zone* or in a state of *flow*. In his classic work, *The Inner Game of Tennis* (1997), W. Timothy Gallwey described the psychological help and hindrance offered by what he labeled Self 1 and Self 2, not only to excel in the game of tennis, but, more importantly, in the game of life:

> "To gain clarity on the mental problems in tennis we introduced the concept of Self 1 and 2. Self 1 was the name given to the conscious ego-mind which likes to tell Self 2, you and your potential, how to hit the tennis ball. The key to spontaneous, high-level tennis is in resolving the lack of harmony which usually exists between these two selves. This requires the learning of several inner skills, chiefly the art of letting go of self judgments, letting Self 2 do the hitting, recognizing and trusting the natural learning process, and above all gaining some practical experience in the art of relaxed concentration...Focus in tennis is fundamentally no different from the focus needed to perform any task or even to enjoy a symphony; learning to let go of the habit of judging yourself on the basis of your backhand is no different from forgetting the habit of judging your child or boss; and learning to welcome obstacles in competition automatically

increases one's ability to find advantage in all the difficulties
one meets in the course of one's life." (pp. 115-116)

An important question to ask in light of these concepts regarding focus
and peak performance, broadly speaking, is this: "How do I apply this
material about improving my focus toward my empowerment?" I'll answer
the question with continued use of a sports metaphor, this time from the game
of golf. Many people (like me) have had the frustrating experience of hitting a
bucket of balls seemingly like a pro at the driving range, only to make errant
golf swings repeatedly during a tournament later in the day—a.k.a. *choking*.
Most of us recognize that our mind is getting in the way of what otherwise
could be and should be a fun game at which we excel, or at least one in which
we experience the joy of playing at our very best. But what is the mind doing
to create such obstacles and related suffering?

The answer: we allow our mind to shift our focus from concentrating with
present-minded awareness to thoughts of our past and/or future performance.
And these thoughts trigger our emotions, either negative or positive, which
have the further effect of distracting our attention away from the task at hand.
At maximum power and effectiveness, there is laser-like focus with freedom
from distraction from any source, internal or external, so that we are fully
oriented toward the *sweet spot* of control that will bring about our best possible
performance—bringing the head of the golf club into effective contact with
the dimpled surface of the white golf ball—nothing more or less than this. It is
the only relevant event over which we have external control, thus our cognitive
bandwidth should be fully focused upon the vision and mechanics of striking
the ball with fluid motion and a relaxed, quiet mind. After making contact
with the club, the ball will go where it will go, and we have no control over
that future event—although most golfers like to think they do—thus it is a
focus that we can ill afford to entertain in the present moment.

However, even when we know these things, many of us stand eagerly
and/or nervously over the golf ball with our focus dispersed toward times
and events over which we have no immediate control, such as how we've been
playing all day, what our partners or competitors are thinking of our golf
game, and how wonderful it would be to make this next shot a great one—
perhaps even a hole-in-one! So, instead of focusing on that very finite area over
which we have maximum control—hitting the golf ball so intently that we

can observe the micro-second during which the metallic face of the club meets the ball, keeping our head down through that point of contact in order not to miss that fleeting but critical event—our mind launches us toward a future focus (e.g., thoughts about the ball landing on the green near the pin, as the best case scenario, or buried in a sand trap or, worst, submerged in the lake). To the degree that our focus has been so diluted by these mental distractions and emotional interruptions, we increase the probability of hitting the ball wrong and producing a less than optimal result.

Of course, harsh criticism levied quickly from Gallwey's Self 1 following such failure serves to set the stage for the next episode of focus-destroying chatter as we approach our next shot, unless we learn and practice the skills of mind management through the three facets of focus presented earlier: *Selection*—what to focus upon in the present moment for the task at hand; *Concentration*—sustaining that focus by maintaining attention without distraction, and *Perspective*—viewing the event either with no interpretation or evaluative judgment (e.g., as being *good* or *bad*), or through a lens that best supports natural and spontaneous action (e.g., a Self 2 offering: "I'm having fun just making solid contact with the ball!").

Mindfulness and Focus

You already recognized a return to mindfulness in the previous section, adding to the discussion of its role in personal power development begun in Chapter 5. In *Unlimiting Mind* (2010), Andrew Olendzki offers keen insights regarding the role of *Focused Action* in determining our quality of life. He advises that we resist the current "penchant for multitasking" as follows:

> "When the mind tries to do several things at once, it does not do any of them very well...It is not that the mind is incapable of such feats of parallel processing, it's just not a very healthy thing to do...Mental energy is finite, and our mind is diminished in direct proportion to how much its attention is fractured. The problem is not so much attention deficit as it is attention *dispersion*, when the available attention is spread thin. Just like water spreading out to cover a surface, the wider the expanse the shallower the depth." (p. 83)

This brings us then to a question of paramount importance: "Since the mechanics of *Focused Action* are essentially equivalent when practiced by those engaged in great good as well as those engaged in acts of evil and destruction, what differentiates acts of *Healthy* and *Unhealthy Power* within this dimension?" This question arises not because there is uncertainty about the ineffectiveness associated with *Fragmented Activity* or the negative ripple effect created by those who fragment the activities of others by dispersing their focus. Instead, we ponder this question in view of people like Adolf Hitler, who apparently met all of the criteria pertaining to the technology of focus—proficiencies in *Selection*, *Concentration*, and *Perspective*—that could have enabled him to demonstrate exceptional *Healthy Power*. But, much to the contrary, we know that his selection of focus (extermination of any inferior race, starting primarily with the Jews in Europe), his sustained, intense concentration (persevering, albeit errantly, with unwavering confidence and determination in spite of counsel from his own military experts), and the self-motivating lenses or perspective through which he viewed his ambitions and plans (believing he was embarked upon a mission for the greater good of Germany and the world) served to create a powerful empire that temporarily wreaked global havoc and mass destruction.

Therefore, the power of focus is revealed not solely through skillful use of the technology behind it, but also—and much more importantly—by the intentions for which the tools are applied and the results the user creates. In short, Hitler's regime ultimately disempowered millions of people, their culture, and their lands. Thus it is the intention and consequences of focus when it is inappropriately channeled —even technically strong focus—that defines it as *Fragmented Activity* and, therefore, as a pathway to *Unhealthy Power*. In a comparable manner, we recognize *Focused Action* in largest part by the positive ripple effect that it makes. Accordingly, leaders among the Allied forces in World War II made use of the same technology involving focus that Hitler and Hirohito used, but the mission for which it was mobilized and the consequences they produced in defeating the Axis forces in Europe and Japan define it historically as a world-changing enactment of *Healthy Power*.

This, then, calls to mind a deepening of the broader framework regarding power being presented throughout this book: that each component of power formation works with the others to create synergy that is either positive or negative. Hitler provides an extreme example to illustrate this point in that he evidently followed each of the preceding pathways toward *Unhealthy Power* that have been covered thus far:

- *Personal Irresponsibility*
- *Orchestrated Suffering*
- *Win-Lose Relationships*
- *Egocentric Pleasure*
- *Regressive Choices*
- *Fragmented Activity*

Think, therefore, of the various facets of focus in the differing ways we might consider a hammer. If it has a broken handle and is missing part of the claw, it will predictably be usable only for *Fragmented Activity* that's secondary to its disorganized makeup. If, on the other hand, it is new and intact, it can be used for *Focused Action* that is productive and healthy, such as building a house, or for *Fragmented Activity*, such as committing murder. What we see in either case, then, more than the tool itself, is the spirit of intention that drives a person at this fork in the road to turn toward empowered behavior that is either positive or negative, health promoting or pathological. Ideally, each of us masters the use of these tools intending to uplift and support each other interdependently, with compassion and loving-kindness, bearing good fruits. When this is the case, fully evolved mindfulness melded with well-managed and skillful focus offers the power to change our world with strength and benevolence, with lasting significance and meaning.

Healthy Power—Prescriptions for Developing *Focused Action* as a Leader in the Workplace:

1) Use the power of focus. Recognize that since our focus on people and things tends to expand, either positively or negatively, it influences how we interact with them. For example, a steady focus on another person's faults only serves to expand our sense of their faults, creating tension as well. Accordingly, we become more effective when we maintain a focus on those things that contribute most to our goals, rather than letting ourselves

become distracted by lesser or counter-productive things. In your communications, therefore, create and maintain a positive outlook and focus. Help your staff to shift their focus in ways that support their successful actions and create a more positive work environment. When, for example, a staff member is complaining about her struggles with problems, whether real or imagined, help her by shifting her attention toward what *is* working, her available resources, potential solutions, and her choices and options, rather than perpetuating the negative focus in which she has become stuck.

2) *Put first things first* each day by first identifying your strategic business priorities and action steps toward attaining them, both as an individual leader and through inspirational guidance and system-wide support of your team. Choose your priorities carefully and remember, *Your car goes where your eyes go!* (*The Art of Racing in the Rain*, Garth Stein, 2008).

3) Develop your *Hedgehog* focus by identifying the intersection of three circles described earlier as part of creating the strategic plan, both short- and long-term, for the organization. Then develop tactical plans that directly support the Strategic plan that can be applied to all your managerial efforts in concert with your administrative team.

4) Uphold the chain of command. The organizational chart defines roles and reporting relationships with an explicit structure through which power and control are to be mobilized. A focus on this chain of command consistently is essential for the support and continued empowerment of every position in the hierarchy. Therefore, ensure in every communication that no manager or supervisor is overlooked or bypassed because doing so renders her less effective, especially in the eyes of anyone who succeeds in nullifying her authority. For example, if someone complains to you without first having broached her complaint with her immediate supervisor, redirect her to her supervisor with the clear expectation that she will handle the situation competently. Should that not be the case, schedule a meeting of all relevant

parties and discuss the matter transparently toward resolution, always supporting the supervisor in question, especially in front of her staff.

PEARLS OF HEALTHY POWER

Ralph Waldo Emerson...
What is life but the angle of vision?

Helen Keller...
Keep your face to the sunshine and you cannot see the shadow.

Charles Hummel...
...with a sense of loss we recall the vital task we pushed aside. We realize we've become slaves to the tyranny of the urgent.

Mahatma Gandhi...
The only tyrant I accept in this world is the still voice within.

Ray Bradbury...
You have to know how to accept rejection and reject acceptance.

Proverbs 25: 28...
Whoever has no rule over his own spirit is like a city broken down, without walls.

CHAPTER 7

U...*Unrelenting Courage* vs. *Unsettling Fear*

Courage is not the absence of fear; it is the making of action in spite of fear, the moving out against the resistance engendered by fear into the unknown and into the future.

M. Scott Peck

UNRELENTING COURAGE AND HEALTHY POWER

As an undergraduate student at Grove City College during the early 1970s—the first child ever to attend college from either side of the family—I suffered tremendous anxiety due to self-doubt and related fears of failure. I majored in Accounting & Business Finance during my freshman year and through the first part of my sophomore year at my mother's prompting, thinking I'd become a CPA. Never having been meant for the field, I became totally bored, physically distressed, and emotionally disillusioned to the point of seriously considering dropping out of college. I even contemplated moving to Alaska to homestead after watching the movie "Jeremiah Johnson" with my father, having heard him verbalize the same dream when he was a younger man with a kind of romantic zeal numerous times throughout my upbringing.

In crisis and extremely fearful of discussing my troubles with my academic advisor, I finally broke down one day in desperation and met with him. He was also the chairperson of the Accounting Department, and he enjoyed a terrible reputation as being mercilessly unsympathetic to student woes like the confusion and despair I was experiencing. Making matters worse, because his nickname was "_____ the gorilla," he became my *monster in the closet* and grew more intimidating in my mind the longer I procrastinated and avoided him.

When we finally sat down together, my hands visibly trembling as I strained to express my despair, he was remarkably helpful by being both compassionate and understanding. In fact, he congratulated me for courageously confronting the truth of my unfitness for such duty before getting into the field as a professional—a point at which turning back would have been much more difficult, he assured me. As my advisor, he strongly (and wisely) suggested that I put my "homesteading in Alaska" plans on the back burner and encouraged me to follow my only identified academic love: Psychology. He told me that I could change my major immediately and—upon my inquiry—even without consulting my parents for approval. I became a Psychology student that same afternoon! This was a developmental milestone for me as it represented the first major decision of my life I would make independently, requiring great courage—taking action amidst fear—for me to do so. I *hugged my monster*—opened the closet door and paid closer attention to it—and it shrank to manageable size.

Courage is often misunderstood as the absence of fear, therein defining a person who experiences fear as a coward. In truth, courage is not the absence of fear, anxiety, doubt, or discomfort. Instead, courage is demonstrated when we take deliberate, effective action in the *presence* of fear and/or other such unpleasant emotions. Derived from the Latin root *cour*, it has its meaning in the word *heart*. Therefore, the emphasis here is placed upon your developing effective personal leadership through the skills of *taking heart* in the presence of fear, etc. in order to initiate undeterred, powerful action steps while being fully cognizant of the risks involved.

It is especially important to our success in leadership that we develop the skills required to confront issues and people courageously, the latter confrontations being more difficult (e.g., addressing behavior and related performance problems). Yet this is the area in which we as leaders most commonly fall short; we demonstrate and/or enable such common practices as avoiding conflicts, procrastinating on projects, minimizing issues, and other means of simply not handling problems. This is so—that we frequently put off doing the very things that are most vital to our success—simply because we are afraid of failure, discomfort, or change (i.e., *Unsettling Fear*). The ripple effects we generate in doing so are similarly unsettling to others, especially to those hoping to witness leadership strengths that will inspire their loyalty and commitment to us, whether in the personal or professional roles we play.

Recognizing fear as the greatest common obstacle we face in confronting major issues in a more direct and timely manner—fear of conflict, fear of failure, fear of repercussion, etc.—John Maxwell described *Failing Forward* as an empowering reframe of fear in order to propel more courageous, perseverant action, and especially for us to embrace more challenging confrontations (*Failing Forward: Turning Mistakes into Stepping Stones for Success*, 2000). Resilience—our ability to bounce back productively following any setback or disheartening experience—is developed by accepting that feelings of fear, hesitation, etc. are normal, rather than indicators of cowardice or our being a failure. A failed attempt we make is just that—a behavioral trial and learning experience to be factored into the next planned and more seasoned effort— rather than evidence that *we* are a failure. We most often tend to get stuck at the first step because of our fears that take shape in a variety of forms: fear of criticism from others and/or ourselves; fear of disappointment; fear of change; and even fear of success. This is when it's good to recall that with increased power comes increased responsibility, ready or not. In the end, we demonstrate courage by taking deliberate steps forward in spite of any accompanying unpleasant thoughts and feelings, moving from the relative comfort of mere intention to the unstable (but rewarding) ground where effective action occurs.

The primary aim of this chapter, therefore, is to raise your consciousness regarding the relationship between courage and personal greatness, because to lack courage even slightly is to miss the opportunity to achieve results and fulfillment that otherwise lie just beyond our reach but potentially within our grasp. Accordingly,

> *…To be fully courageous is to awaken each morning with an outlook and perspective that when verbalized cry out: the world is my oyster…damn the torpedoes, full speed ahead…my life is an adventure to be lived, not a problem to be solved!…*

Living our lives courageously does not mean acting on impulse or without seeing the risks and consequences. Instead, it means approaching our life challenges and opportunities fully engaged and with a zest for living. If we apply the metaphor of an automobile sitting at a red light with a foot on the brake, then being fully courageous means removing the foot from the brake completely and throttling forward when the green light appears. There is no resistance to the moment, partial braking, or labored acceleration once the decision is made to move forward. Our steps are then energized with confidence and commitment, enabling our best efforts and maximizing the results we obtain.

Passages to Adulthood in Hawaii

Among the many stories my father told me as a child, this one about his youthful adventures in the Hawaiian Islands at the start of World War II is one of my favorites. I want to share it with you especially because it exemplifies extraordinary courage under harsh conditions and is thus well-suited to this chapter.

In the year following the Japanese bombing of Pearl Harbor on December 7, 1941, both U.S. Naval and civilian forces were deployed in concert for massive salvage operations—raising sunken ships, salvaging weapons and munitions, and recovering deceased military personnel—meaningful and dangerous work as our nation struggled to regroup upon entering the war against the Axis powers. At the time of the bombing, my father was completing his senior year at a trade school in Pittsburgh, Pennsylvania where he studied to become a machinist and welder. After turning 18 during the spring of 1942 and graduating shortly thereafter, he enlisted in the Civil Service to embark on an adventure that took him by train across the country to San Francisco, California and from there aboard ship to Oahu, Hawaii, where Pearl Harbor Naval Yard lay in ruins. Being a great swimmer and fairly fearless in general, he volunteered for training in underwater salvage duty wearing the traditional diver suit and brass bell helmet with tethering air hoses connecting him to those supporting his air supply and safety at the surface. The waters were described as being murky and dark, billowing with diesel fuel and oil from the massive wreckage—a dangerous undertaking with numerous physical and emotional challenges. Like so many civilian soldiers of that era, he performed his duties admirably; but he had difficulty talking about the horrors that he encountered, such as reaching out to discover a body by the touch of his hand that was hidden in watery blackness. At 18, he came to understand the undeniable grimness of evil and its terrifying wake.

When not working undersea in the gloom and peril that was his daily fare, my father was intrigued by the beauty in which he was immersed in that Hawaiian paradise—then quite pristine and not so commercially developed, 17 years before its statehood in 1959. As an outstanding athlete, he formed the habit of swimming daily after work hours. As part of my father's passage into adulthood, he became inspired by the challenge of some day crossing the channel in a solo swim to a nearby island he could see plainly from the beach where he was stationed. Moreover, he dreamed of reaching his personal *Bali Hai*, longing to test his limits during his journey toward the greater life he imagined for himself. Knowing that it would be quite a risky challenge with many perils, he continued to swim for a number of months to become stronger and more conditioned for his planned adventure.

As he told his story, one especially beautiful weekend morning he knew it was his long-awaited day to swim the channel since the water and weather conditions were just right. So he left the beach and entered the calm inviting waters in the direction of the opposing island. After swimming approximately one mile, he became disoriented and confused because the swim was apparently a much greater distance than he had calculated from afar. He had not taken into account the optical illusion that led to his gross underestimation of distance between islands, nor had he confirmed the distance as part of his preparations. Initially he began to panic, but quickly understood that failure was not an option, and thus he went into a survival mode by floating on his back. Thinking then that he was about halfway across the channel, he deliberated whether to proceed or return to shore. Wanting to complete his adventure successfully and thinking that it was equidistant either way, he continued to swim in a survivor mode—alternating a very slow breast stroke and floating for recovery—in the direction of the original target island.

Undeterred by numerous potentially fatal risks—strong currents, predatory sharks, giant jellyfish, and unforeseen storms—my father spent several additional hours slowly making his way toward the shore. Upon making the beach, a shocked onlooker greeted him with the question, "Where did *you* come from?" Upon learning the answer, the amazed bystander blurted, "That's a seven-mile swim!" Happy to be on dry land late that afternoon and very fatigued, Dad humbly made the return trip by boat—mission accomplished. As a side note, I remember my parents returning home after watching the movie *South Pacific* (based upon James Michener's World War II era book, *Tales of the South Pacific*) when it was first released in 1959 when I was just five years old. My father (then 35) could not stop speaking about it with youthful exuberance since the backdrop and storyline—having been filmed on location on the island of Kauai, Hawaii—immediately took him back to his passages and adventures as a blossoming and courageous man of that same era.

You could certainly argue that my father was ill-prepared for such a dangerous mission and was quite fortunate to survive the swim, and you would be right. I share the story with you here with a certain pride not only for the courage my father demonstrated both in his salvage work and this athletic adventure (albeit with a wake-up call not to enter harm's way without being fully prepared), but also for the spirit that characterized so much of our nation's behavior during the years of World War II and beyond. Upon returning from Hawaii following his Civil Service duties, my father enlisted in the Army and was stationed in Korea during the years leading up to the Korean War, where he continued to demonstrate dutiful courage in the face of peril.

Later in this chapter, I'll describe the key components of *Unrelenting Courage* development in order that any person so inclined will be able to follow the pathway leading to exceptional *Healthy Power* within this dimension. But first, let's examine the pathway leading to *Unsettling Fear* and its impact upon individuals and systems.

UNSETTLING FEAR AND UNHEALTHY POWER

We have a choice: to plow new ground or let the weeds grow.

Jonathan Westover

Fear and anxiety are complex emotions, not simply negative in character or effect. Hitting the sweet spot for anxiety—a *Goldilocks* principle of not too much, not too little—maximizes our ability to succeed at tasks at our very best. Similarly, healthy fear guides our prudent behavior for our safety and otherwise to help us avert unwanted—even fatal—consequences, thus we slow down at the sight of a State Trooper parked at the side of the road. While it might be unpleasant subjectively, such healthy fear allows us to follow rules, obey laws, and generally color inside the lines where such compliance is important to our well-being.

Normally, when any one of our strengths is overdone it becomes our weakness. So, too, is the effect of our excessive fear and anxiety when poorly managed. The particular focus here, however, is not upon the intensity of fear inducing events, such as those that traumatize us. Instead, the focus is upon our core strength (or weakness) as the primary determinant of fear management and its impact upon our personal ability to function. And what is especially important for consideration also is the degree to which we might embody a fragile ego as our primary core weakness. Earlier I wrote that core strength enables outward flexibility, openness, and our ability to make adaptive changes. Conversely, core weakness usually shows itself as external rigidity, exaggerated needs for control over our external world, and through resistance to change. These core weaknesses and how they manifest in our outward behavior make a lack of courage most evident.

Let's consider that fearfulness is an instinctive reaction to perceived threat—whether we're responding to a nearby hooded cobra or to the challenge of a public speaking event with risk of embarrassment or failure—where our primitive fight or flight response comes into play. However, when we have a fragile sense of self with wavering self-esteem, they both must be heavily guarded and defended in order to prevent emotional injury and pain. Accordingly, we then learn to develop ego-driven defenses. Such defenses are then maintained through one or more of the following behaviors:

We either cannot or will not...

- Change direction in deference to authority
- Follow rules or obey laws consistently
- Take criticism in a constructive manner
- Empower others and/or celebrate their success
- Accept blame, take responsibility, or acknowledge failure
- Demonstrate loyalty and followership without feeling diminished
- Think flexibly with creativity

If you hearken back to the analogy of the automobile at the red light, then you'll recognize that when we are fraught with *Unsettling Fear*—applying all necessary defense mechanisms to protect our fragile ego and other aspects of core weakness—then we essentially keep our foot on the brake when it's normally time to go. Further, we can understand this dynamic through two related but qualitatively different processes.

In the first process, think of yourself literally moving forward by depressing the gas pedal while simultaneously applying enough brake to create a drag effect—a very common phenomenon, metaphorically speaking. We make forward progress in our movement, but it is certainly less than ideal both in terms of efficiency and performance. Related to how we function, to move forward by taking only partly courageous action steps while guarding against failure—essentially hedging our bet—not only interferes with optimal performance, it also takes a toll by depleting our energy and creating self-imposed stress. Moreover, in contrast to how we function when we are engaged in goal-directed activity with *Unrelenting Courage*—throttling forward without drag or energy waste—when we are impeded by fear we are not fully functioning, not only because our energies are being invested in opposing directions, but also because of the wear and tear on the chassis, so to speak. This is self-defeating behavior, and we're simply not built to work against ourselves, although often we do. In other words, it's helpful for us to recognize that an element of resistance (braking) is spawned by fearfulness as an ego defense—a kind of holding back akin to a turtle only partially peering out from her shell as she moves—and it is our fear-based defensiveness that impedes our progress along the action path we have consciously accepted and toward which we strive to go (accelerating). Our forward progress is made only haltingly in this painstaking manner, thus it comes with wasteful costs. As my high school driving instructor once insisted when I was initially timid at the wheel, *please, don't ride the brake!*

In the second process, which represents the most extreme form of *Unsettling Fear*, we simply remain comfortably braked at the red light and keep our foot off the accelerator. The priority is to maintain comfort—comfort derived from the illusion of enjoying good control—while being blind to the underlying truth that weakness is, in fact, the driver. Along with this comes resistance to change, reticence to cooperate, rebellion against authority, defiance against rules and laws, and a general sense of rigidity in both thinking and behavior.

When attempting to function in this impaired state, we cannot ever afford to lose, be found at fault, or proven wrong because any such event shatters our self-image. Our magnified fears must be assuaged. Given the accompanying ego fragility that drives such fear-based behavior, we can recognize some of the *Unhealthy Power* described in previous dimensions: *Personal Irresponsibility*, *Win-Lose Relationships*, and *Fragmented Activity*. Accordingly, we tend to recruit others to follow suit in order to validate our predominantly negative stance. On either side of the power ledger, we recognize that there is strength in numbers.

Perhaps the most insidious aspect of *Unhealthy Power* within this dimension is deliberate provocation of fear among others in order to manipulate them. We commonly recognize this in government politics, corporate maneuvering, marketing/sales strategies, and otherwise in those situations that become empowered through the inducement of fear among those whose support and/or money is being sought. For example, those with a financial interest in selling pharmaceuticals—both over-the-counter and by prescription—invest heavily in advertising and other communications intended to amplify our concern about a particular disease, disorder, or abnormality. They know there is a tipping point they gain because of sufficient public fear and anxiety. Just as sex and violence in the media are well recognized for their potency in attracting attention and supporting sales from a hedonistic standpoint—the lures of *Egocentric Pleasure*—we should also recognize that fear and anxiety are key components of certain political campaigns, marketing plans, and sales activities. Whenever we react with *Unsettling Fear* as individuals or as a group (especially as a nation), we empower those who stand to gain through our lack of courage.

THE PATHWAY TO UNRELENTING COURAGE

> *Those who try to do something and fail are infinitely better than those who try to do nothing and succeed.*
>
> Lloyd Jones

This version of the poem, *Do It Anyway* is credited to Mother Teresa. Reportedly, the verses were written on the wall of her home for children in Calcutta, India. It provides us with an inspiring roadmap for applying

Unrelenting Courage melded with awareness and decisiveness, instructing us to act with commitment and confidence in the face of varied life adversities:

People are often unreasonable, irrational, and self-centered…
   Forgive them anyway.

If you are kind, people may accuse you of selfish, ulterior motives…
   Be kind anyway.

If you are successful, you will win some unfaithful friends and some genuine enemies…
   Succeed anyway.

If you are honest and sincere people may deceive you…
   Be honest and sincere anyway.

What you spend years creating, others could destroy overnight…
   Create anyway.

If you find serenity and happiness, some may be jealous…
   Be happy anyway.

The good you do today, will often be forgotten…
   Do good anyway.

Give the best you have, and it will never be enough…
   Give your best anyway.

In the final analysis, it is between you and God…
   It was never between you and them anyway.

Courage = Commitment + Confidence

After reading the inspiring words above by Mother Teresa, you as the reader at this point might be asking, "Since I'd like to be able to do everything she described courageously, how do I develop my own courage in the first place?" The answer lies in the formula introduced here in which the combination of *commitment* and *confidence* generates the upwelling of courage. Accordingly, let's explore both of these components in order to apply them to how we face our daily challenges.

If you were to ask me what I would do if either of my sons was to step unknowingly into the path of an oncoming vehicle—even today as adults in their early 30s—I know I would do everything within my power to protect them from the danger, even if it meant sacrificing my own life. As you know, it is not an uncommon commitment or instinct for parents to protect their children. The combination of my love for my children and the dread of losing either one of them would propel my courageous behavior primarily because of my commitment to them as my progeny, along with my commitment to myself to be a good parent. By contrast, if I witnessed my neighbor's cat streaking across the road into the path of the same oncoming vehicle, I would not likely muster the courage to take protective action because my commitment in that situation pales by comparison with the commitment I have for my children. Even if I was fairly confident that I could rescue the cat from a collision, I would not be mobilized to face the risk to my own life without sufficient commitment to that animal. My courage to take action would simply not be there.

And that last point brings us to the second key variable that determines our level of courage: confidence in our ability to take effective action. Confidence is the second of these necessary but insufficient conditions that produces courage. Returning to the example of one of my sons facing imminent danger in the path of an approaching vehicle, I would not be likely to take any courageous action to protect him if I had absolutely no confidence that I could succeed on his behalf, in spite of my extremely strong parental love for and commitment to him. This does not mean that I'd be technically correct in my conclusion that I couldn't succeed, especially because a snap decision is being made while under duress, making objective assessment all the more difficult. It *does* mean that my *perception* of my capabilities comes into play when calculating the probability of being successful in a dangerous situation, and that level of confidence is a primary driver (along with my level of commitment) affecting my decision whether to act or to remain passive—to lunge forward in an effort to save my son, or to watch him helplessly from afar.

To summarize, we develop the courage to take effective action in spite of our fears and other barriers to success when we experience both sufficient commitment and confidence to embrace the risks involved in completing any task—both are necessary but insufficient alone for mustering our courage. Moreover, the greater the perceived risks, the greater the thresholds that must be reached in both commitment and confidence before we pull the trigger and knowingly make ourselves more vulnerable. We tend to struggle whenever we feel strong commitment to a goal while lacking confidence that we can attain it—inadequate confidence is thus immobilizing. Conversely, whenever we feel sufficiently confident regarding a goal but are lacking in our commitment to it we become prone to making either incomplete effort or no effort whatsoever. Therefore, the pathway leading to *Unrelenting Courage* involves the conscious work of building both commitment and confidence for a particular goal so that we can answer the call to take action with appropriate discernment and effectiveness.

Building Resilience

Unrelenting Courage is driven at a deeper level by our resilience—resilience being a key component of core strength—because it affects both our commitment and confidence during risk-taking activities. Knowing that we can bounce back even when we've failed at something reduces our vulnerability—we get to try again with *Plan B*—and with reduced vulnerability we can more readily make commitment to our goals with increased confidence. Since resilience can be developed through practice, material is presented here so that you can better understand and develop your resilience in pursuit of courage and greater personal power.

Factors Affecting Resilience

- Having a network of family and friends who will be there to support us during difficult life events—having people close to us that we can trust and depend upon when the going gets tough
- Having one or more people who love us, care about us, and, if necessary, willing to protect us from harm and danger
- Having adult mentors, whether family, teachers, church members, etc. who guide and teach us how to find the right path for our

lives, both before life struggles and afterward, so as to get back on track when we've gone awry and/or fallen somehow

- Developing the skills for making realistic plans, and then taking the necessary steps in order to transform our plans into reality
- Developing a realistic and positive view of ourselves—one in which we see both our strengths and limitations humbly within the light of being worthwhile and capable
- Developing effective interpersonal skills for communicating and problem solving
- Practicing the skills of self-discipline, including behavioral self-regulation and emotion management

Ten Ways to Build Resilience

1) *Make Connections...* By making deposits into the *emotional bank account* with others, we are better prepared to handle difficult problems—we're able to make withdrawals from those same people when we are in need. This means accepting that we should not think of ourselves as an island—that we can live alone in complete independence or isolation. Rather, we do better in life by having the humility to accept our weaknesses, especially our need to have help from others at important times. The more people we can call upon for help during tough times, the lighter will be the weight of any problems we face. Just as the saying applies during tasks, "Many hands make light work," having meaningfully connected people at our side during hardship makes our suffering more bearable. Also, there are great rewards that come from helping others during *their* times of need. Such *Win-Win Relationships* are especially helpful because we are comforted through our unselfish and heartfelt acts of kindness toward others in altruistic giving (to be discussed further in Chapter 8).

2) *Avoid Seeing Crises as Insurmountable Problems...* This is the skill of *reframing*— putting a new frame or perspective around something in order to see it differently. It can involve both

decreasing its importance and changing its value. Sometimes all we need to do is keep things in proper perspective—not make *mountains out of molehills.* And at other times we do well to see the *silver lining* behind the dark cloud—recognizing that there often can be great opportunity in the problems we face. There is a normal tendency to see things in the light of any feelings that we have at the moment of trouble, so that our anger, fear, and sadness make our problems seem much worse than they really are. One way to keep things in perspective is to ask ourselves how we'll feel about a situation or problem years into the future. Most things seem to be far less important or difficult when we see them this way, especially if we have confidence that our problems will be behind us then. Another aspect of this skill is learning how to reframe problems as gifts or opportunities. For example, sometimes having to wait is very hard because we are eager and impatient; but that very same situation might prompt us to practice patience, thereby helping us cope in the future without as much distress once greater patience has been developed.

3) *Accept That Change Is a Part of Living...*First, we need to accept that change is the only thing that is predictable and that it cannot be avoided since *permanence* on this earthly plane is merely an illusion. Therefore, clinging to anyone or anything as if permanent—and being deceived—is a root cause of suffering. Second, accept that change often represents the opening of a previously closed door. Third, accept what we truly cannot change instead of engaging in self-defeating battles that increase our distress through the experience of futility or *learned helplessness.* The fact that changes go on constantly in spite of any efforts to stop them from happening highlights the wisdom of following the *Serenity Prayer* since it serves as an empowering pathway toward peace and, therefore, greater resilience in the face of difficulties. Once we accept those things we cannot control and shift our *focus* (the subject of Chapter 6) toward alternative things where we *can* make a difference, we become liberated to better invest our time, energy, and resources. Accordingly, we also

become more adept at coping with and solving our problems with increased confidence and, therefore, with decreased emotional and physical distress.

4) *Move Toward Your Goals...*By staying focused upon our goals— the realistic plans we've made—with steady, persistent efforts over time, we see regular results that provide evidence that we are capable and strong. Of course, this requires patience and perseverance—the skill of sticking to our goals and having faith that we will be successful some time later. Forming helpful habits—planning ahead, staying focused, maintaining faith and hope, and visualizing ourselves reaching our goals—are invaluable means of developing resilience, especially when the challenge we face requires long, sustained effort. We learn to put first things first, and then spend our time wisely each day doing the things that contribute the most toward reaching our goals. Time and efforts well spent today lead to successful achievements that, while seemingly far off, often await us around the next bend.

5) *Take Decisive Actions...*We do well to practice the skill of facing problems head on, rather than avoiding them, running away from them, or denying they exist. As stated earlier, too often we put off doing the things that are most important for our success and happiness, simply because we are afraid of failure, difficulty, or change. As healthy, resilient people, we commit to the habit of acting in real time to solve problems and complete tasks, rather than procrastinating or wishing our problems and work away. Although it seems to be easier to *live for today* without concern for tomorrow, when we are indecisive or shirk our responsibilities in the near term we pay a high price later for our shortsightedness. Therefore, let's aspire to act with such decisiveness that we won't later say, "If only I had done...," "I wish that I would have...," or "Now it's too late for me to...." Our intent is to live and to work without later regrets. We know our goals and plans, we stay focused on them daily, and we say "No" to anyone or anything that could throw us off track, including any negative self talk.

6) *Look for Opportunities for Self-discovery*...Even a crisis can be a blessing in disguise. Serious life challenges usually provide us with rare chances to learn about ourselves and to grow from self-discovery. As a result, many of us who've endured stressful, even life-threatening events have become more self-aware and attuned to others, thereby developing a better appreciation for living. The expression that we often hear about exercise, *No pain no gain*, also appears to be true about developing resilience: the process of being challenged by difficulties can help us to be rebuilt even stronger than before. On the other hand, viewing difficulties as nothing other than painful events to be avoided tends to keep us from learning about ourselves during our trials of living, thereby missing potential opportunities for maturation and growth.

7) *Nurture a Positive Self-image*...We usually behave in ways that reflect how we truly think of ourselves—with positive or negative energy—depending upon our attitudes toward ourselves. For example, a positive, confident attitude about our ability to cope with problems—and perhaps even to benefit from them—tends to make us less reactive to even the most challenging problems. Being less reactive means less stress, and, therefore, greater resilience in facing the challenge. Similarly, confidence about tolerating pain—while minimizing the *second arrow* of suffering, enduring hardship, and managing difficulty—helps us to persevere, usually toward more successful results.

8) *Keep Things in Perspective*...As suggested in Chapter 6 in the discussion about focus, the lens through which we view problems—our emotional response and view of them—has the potential to expand our problems, making them feel much greater and more serious than they really are. Instead, by allowing ourselves time to calm down and look at the situation more rationally, we then can see the problem more realistically, and we are then better able to think through the solutions that are available to us. Often, the solution is right in front of us, but we cannot see it in the haze of being upset and distressed—recall here my problematic encounter in the story of *The* Printer, also

in Chapter 6. Remember also that imagining ourselves far into our own future with the particular problem behind us is another method for keeping things within a helpful perspective.

9) *Maintain a Hopeful Outlook*...What we focus upon tends to expand, whether it is a good thing or a bad thing. That is, what we expect to happen often does happen, in large part because we work to make our expectations come true. People with negative attitudes and expectations usually find that their lives are filled with the negative things that filled their minds, even though they might have hoped for something better. On the other hand, people with positive attitudes and expectations usually find that their lives become filled with the positive things for which they dreamed. This was presented in Chapter 2 where *self-fulfilling prophecy* was discussed as a powerful tool for creating the best (or worst) that we want out of life, including how others tend to relate to us. Therefore, a helpful method for experiencing positive, healthy, and supportive peer relationships is by first maintaining a positive attitude about others—expecting that they will treat us more often than not the same as we treat them.

10) *Practicing Good Self-care*...Since the most important tools we have to combat stress are our mind, body, and spirit, it is vital that we develop healthy lifestyle habits to keep them in great shape. For example, eating well, exercising regularly and safely, and getting enough restful sleep are keys to creating a healthy, more functional and resilient body. Also, it's just as important that we exercise the mind through selective reading and ongoing quality education as lifelong learners. The expression, *garbage in–garbage out*, not only applies to computers, but also to keeping our minds free of unhealthy ideas and attitudes. Our quality of life is determined to a very large extent by following these suggestions, and our ability to bounce back from devastating life events is also dependent upon our inner core strength-conditioning when misfortune strikes. Additionally, we need to understand the role of spirituality in our preparedness for life challenges because having faith in something or someone greater than ourselves is a

critical part of life sustaining energy when facing a crisis or when assisting others to do the same.

Learning and Growing from Difficult Experiences

We can develop greater resilience for future challenges by learning from our past and/or current difficulties, so consider these questions:

- What kinds of life events have been most stressful for me?
- How have those events typically affected me, both physically and emotionally?
- Have I found it helpful to think of an important person in my life when I am distressed? What would she do in order to cope better?
- To who have I reached out for support in working through a traumatic or distressing experience? Who has been most helpful?
- What have I learned about myself and my interactions with others during difficult times—my strengths and my weaknesses?
- Has it been helpful for me to assist someone else going through a similar experience? How so?
- Have I been able to overcome obstacles, and if so, how? What usually seems to work for me?
- What has helped make me feel more hopeful about the future? What thoughts seem to block my hope and energy? How can I get unstuck?
- What have I stopped doing that is generally helpful for me when I do it? What can I start doing again that will be likely to renew my inner energy and vigor so that I can feel like myself again?

Skills for Healthy Risk-Taking

- Understand that our fears, discomfort, and doubt (especially self-doubt) are the most common factors that hold us back from trying new things, stretching toward greater goals, and embracing change, even when we, in fact, are capable of doing such things.

- Recognize and accept that no significant change ever occurs without a period of transition that involves sacrifice and/or discomfort, and that difficult challenges involve risk of failure and disappointment.
- Reframe failure before it might happen—and especially after it has happened—as a stepping stone toward eventual success, thus as a learning opportunity, rather than as evidence of deficiency or of being a *failure*.

Healthy Power—Prescriptions for Developing *Unrelenting Courage* as a Leader in the Workplace:

1) Become a stronger, more courageous leader by practicing the habit of acting in real time to solve problems and to complete key tasks first, rather than procrastinating about jugular issues (i.e., *open the closet and hug your monster*).

2) Reframe challenges and adversity as opportunities to develop resilience while maintaining faith that you and/or your staff will prevail in the end, thereby showing and engendering confidence among your team—a foundation of core strength—while not being wedded to the details of your eventual success.

3) Expect and teach your staff to find the courage to follow your good example in order to meet the challenges they face, insisting that courage is not the absence of fear but, instead, taking decisive action in the *presence* of fear.

4) Influence open and courageous interpersonal exchanges. Expressing empathy and understanding with staff is the most important communication skill that you can demonstrate in order to influence the courageous communication exchanges you desire. This begins with the willingness to listen to what others have to say and giving genuine respect to their ideas and opinions, even when they are quite different from your own. It means meeting your people where they are—listening with empathy to gain deeper understanding—before attempting to move them where you want them to go. This has a profound impact upon others because it gives them a sense of being safely

157

valued and understood, two of the most important factors that determine how secure your people will feel working under your direction. By having first validated the other person's right to her opinions and feelings, even if you strongly disagree with them, you have reduced the tension that otherwise would stand in the way of more open communication. By patiently and respectfully understanding the person, you help her to take heart and more openly express her voice with courage.

5) Understand that *Unrelenting Courage* is both the roadmap (i.e., moving from point A through transition at point B and ultimately to point C) and the heart strength that drives positive change.

6) Remember: you'll fail sometimes when you try your best, but you'll fail *every* time you don't try. Since failed efforts are inevitable—highly successful people providing evidence of this—decide that if you fail it will be while trying to succeed, instead of failing by not trying. As an important corollary: putting forth good effort with courage (commitment and confidence) already makes you a success, regardless of the outcome.

PEARLS OF HEALTHY POWER

George Bernard Shaw...

You see things; and you say 'Why?' But I dream things that never were; and I say 'Why not?'

Author unknown...

What would you attempt to do if you knew you could not fail?

Carolyn MacKenzie...

If you have a skeleton in your closet, take it out and dance with it.

Amy Bloom...

Intimacy is being seen and known as the person you truly are.

Ralph Waldo Emerson...

If I have lost confidence in myself, I have the universe against me...What lies behind us and what lies before us are tiny matters compared to what lies within us.

Beverly Sills...

You may be disappointed if you fail, but you are doomed if you don't try.

Bill Purdin...

One of the secrets of life is to be honestly who you are. Who others want you to be, who you used to be, and who you may someday become...these are fantasies. To be honestly who you are is to give up your illusions and face today with courage.

Henry David Thoreau...

If one advances confidently in the direction of his dreams, and endeavors to live the life which he has imagined, he will meet with a success unexpected in common hours.

Dr. Seuss...

Be who you are and say what you feel, because those who mind don't matter and those who matter don't mind.

Judy Garland...

Be a first rate version of yourself, not a second rate version of someone else.

Wayne Gretzky...

You miss 100% of the shots you don't take.

CHAPTER 8

L...*Lifelong Purpose* vs. *Lifelong Grasping*

Man is born to live, not to prepare for life.

Boris Pasternak

LIFELONG PURPOSE AND HEALTHY POWER

Purposeful, values-driven leadership is the most important root principle driving *Healthy Power* among the eight dimensions presented in this book. As Rick Warren has written, "When life has meaning, you can bear almost anything; without it, nothing is bearable." (*The Purpose Driven Life*, 2002, p. 30) Leadership that embodies such perspective infuses positive energy into both our personal and work lives. Obstacles then turn into helpful challenges, problems into opportunities, and setbacks into stepping stones that become equity in your bank toward eventual success. What, then, are the qualities of such values-driven leadership that galvanize our mind-body-spirit with *Lifelong Purpose* and empower our fullness of living?

Inspirational healthy leaders (e.g., Dr. Martin Luther King, Jr.) always evoke deep, positively transforming emotions in others through their commitment to a higher calling—to an ennobling purpose greater than themselves. By having such an effect, they generate the power of aligned and loyal followership and then use their supports and resources to mobilize purpose-driven effort, sometimes changing the world in which we live. Achieving this pinnacle of leadership success begins with a clear and passionate commitment to our dreams—visions that are so transparently benevolent and health-promoting that most people who hear of them cannot help but identify with their importance and lend their support.

Leadership that engenders positive, lasting results must embody the intangible qualities of *spirit* in order to create an atmosphere of purposeful excellence. When, for example, purpose-driven behavior characterizes a medical practice, Thomas Moore asserts, "You are not just doing a job, and you're not just a technician. Your whole being is involved in your work. People see it in the air around you." (*Care of the Soul in Medicine*, 2010, p. 56)

However, there is a caveat: some who ascribe primarily to a self-serving, primitive agenda either cannot or will not fathom such benevolence, and they will predictably resist and undermine its enactment within the group. The most effective leaders, therefore, recognize this archetypal conflict between *Healthy* and *Unhealthy Power*. They intervene to protect and preserve the group through all necessary and appropriate efforts.

Perhaps no one ever demonstrated more purposeful *Healthy Power* in leadership during challenging circumstances and then emerged more inspirationally than Viktor Frankl, who, as an Austrian Jew and psychiatrist, spent almost all of World War II in Nazi concentration camps, including three years at Auschwitz. Through his prolonged and tortuous trials, including the murder of his entire immediate family, he discovered many of the keys to psychological thriving beyond mere survival. He not only applied such strategies toward his own survival, but also played the roles of physician and spiritual guide to bolster the physical and emotional resilience of his fellow prisoners wherever he was held in captivity. Because Frankl's messages are timeless in their relevance to human struggles, we note his triumph of personal power because the modern day challenges we now face within economic, political, educational, and health care arenas require us to develop the same fundamental, purpose-driven leadership:

> "As we said before, any attempt to restore a man's inner strength in the camp had first to succeed in showing him some future goal. Nietzsche's words, 'He who has a *why* to live for can bear with almost any *how*,' could be the guiding motto for almost all psychotherapeutic and psychohygienic efforts regarding prisoners. Whenever there was an opportunity for it, one had to give them a why—an aim—for their lives,

in order to strengthen them to bear the terrible *how* of their existence. Woe to him who saw no more sense in his life, no aim, no purpose, and therefore no point in carrying on. He was soon lost."

(*Man's Search for Meaning*, 1959, pp. 84-85)

Purpose-Driven Leadership

Whether working productively with loyalty and commitment for a servant leader with whom we have an intimate yet deferential connection or merely toeing the line because we fear for our survival under a dictatorial boss, the underlying dynamic is the same: we are emotionally and behaviorally responsive in direct proportion to the magnitude of power we ascribe to another. Just as in effective parenting, a supervisor who is perceived as lacking power and, therefore, evoking little or no fear in her staff, receives proportionately little or no respect.

The key to creating enduring organizational or family strength and effectiveness that together generate healthy results, however, is not simply a matter of growing our arsenal of power without regard for interpersonal fairness or individual well-being. If it were truly the case that *might makes right*, then we would do well to rule dispassionately with a dictatorial iron fist. However, we know this is clearly not the case since the mere *quantity* of our power is not the only prerequisite to leadership effectiveness: the *quality* of our power and its perceived expression are much more important.

We become effective leaders to the degree we can influence others to follow our lead—aligning and engaging others so they strive together successfully toward outcomes we identify. Moreover, the authentically wholesome purposes we strive for are instrumental in invoking such loyalty and commitment. The admirable purposes which others can rightly identify with thereby create the ripple effect of our personal power when leading people. Accordingly, it cannot be expected, in general, that others will readily follow our directions, make adjustments, or embrace even moderately difficult changes we request without first having respect for the purposes that comprise our story—how others understand the most meaningful dreams that enliven us. People generally offer us respect in response to how they perceive our personhood—especially the strength of our character—more than to our position in the chain of command. It is part of our innate wiring to respond most to those people who carry sufficient power to make meaningful differences in our lives—who wield rewards and punishments—and to be especially attuned to those whom we fear, be it healthy fear or destructive dread. However, the most effective, influential leaders make their purposes transparently clear and altogether inviting, especially to those with good integrity. And while people at all levels of maturity become more willing followers in response to stronger, more powerful leaders—those who can impact their lives most meaningfully, regardless of their benevolent or malevolent intentions—truly great leaders understand and convey their commitment to purposes even greater than themselves, setting the stage compellingly for others also to play their part.

A Gift Filled with Purpose: *The Coin Purse*

My great-grandmother on my mother's side made an indelible impression upon me as a young boy about the value and importance of living with purpose, a purpose greater than oneself. Born in Bavaria during the late 1800s, she came from poor but proud German stock and spoke English with a bit of an accent. She lived alone as a widow in a small, old wooden shanty well into her 80s during a time when my family would visit her on Sunday afternoons following church services in the part of Pittsburgh where my mother had been raised. Her daily life was primitive, depending upon hand pumped well water and similarly old-fashioned coal stoves for both heating and cooking, and she was literally *dirt poor*. She always wore an old cotton dress with an apron, both habitually covered with coal smudges, traces of which also marked her face and hands. But what still impresses me most about this petite but hearty woman we affectionately called our *Little Grandma*, long after she passed away in her 90s, was the generous, heartfelt love that she always expressed with a warm smile, strong but gentle hands, and beautiful spirit.

She was always joyful and upbeat—never complaining—even though her lifestyle required daily arduous labor, she had minimal economic and social supports, and she weathered the most humble of living conditions. Being a person of strong faith, she frequently read her Bible and prayed as she gently rocked her old wooden chair next to her potbelly coal stove, especially when shut in on cold winter days. She also related stories to us children about her experiences of spiritual encounters with God, which at the time seemed both miraculous and frightening. Little Grandma was the embodiment of love, never speaking an unkind word, and dedicating herself to the betterment of others, as well as stray animals and those injured on the highway that ran along the modest front yard of her shanty.

By comparison, the suburban middle-class house in which we lived was much more spacious, clean, and physically comfortable. Little Grandma's shanty was chronically filled with coal dust, cramped and cluttered, and filled with the pungent smells of the dogs and cats she safeguarded from bad weather and nurtured back to health when hurt. In spite of these cosmetically unattractive features, I always felt that I was safe and loved in her presence— as if she had an aura about her that was powerful and sacred—making the stage on which she enacted her part secondary, even irrelevant.

During one particularly memorable visit to Little Grandma's shanty when I was about six years old (circa 1960), she eagerly took me to the side and firmly placed a small, black rectangular leather coin purse into my hands. The tiny pouch was old even then—having a rounded top with a strong brass zipper—and both sides bulged outward from the coins she had been saving for quite some time. She gave it to me wholeheartedly with astonishing energy and brightness in her eyes that can best be described as the emanation of pure love. Even at the time I understood that I should not accept this monetary gift because the 86 cents it contained was for her a significant portion of her food budget. She insisted, however, that I keep it in a manner that was clearly not negotiable. I fairly quickly relented, each coin looking to me like a precious gold piece, feeling that I had received a treasure chest because it was the most money I had ever held my little hands. And, I had already imagined *86* pieces of penny candy to follow: *heaven on earth!*

When my father spied how I delighted I'd become in receiving her gift, he insisted that she keep the money for all obvious reasons, thinking that she would go hungry without it and that I certainly would not. Then she declared something that profoundly shaped my future. Bracing her unimposing but hearty frame, she looked up at my father squarely in the face and fervently explained that this monetary gift she had saved was to be put aside for later college education. Further, she wanted my father (and me) to believe that I was destined one day to become a *scientist*—the term she used to define someone who could make positive contributions to society through knowledge and skills. Little Grandma implored my father to recognize my potential in this regard and, therefore, to allow her modest but significant investment in my future—a future she understood she would not likely witness but could support enthusiastically nonetheless. Dad finally appeased her by agreeing to permit me to receive her gift, but later in another room he quietly emptied the coins into a kitchen drawer, still believing that her immediate practical needs were much greater than her need to invest in my future. He then gave me the empty coin purse, now light and unimpressive—deflated, just like me—much to my heartbreak and disappointment.

In Chapter 7, I related the story of my early college struggles and the final resolution I made to major in Psychology following a helpful encounter with my intimidating but compassionate academic advisor. What I didn't include in the story then—emphasizing the role of *Unrelenting Courage* as part of core strength and personal empowerment—was the pivotal role played by the same leather coin purse during my strife. Little Grandma had recently passed away, and I had taken her coin purse with me to college as a sentimental keepsake, a remembrance of her loving spirit. During long, lonely walks at night across the campus, depressed and considering whether I should stay in college or pursue another path, I held the coin purse in my hand and recalled her words to me and my father that I would one day become a scientist. It was late into one such brightly moonlit walk that her words inspired me to find a way, if at all possible, to fulfill the dream she had instilled in me so long ago. She had defined for me a noble purpose—one in which I could be valuable through my knowledge and skills—so with a little help I subsequently became a psychologist, a *social scientist*. Once my path became clear, I felt imbued with her spirit and developed an unrelenting passion for helping others, fundamentally in much the same manner that Little Grandma demonstrated heartfelt compassion and generous service at every opportunity. Even during subsequent periods of professional turmoil and career crisis, the spirit of her intention for my work has brought me back to a confident focus on the higher purposes for which my education, training, and life experiences have prepared me.

Such is the role of *Lifelong Purpose* in providing both direction and energy to our lives, especially during periods of confusion, setback, and struggle. It doesn't matter if the purpose you choose (or in my case adopt) is one spiritually ordained or merely a random selection from our conscious mind having no other basis, the role and influence of purposeful living are always extraordinary. Accordingly, it has long been a mainstay approach of mine in working with a person struggling with what might be described as an *existential dilemma*—most often during early adulthood or mid-life—to encourage her to examine and discover a personally meaningful purpose for her life. For it is with an inspired sense of purpose that our lives take on meaning, and with such meaning we more readily become validated, energized, and focused. *Healthy Power* within this dimension—an authentic commitment to our *Lifelong Purpose* in accordance with the higher calling for which each of us is uniquely suited—synergizies with and amplifies each of the other seven dimensions presented earlier. While I'm tempted to go further down that path here, the integration of all eight of the *Healthy Power* dimensions working in concert will be presented in Chapter 9.

In the remainder of this chapter we'll examine the pitfalls of living without healthy purpose and meaning—*Lifelong Grasping*—followed by the keys to developing *Lifelong Purpose*. In case you're wondering, I keep Little Grandma's coin purse in her hall tree—built in 1865, as I discovered when I replaced its mirror shattered in transport and found newspaper clippings behind the glass. I keep a picture of her in her cotton dress and apron carrying a pail outside her shanty atop the drawer containing that precious gift, next to an antique wooden rocker where I sit and do most of my reading and meditating. I can still see her loving goodwill and *Optimistic Expectations* for me in her face. She continues to support the dream for which she made that inspiring investment many years ago. I'm reminded in writing these words how often the smallest gestures make the biggest impact—that mighty oaks grow from little acorns—and that *Healthy Power* is nurtured most effectively through our heartfelt acts of love.

LIFELONG GRASPING AND UNHEALTHY POWER

> *The irony of man's condition is that the deepest need is to be free*
> *of the anxiety of death and annihilation; but it is life itself which*
> *awakens it, and so we must shrink from being fully alive.*
>
> Ernest Becker

Modern history continues to be written with tragic stories of charismatic leaders (e.g., Francisco Franco, Jim Jones, Saddam Hussein, Moammar Gadhafi) who fundamentally enjoyed the same dynamics of power I just described—loyal followers imbued with a noble sense of purpose making committed efforts toward ambitious goals—but who caused mass suffering and brought devastation to the very people who empowered them. And while we celebrate the noble achievements of truly benevolent movements for both their intentions and the fruits they bear, too often inspired followers of their beloved leader's movement don't realize until after the fact that they were recruited for a dark and destructive purpose, even toward themselves. They discover too late in the game they've been deceived and/or ensnared by carefully hidden intentions, and then fall prey to well guarded weapons of *Unhealthy Power* they believed were part of the machinery geared for another mission. Although inevitably such reigns fall apart, they do so only after creating a destructive, often deadly wake. Like the character Lonesome Rhodes, portrayed convincingly by Andy Griffith in *A Face in the Crowd* (Warner Brothers, 1957), such leaders can influence millions by gaining their trust and support while at the same time holding them in disdain and tolerating them only as long as they are useful. What, then, differentiates leaders who follow the darker, more sinister path toward *Unhealthy Power*— characterized within this dimension as *Lifelong Grasping*—from those who follow the path toward *Healthy Power* in pursuit of *Lifelong Purpose*?

The Existential Dilemma: Failure to Make Resolution

M. Scott Peck began *The Road Less Traveled* with the assertion, "Life is difficult," resonating well with most readers because of its universal truth. And while many volumes of self-help literature provide information about how we can better cope with stress en route to thriving—making life less difficult, even joyful—the indisputable fact remains that each of us eventually will die, no matter how well or how poorly we cope during our life's journey. I believe there is no more important fact of life we must accept than this. At the risk of making light of a serious subject, the popular cliché about death certainly fits: *it is what it is.*

The fact that we are mortals and each of us will one day die is incredibly difficult to acknowledge because it cuts across the grain of our natural instincts, desires, and life energies. We are genetically endowed with powerful life-producing drives, including urges to propagate ourselves. Accordingly, we become predisposed during our formative years toward thinking that we are especially important and powerful, that we are destined to become winners and not losers, and that we and our offspring should rightly take charge of things: determining who should run our country, our corporations, and our key institutions. Attitudes and perspectives like "We're number 1" are highly supportive of fierce competition and superior achievement—winning in sports, in business, in the game of life—so facing our own eventual death runs counter to the primordial expectation that we are destined for unstoppable and eternal greatness, even though we are surrounded by evidence daily that points without exception the opposite direction. In spite of our denying reality, the facts remain that our bodies are mortal, that no material thing we acquire will be retained personally, and that nothing we achieve through a lifetime of effort will endure forever. Angst and despair are the normal initial reactions to this sobering realization. Moreover, most of us become so dismayed that we find it unthinkable that Shakespeare's Macbeth echoes theses same grim truths in lamenting:

> "Out, out, brief candle! Life's but a walking shadow, a poor player that struts and frets his hour upon the stage and then is heard no more: it is a tale told by an idiot, full of sound and fury, signifying nothing." (Act V, Scene V)

In light of the above, I invite you to consider the following paradoxical, seemingly contradictory truth: that only by understanding and accepting our own mortality can we remove the greatest barrier to living our lives to our fullest potential. We can attain our personal greatness only by first making this resolution—by accepting this fact of life that is wholly nonnegotiable. Remembering that *information is power* (when it is accurate and truthful) and that *Reality-Based Choices* are thus further empowering, accepting the fact of our guaranteed eventual passing frees us to live our lives within the light of this initially difficult truth. To do otherwise—to avoid and deny this truth—is to make it into a *monster in the closet* that grows from our inattention and haunts us by scratching at the door of our unconscious awareness. While popularly tempting and widespread, such monster making is a *Regressive Choice*, representing self-deception and disempowerment through magical thinking that is perpetuated by our *Unsettling Fear*.

I hope as you're reading this material it stirs you to wrestle with some difficult feelings and tough questions, such as: "All this talk about my own death makes me nervous and depressed! I know it's true, but how can accepting my mortality and coming to grips with it help me live my life more powerfully? I feel better and certainly do better when I just don't think about it. After all, even if I thought it was worthwhile, how *can* I resolve this haunting issue about my eventual death?" While I'll say more about this in the section on *Lifelong Purpose*, let's consider further here the disempowering effects we experience when we fail to resolve this key dilemma.

Denial of Death: *Running to Keep One Step Ahead of the Bear*

We generally feel most comfortable pursuing an expanded life without an anticipated or palpable end, thereby following our basic instincts, since after all, *ignorance is bliss*. However, this preference for comfort over facing the otherwise harrowing truth requires some means to maintain and perpetuate the inherent self-deception. Some of us avoid conscious realization of our own death as if we were running from a ravenous grizzly bear chasing us from afar. Terrified and seeing no other solution—believing we have no chance of survival unless we keep running—we continue to run desperately to stay one step ahead of the bear, too terrified even to glance backward for fear it will finally catch us, to our awful demise.

Many of us adopt this coping strategy to make it through life without dreading our looming death sentence. That is, we simply don't face the most jugular issue head-on, preferring instead to keep moving forward, persistently keeping the relentless grizzly out of sight and out of mind as much as possible by staying busy. We become preoccupied with day-to-day challenges and set our sights on future plans and goals, believing somehow that the importance of what we're doing supplants and nullifies anything else that could happen. Moreover, this strategy might even convince us for most of a lifetime that we have been able to *dodge the bullet* through hard work and achievements.

But deep inside our minds, of course, we are not fooled—the truth is irrefutable—even though we have set a pace to stay one step ahead of the bear, fearfully keeping our backs to it all the while. Ironically, the unconscious awareness that we have made a *Regressive Choice* of staggering proportions in denying our death limits the authenticity and depth to which we can commit ourselves to life itself. Without having resolved the question of our death, we block ourselves from making a full commitment to life, especially toward a purpose greater than our self. We go through life half-baked, knowing that we still need time and attention before we're complete, but we remain incomplete (and unfulfilled) until and unless we break the addiction that has emerged from preoccupation with our primitive self—the grand self who somehow certainly deserves to live forever. Like any addiction, based largely on denial and self-deception, our habitual pursuit of hedonistic comfort as a short-term substitute for the difficult task of wrestling with our eventual death requires progressively greater doses to have the same distracting and/ or numbing effect. We ascribe meaning to accomplishments and acquisitions that are both conscious and unconscious efforts to deny our mortality, such as reaching a pinnacle of success in our career, amassing a predetermined financial fortune, owning an idealized material prize, etc.—ultimately futile efforts to satisfy our craving.

Eventually, of course, we realize that there is no escaping the ever faster approaching bear, and that each accomplishment and acquisition has merely delayed our awakening to this truth. Usually late in our career, when we're less likely to achieve further upward mobility or acquire more assets, and we face failing health and a growing awareness that friends and family are passing away, most of us finally begin the hard work of making peace with death. Painfully, however, we often do this with a sense of regret—regret for having run so hard to stay ahead of the bear, instead of making peace with it before the run and chase event began. For some, better late than never, they achieve such a resolution, albeit with some degree of regret. However, for far too many others, the latter portion of life is lived in despair without ever making a healthy resolution.

In his classic, *Childhood and Society* (1963), Erik Erikson described the final two developmental challenges—*psychosocial conflicts*—we must resolve in order to live our lives with fullness and grace during our later years, including grace in how we manage our death as the final task of living:

...Generativity versus *Stagnation...*

...Ego Integrity versus *Despair...*

Resolving these conflicts is vitally important since they represent milestones of our personal development. Such resolution requires us to accept that our lives—no matter how masterfully orchestrated—end with the same predetermined crescendo, and to humbly accept this natural way of all living creatures. We cannot demonstrate *Generativity*—a conscious and altruistic commitment to the well-being of others, including future generations—without first having accepted the limitations of our time and opportunity on Earth. Failure to make such resolution leaves us either running on a treadmill of compulsive effort to convince ourselves that the race goes on forever, or we simply embody *Stagnation*—arrested in growth, resigned, and bitter. Of course, the final milestone we do well to attain—*Ego Integrity*—also requires coming to grips with our eventual end, for if we fail to do so we're likely to feel cheated, victimized, misled, and betrayed. We then *Despair* the opportunities missed, the brevity of life itself, and the foolishness with which we spent our most precious gift other than life itself: our time!

Avoiding the Shock: *Learned Helplessness*

Martin Seligman is a behavioral psychologist who conducted research with dogs in the 1960s to better understand depression en route to popularizing what has become known today as *Positive Psychology*. As part of his studies, he observed dogs that were placed in long raised cages with wire mesh floors through which mild electric shock could be sent. Shocking the dogs on only one half of the cage floor sent them scampering to the other side to escape the discomfort. But when they were shocked throughout the cage floor and had no chance to escape, many gave indications of depression—no longer eating or sleeping—and most simply gave up. The majority of such ill-fated dogs continued to lie helplessly in their cages receiving shocks believing that no escape was possible, even when they would have been spared by moving to the other side after the conditions were altered. Like us, their perception became their reality, even though they were wrong, and they gave up hope when they could not face what they perceived as inescapable reality. Seligman then coined the phrase *learned helplessness* to describe this phenomenon of disempowered thinking, feeling, and behaving, and we have since come to recognize how vulnerable each of us is to this phenomenon, especially when we *perceive* that no escape from our torment is possible.

The disquieting lessons learned with these experimental dogs apply directly to our struggles to resolve the torment posed by questions regarding our death. We must face the shock inherent in this fact of life with courage, resolved that each of us can become free to live life without either trying to escape it—staying one step ahead of the bear—or depressed with a sense of resignation and helplessness. This latter sense of sub-acute depression characterizes the popular malaise in our society today. Rather than facing the challenge of finding purpose in life, in spite of the fact that it always ends in death, too many of us abdicate our power to death either by avoiding it or settling for a life of diminished vigor because we judge it was unfairly scripted before we were born.

Recognize that *Lifelong Grasping* stems largely from two different failures regarding locus of control. In the first, although we maintain an internal locus of control regarding death, we take an arrogant stance by resisting and denying it, blocking healthy resolution. We then stumble forward through life staying necessarily half asleep, only to be awakened to the truth late in the game when regret is the predictable outcome. In the second type—this time from an external force—we acknowledge death as being inevitable, but again we fail to make adequate resolution: we resign ourselves to being trapped as if helpless victims, like the dogs who erringly gave up hope/effort, squandering our lives in *Stagnation* and *Despair*.

The other factor that makes it difficult, if not impossible to make peace with death en route to finding purpose in living is the direction we invest our energies and resources—the mission that gives our life meaning. When we remain self-absorbed and essentially egocentric, we attract people and resources toward ourselves as if we are the final mission. In our relative immaturity we then define ourselves as the endpoint in the journey—a mission to serve and perpetuate our ego indefinitely. Progressively developing an addiction to self, we live according to numerous lies, such as, "She who dies with the most toys wins!" Any mission that begins and ends with such shortsightedness based upon self deception is destined to fail. This failure stems from our magical thinking about death—another *monster in the closet* from which we can run but not hide. Haunted by the same truth we're trying to avoid, we run scared through life, being scared of life itself, arrested developmentally. And thus we remain stuck in our personal mission focus, one in which *more is better*. Tragically, this represents a vicious downward spiral because—like any addiction—no amount of people, energy, and resources invested in the self as the final mission brings joy or lasting happiness. Instead of living in the present moment with mindfulness gained via healthy acceptance of the future endpoint, we have a desperate need to live *for* the moment as a way to avoid even thinking about that endpoint. And when we enter into that downward spiral, we simply continue to grasp for the elusive brass ring hanging just beyond our reach, or in reaching it we despair anyway.

Such is the character, Ryan Bingham, portrayed wonderfully by George Clooney in the movie *Up in the Air* (Paramount Pictures, 2010). His espoused major purpose driving him ever forward is to become only the seventh person ever to accumulate 10 million air miles and thereby be granted "elite status" by an iconic figure from the airline he frequents. Because he is a business consultant who enables employers to downsize their workforce, he travels incessantly across the country to deliver bad news to those being let go, preferring life as a road warrior over any home base. He also freelances as a motivational speaker in which he prescribes a superficial yet seemingly attractive philosophy of life in which you "empty your backpack"—making minimal meaningful connections in order to travel light, emotionally speaking. After a passionate affair with a fellow traveler who ascribes to his same basic philosophy, Clooney makes an uncharacteristic gesture to come in for a landing with her, so to speak, after having spent many years leaving deeper personal connections in a holding pattern. But when he discovers that she is married with a family and has only superficial interest in him—confessing, "You're a break from our normal lives...a parenthesis!"—he simply returns to the lifestyle he knows: flying high, relentlessly grasping for special recognition and temporal rewards, keeping his backpack as light as possible.

So we don't leave you also up in the air, let's now focus on the development of *Healthy Power* we obtain first by making resolution regarding our mortality on the way to finding our *Lifelong Purpose*.

THE PATHWAY TO LIFELONG PURPOSE

*To live fully is to live with an awareness of the
rumble of terror that underlies everything.*

Ernest Becker

The *Candy Dish*

Imagine that when we're first born, fresh out of the womb, not yet having been subjected to the influences of the external world and the environment that greets us, we are the equivalent of an empty candy dish—as opposed to the common image of a blank slate or *tabula rasa*. Further, if we think of basic parenting during infancy as providing sustenance, both physically and emotionally, that enables us to develop normally, we can liken a child's early nurturing to the experience of receiving candy in our dish, one piece at a time. Again, when exposed to at least adequate care and nurturing, we grow and develop year after year having our dependency needs met, and our candy dish grows ever fuller. We begin to grow then in the building blocks of core strength, including more confident actions and accompanying self-esteem, setting the stage for a solid, realistic sense of self. Once we develop greater autonomy—the ability to stand on our own two feet and to nurture ourselves interdependently through loving attachments outside the home—we discover that we can bring even more delicious treats into our candy dish on our own accord.

Once we become sufficiently strong and independent that the flow of candy brings us to the brim of fullness—having core strength with contentment and appreciation for all that we have or ever expect to have—something miraculously transformative takes place: we shift from being inner-directed to other-directed. That is, we become unstuck, no longer preoccupied with preserving and perpetuating our self as our ultimate life mission. Instead, we turn our attention, energies, and resources outwardly to consider the needs and well-being of others while, at the same time, continuing to provide for our personal needs—a *Win-Win Relationship* with the world. Like a child free to eat her fill in a candy shop who discovers way too soon there's just too much to hold, we find a purpose greater than ourselves once we're full and satiated. Operating at that point from an abundance mentality, wholly satisfied with the richness we've enjoyed, we become altruistic—showing unconditional, generous goodwill toward others, as described earlier in this book. And it is through our altruistic acts that we derive the highest forms of fulfillment, including *Energizing Joy.*

Recognize in the scenario above, however, that in order to arrive at the point of appreciation, fullness, and contentment that enable the joy of altruistic behavior there is a caveat: this highest ideal requires a combination of adequate early developmental nurturing/support and core strength formation that leads to our independent functioning and personal satisfaction. Tragically, the scenario follows a very different path when the newborn does not receive adequate nurturing and support. And when her life story is characterized by trauma, abuse, and/or negligence, she struggles in her core strength development, compromising her ability to function independently or to become personally contented. Her candy dish then not only remains woefully sparse, she does not discover how to fill her own dish when her more fortunate peers are learning to do so successfully. Addiction treatment professionals consider this is the equivalent experience of producing a *hole in the soul*—an emptiness that impedes forward progress and growth, amplifying dependency needs, and generating some form or another of craving. Until and unless we make developmental progress in this respect, we remain fixated upon ourselves as the primary object of personal investment and importance. Amid such arrested development, it is fairly inconceivable that we can become genuinely committed to the welfare of others, even though the idea is inviting and seemingly noble, because we experience a sense of being diminished or cheated whenever someone else has good fortune or is somehow blessed—as if we've been cheated of our fair share the candy.

While there is relatively little we can do to change our past, except to learn from our personal history and view it through a more helpful lens, there is a great deal we can do to increase our core strength and, therefore, to make the developmental progress that liberates us from a self-serving focus and life mission to one that can become truly generative. In fact, this entire book has been devoted to such core strength development through each of the preceding seven dimensions. Moreover, I hope you now recognize how making progress in each of the preceding pathways toward *Healthy Power* sets the stage for this major life transition—for us to gain the strength, resilience, and insight to recognize our higher purpose as living creatures. Such core strength development—including the humility required to make *Reality-Based Choices*—brings our own mortality into full view where we can grapple with the seemingly insurmountable issues it first presents.

Again, our struggle to make peace with death is an arduous one—one in which we naturally experience the stages of death and dying identified by Elisabeth Kubler-Ross in *On Death and Dying* (1969). We initially react to the news about the grim reaper coming one day for us in shock and disbelief, denying the veracity of this reported fact. If we move forward to the next stage, we protest in anger and/or become depressed, and this is where the maladaptive defense mechanisms described earlier too often come into play that stunt our further maturation and growth. But if we have sufficient core strength, including a commitment to truth and the courage to understand and accept it no matter how difficult to believe, then our initially horrifying realization of death provides the energy to make sense of our lives. In our struggle, from which we refuse to retreat in pursuit of greater comfort, we have no reasonable healthy alternative but to find a purpose even greater than our time-limited mortal selves—one that then gives our lives deeper meaning. And it is critical that we eventually identify this sense of dharma—higher calling—to ignite the hope and energy that enable us to live our lives wide-awake, focused, and at peace with its inevitable ending. Such is the only empowering stance we can take. In making a healthy resolution with death we discover, ironically, that it serves as the critical linchpin connecting us back to our daily lives, then and only then with opportunity for fullness of living toward our unique personal greatness. Moreover, our lives become reinvented as an adventure to be lived, no longer a problem to be solved. After all, it is impossible to experience deep, lasting peace and uninterrupted productive focus as long as we are haunted—and thus diminished and distracted—by the back story of death ever more persistently robbing us of energy for living.

Daniel Pink underscores the importance of resolving this existential dilemma so we can spawn and liberate our energies to find our deeper, fulfilling life purpose acknowledging that it usually happens much later in life than would be ideal, according to the research he cites:

> "Failing to understand this conundrum—that satisfaction
> depends not merely on having goals, but on having the

right goals—can lead sensible people down self-destructive paths…Being able to contemplate the big picture, to ponder one's own mortality, to understand the paradox that attaining certain goals isn't the answer seemed to require having spent a few years on the planet."

(Drive, 2009, pp. 143-144)

Connection via Purpose

Each of us carries a profoundly important need to feel connected in meaningful ways, especially with other people, instead of feeling isolated and alone. At the same time, however, in our relative immaturity we remain fixated upon ourselves as the primary purpose for which we strive day-to-day. And so there is a catch: the primary purpose for which we strive enables a sense of connection, since we value and embrace the objects of our emotional investment. However, once we recognize the truth of our mortality—that our bodies will eventually get sick and die—we understand that our life's purpose has become futile, and we lose life energy because we've lost hope. Even in our denial and other defensiveness about death described earlier, there can be no lasting enthusiasm about a mission—albeit a recurrently pleasurable one—that ends abruptly by falling into a bottomless pit and utter darkness. We then lose meaningful connection, regenerating *The Nothing* described in Chapter 2. We also face a wonderful opportunity to become transformed in response to this intriguing paradox. Facing mortality, we shrink into infinite smallness as a singular, time-limited being on Earth. But we recover from this crisis by finding a purpose greater than ourselves—one in which we extend ourselves toward others and our planet with loving kindness—thereby becoming inclusively connected with the universe. And in this intimate and inextricable connection with the universe—comprising infinite time and space—we embrace our purposeful action to leave a legacy with a sense of immortality.

In his intriguing book, *The Shift*, Wayne Dyer suggests that the *afternoon of life* differs from the *morning* in that we experience the compelling drive (i.e., *future pull*) to discover the unique purpose of our lives. It is a shift *from ambition to meaning* through which we can enjoy lasting fulfillment and joy. As Joseph Campbell said, "The big question is whether you are going to be able to say a hearty yes to your adventure." As Americans enter their mid- to late-50s and consider retirement options for their not-too-distant future, often having amassed significant material wealth, new challenges emerge apart from those of career and family management. Specifically, they face developmental challenges of personal growth and fulfillment that tend to creep into consciousness more intensely at this time, often leading to mid-life crises.

Once we finally come to grips with our own mortality, having mustered the core strength through humility and courage to do so, we resolve to find purpose and meaning in our lives by focusing outside ourselves. In the transition of priorities we become other-directed and altruistic, assuming our candy dish has become sufficiently full to afford us an unselfish investment of our time, energy, and resources. As a forerunner to this shift in focus, we learn to pace and nurture ourselves first in order to be ready and in shape when we have the opportunity to serve others with any significance or to bring them something of lasting value—to bring candy for *their* dish. Forming and maintaining lifestyle habits for effective self-care are, therefore, prerequisites to experiencing the joy of acting with altruism. That our gifts are not always abundantly available becomes acutely apparent when we're wounded, exhausted, and otherwise depleted through our *Regressive Choices*. Altruism at such times is a luxury we basically cannot afford. We either feel no desire to serve others due to our personal deficits or we deplete ourselves further in a lose-win proposition while striving, perhaps nobly, to do so in a kind of martyrdom. Such self-defeating sacrifices over time render even the most hearty souls among us weakened and diminished, no longer feeling of value to self or others—a lose-lose outcome. While genuinely altruistic behavior feeds the soul with joy, the body and mind must also be fed and strengthened in order to maintain our vitality over the long term. Therefore, make daily efforts at personal empowerment in every form, reflecting not only your healthy self-love in doing so, but also a deep desire to express that well of caring in serving others—creating a beautiful win-win.

In the classic film, *You Can't Take It With You* (Columbia Pictures, 1938), Lionel Barrymore (Grandpa) beautifully sums up seeking *Lifelong Purpose* when speaking to Edward Arnold (portraying wealthy business mogul, Mr. Kirby) instead of simply amassing great fortune at the cost of his family and friends:

> "You can't take it with you, Mr. Kirby, so what good is it? As near as I can see, the only thing you *can* take with you is the love of your friends!"

Healthy Power—Prescriptions for Developing *Lifelong Purpose* as a Leader in the Workplace:

1) Strengthen your commitment to building meaningful interpersonal and professional relationships toward the achievement of worthy goals. Nurturing healthy interdependence between yourself, your co-workers/staff, and your family/friends/community is important for living with a sense of wholeness, safety, and purpose.

2) Develop and consistently demonstrate your *integrity*—the depth and degree to which your values align with your observable actions—so that you embody internal harmony and core strength. Accordingly, lead others with transparency, authenticity, and trustworthiness—the keys to empowerment of others and, thus, to gaining their following in support of your leadership.

3) In parallel fashion, determine to build a culture of integrity within your organization that is forward-thinking, results-oriented, and values-driven. Toward those ends, create meaningful *Vision*, *Mission*, and *Values Statements* aligned with and supportive of both business and cultural development goals, and then make them palpable in everything you do.

PEARLS OF HEALTHY POWER

Ernest Becker...

Man cannot endure his own littleness unless he can translate it into meaningfulness on the largest possible level.

Max DePree...

When we think about leaders and the variety of gifts people bring to corporations and institutions, we see that the art of leadership lies in polishing and liberating and enabling those gifts.

Joseph Campbell...

I think the person who takes a job in order to live—that is to say, for the money—has turned himself into a slave.

Gail Sheehy...

No sooner do we think we have assembled a comfortable life than we find a piece of ourselves that has no place to fit in.

Abraham Maslow...

He that is good with a hammer tends to think everything is a nail...What a man can be, he must be. This need we call self-actualization.

Carl Rogers...

The good life is a process, not a state of being...It is a direction, not a destination.

Viktor E. Frankl...

Ever more people today have the means to live, but no meaning to live for.

Elisabeth Kubler-Ross...

As far as service goes, it can take the form of a million things. To do service, you don't have to be a doctor working in the slums for free, or become a social worker. Your position in life and what you do doesn't matter as much as how you do what you do.

Matthew 5: 14-16...

You are the light of the world. A city set on a hill cannot be hid. Nor do men light a lamp and put it under a bushel, but on a stand, and it gives light to all in the house. *Let your light so shine before men, that they may see your good works and give glory to your Father who is in heaven.*

Buddha...
Even death is not to be feared by one who has lived wisely.

Stephen R. Covey...
It's incredibly easy to get caught up in an activity trap, in the business of life, to work harder and harder at climbing the ladder of success only to discover it's leaning against the wrong wall. If there is one message to glean from this wisdom, it is that a meaningful life is not a matter of speed or efficiency. It's much more a matter of what you do and why you do it, than how fast you get it done.

CHAPTER 9

Conclusion

Have you died to your animal nature and come to life as a human incarnation? That's the beginning of humanity!

Joseph Campbell

Power: *The Interplay of Light and Shadow*

At its deepest essence, this book has been about the interplay of light and shadow—good and evil—in constant motion throughout our lives. Like the ebb and flow of oceanic tides, rising and falling in concert with the moon, we move constantly back-and-forth between admirable and ignoble behavior. We are not fixed, and we're never perfect. No one is exempt—we are mercurial and ever-changing—thus any sense of permanence is merely an illusion. Each of us is born with an animalistic nature that is our ancient heritage and has served our species well through the millennia for basic survival. Since it appears that we are the only creatures endowed with higher consciousness, we are uniquely capable of contemplating our existence, thus we have evolved to the point that we can make choices above and beyond our mere survival. Moreover, through self-mastery, evolution has presented us opportunity to go beyond the reactivity that characterizes most other living things. Our species governs and reigns supreme over the planet with advanced reasoning and execution skills combined with skills in emotion management and impulse regulation—also setting our species apart from the animal world. However, the *nature* of our power depends not primarily upon this superior raw potential. Ultimately, our power is determined by the operating system we apply in self-governance, and that has been the focus of this book.

Speaking in behavioral terms, we can mature in a manner that affords us the power to choose our responses to most any situation, rather than simply react in knee-jerk fashion. That is, while animals predictably demonstrate *stimulus–response* ("S-R") behavior, we have the power to make conscious choices as the *organism* functioning in between stimuli and the responses we generate ("S-O-R"). Accordingly, the framework for understanding power within the eight dimensions described throughout this book has been an attempt to illuminate those key forks in the road where choices are made in our pursuit of power, both healthy and destructive.

Perhaps the most fitting way to capture the essence of the lessons provided throughout this book is to cite a quote from Erich Fromm's work, *The Heart of Man: Its Genius for Good and Evil* (1964):

> "Most people fail in the art of living not because they are inherently bad or so without will that they cannot lead a better life; they fail because they do not wake up and see that they stand at a fork in the road and have to decide. They are not aware when life asks them a question, and when they still have alternative answers. Then with each step along the wrong road it becomes increasingly difficult for them to admit that they *are* on the wrong road, often only because they have to admit that they must go back to the first wrong turn, and must accept the fact that they have wasted energy and time." (pp. 173-178)

In Robert Louis Stevenson's *Strange Case of Dr. Jekyll and Mr. Hyde* (1886), the basic coexistence of light and shadow in each of us is poignantly portrayed. Written by the author during Victorian era Scotland—which is characterized historically by pervasive repression of primitive emotions and impulses, sexuality in particular—Dr. Jekyll exemplifies the admirable qualities of a man striving to separate from and conquer the evil that lies within our species in order to liberate the spirit and thereby fully empower our better selves. However, he discovers tragically that the more he endeavors to split away and extinguish this part of his basic nature, the more power his dark side acquires, leading him as Mr. Hyde into the most hedonistic and horrific acts of self-indulgence and violence at others' expense. Ultimately, he brings about his own destruction after having become progressively more out of control in pursuit of self-serving goals having no other purpose than to persist in personal pleasure while avoiding pain and discomfort.

Moreover, it amplifies the point that *what we resist persists*. That is, when we strive to split away any portion of our being deemed to be alien to our self-image—thereby denying the truth to ourselves—we lose touch with that portion of ourselves and, therefore, sacrifice whatever controls we had over it. There is an adage which states, "Keep your friends close and your enemies closer!" This certainly pertains as well to the management of various unbecoming facets of our personality. So, instead of attempting to deny or split away the shadow aspect of our being—which tends only to amplify it beyond our conscious control—we do well to accept and embrace even the most primitive and unattractive features of which we are comprised. Ironically, then, it is from this self acceptance and personal inclusiveness— through assimilation of our most animalistic urges and impulses—that we develop the strongest possible integration and self mastery.

Rather than thinking of this process as one of repression and restraint—like struggling to hold a beach ball beneath the surface of the water—think of this as acknowledging every aspect of our being in the light of day, thereby channeling its energy for expression and sublimating it into constructive choices. After all, the beach ball above the water becomes lighter and more easily managed, even fun to play with at times. When we develop this more realistic and inclusive sense of self—gaining mastery in self-control in the face of internal or external stimulation—it also becomes easier to acknowledge the coexistence of light and shadow in others. By contrast, if we are limited to creating an all-or-none dichotomy in which we only recognize inherent good in ourselves and split away the not so good, we will tend to view others and the world in similar fashion. There will be those we judge to be good, with whom we feel safe and well identified, and those we judge to be evil, so unlike ourselves that we lack identification, empathy, and compassion, even for their existence. When such is our worldview, a view based upon lower consciousness and self deception, we are destined to experience conflict and to create suffering. So, the question you might rightly ask at this point is, "How do I grow and mature into a person with sufficient integration of *light* and *shadow* that I can develop the mastery and skills I desire?" Let's explore this question more fully in view of power.

Corruption through Power

In J. R. R. Tolkien's classic trilogy, *The Lord of the Rings* (1954), Frodo Baggins, a humble and unassuming little hobbit, undertakes a mythological and perilous journey. It is an epic tale of the hero's quest for *Healthy Power* amidst the archetypal challenges posed by *Unhealthy Power*, like so many enduring myths and stories over the centuries. He has accepted the challenge to destroy the Ring—the most powerful of all other rings being sought by the Dark Lord, Sauron, who is striving to conquer Middle Earth. Frodo must take the Ring to its place of origin, Mount Doom, and cast it into a molten river to destroy it so that the forces of darkness under Sauron will not prevail. Symbolizing each of us at our best, he is at the same time virtuous and flawed as the Ring's bearer. Frodo receives assistance from a wide variety of mortal and supernatural beings in fellowship with him as like-minded travelers who share the purpose of supporting his journey. The external challenges he encounters are both arduous and life-threatening, but his greatest challenge is internal. That is, the Ring compels its holder to acquire its intrinsic power— the power of darkness—and that part of Frodo which is also shadow-like becomes entranced and drawn by its lure. At such times of corruption arising within him, Frodo becomes suspicious, critical, and competitive, even toward his closest friends. His uncharacteristically animal nature and primitive, self-absorbed behavior make him all the more susceptible to serving the interests of the Ring and its would-be master.

No one falls under the spell of the Ring more tragically than another hobbit, originally named Sméagol. Thousands of years after it was lost, the ancient Ring was found by a river-dwelling hobbit called Déagol after falling into a pond where he and his friend, Sméagol, had been fishing. Sméagol falls under the Ring's spell immediately and kills Deagol during a violent fight to seize it. Hiding from his crime in seclusion under the Misty Mountains, Sméagol becomes transformed over the course of several hundred years through the Ring's unholy power into a misshapen and corrupted creature called Gollum. Eventually, Gollum also loses the ring, only to become preoccupied with finding and reclaiming it at any cost. He refers to the ring as *my precious*, showing absolute devotion toward and dependency upon it, much as you would expect a chronic drug addict to describe her daily drug of choice. Gollum can think of nothing else. In his compulsion to reclaim the Ring, he lies, steals, manipulates, and attempts to kill others without hesitation or remorse.

At the climax of the story, Frodo is unable to fend off the dark power of the Ring any longer and claims it selfishly as his own. Perched along the cliff overlooking the molten River at the Cracks of Doom, Gollum reemerges and struggles wildly with Frodo in pursuit of the Ring he is wearing. Gollum then bites off Frodo's finger, Ring and all. In wild celebration, oblivious to the danger, Gollum falls over the cliff into the river of fire to his death, unwittingly destroying the Ring along with him.

In the end, Frodo is victorious, having mustered sufficient self-discipline to see the Ring destroyed—rather than succumbing to it entirely—permitting light to prevail by keeping darkness from overwhelming it. The deeper message is that private victory over his own dark leanings was required before he could experience a public victory, as is usually the case with each of us. Others briefly holding the Ring along the way had become untrustworthy and then jeopardized the greater mission because they were transformed by the Ring's seductive power. We also come to appreciate that Frodo, like each of us, had to make significant sacrifice in order to complete the heroic challenge. It took Gollum biting off his finger holding the Ring to awaken his consciousness before he could let it go, much like the monkeys described earlier who could only find freedom by releasing that to which they clung at the bottom of the gourd (see Chapter 4).

"Power corrupts, and absolute power corrupts absolutely" holds true, except for those with an effective operating system. We all face difficult forks in the road repeatedly, just as every hero throughout history has faced and forever will. In our own journey, how do we gain the victory in pursuit of our highest purposes, and what are the roadmaps we can follow?

All Roads Lead to Power

...Following Pathways toward Healthy Power

In Figure 1, five phases of human development are depicted as they relate to our personal power. In Phase I, the child is dependent upon protection and nurturance from her environment to ensure healthy growth and development, metaphorically described as a *candy dish* in Chapter 8. Accordingly, energy and resources are invested within the child, enabling her to grow and to complete passages toward core strength development successfully. In Phase II, she has developed sufficient core strength to engage in further struggle effectively with necessary features of safety, stability, and a cohesive sense of self. With continued maturation and growth, she enters Phase III and gains the ability to subordinate her ego with a realistic sense of self, humility, and an appreciation for others. The subordination of the ego can be likened to dying to oneself, so it thus serves as a critical developmental milestone that must be attained in order to enter Phase IV: feeling an intimate connection with the world as a viable creature within it. The experience of such intimate connection and appreciation for the world, including all living things and the universe, itself, sets the stage for resolution of the challenge posed by mortality, also discussed in Chapter 8. Having developed the prerequisite core strength to accept our death, in Phase V we resolve the existential dilemma ultimately by finding a purpose greater than ourselves, and in doing so we invest our energies and resources outwardly, no longer preoccupied with a self-serving mission. This leads to the highest level of consciousness and fulfillment through altruistic behavior and consequent joy. Rather than bemoaning the injustice of living only a century or less, we celebrate our lives with an immortal sense of presence, appreciating our best contribution to the universe, finding contentment and peace in the process.

Figure 1: *Healthy Power...*

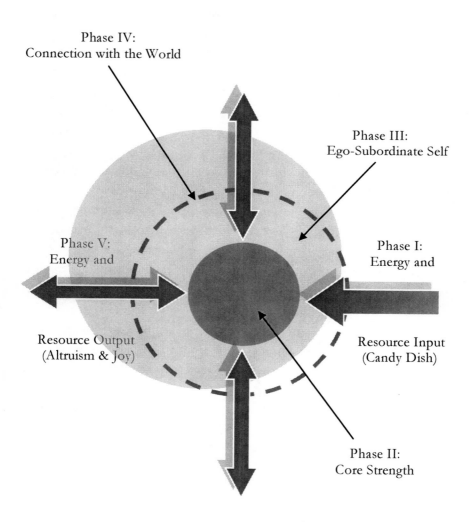

Phase IV:
Connection with the World

Phase III:
Ego-Subordinate Self

Phase V:
Energy and

Phase I:
Energy and

Resource Output
(Altruism & Joy)

Resource Input
(Candy Dish)

Phase II:
Core Strength

Personal Greatness in Harmony with the World

...Following Pathways toward *Unhealthy Power*

In Figure 2, the same five phases of human development are depicted in our quest for power; but, unlike the first scenario described in Figure 1 above, we become predisposed toward following pathways leading to *Unhealthy Power* instead. In Phase I, conditions either too harsh or too comfortable impede early growth and maturation, predisposing the child to remain weak, unstable, insecure, and thus slow to develop, if not arrested altogether. Accordingly, core weakness becomes apparent in Phase II, characterized by continued preoccupation with self, specifically around issues of physical safety, emotional security, and psychological wholeness. There is exaggerated and prolonged dependency, and this carries over into Phase III by perpetuating an egocentric self, one who lacks empathy and regard for others. Interpersonal relationships remain conflicted, further compounding the struggle toward healthy maturation. She develops a thick and rigid defensive shell to safeguard a fragile sense of self at her core, having the effect of creating a lonely separation from the world—one in which deep, meaningful relationships cannot be established or maintained—while hungering for intimacy and loving attachments. In her continued struggle for power, she seeks energy and resources from people and the world otherwise, often in addictive fashion. Phase V is then characterized by her inability to shift focus outside of her or to invest in others in meaningful ways while consuming everything around her incessantly, much like the *black hole* from which nothing re-emerges. Consequently, she remains essentially addicted to herself, craving energy and resources to fill the hole in her soul, fixated upon a personal mission—rather than an outer-directed one—while remaining unfulfilled in *Lifelong Grasping*. Whereas in Figure 1 the pinnacle of development is characterized by personal greatness in harmony with the world, the road to *Unhealthy Power* always generates personal struggle in conflict with the world.

Figure 2: *Unhealthy Power...*

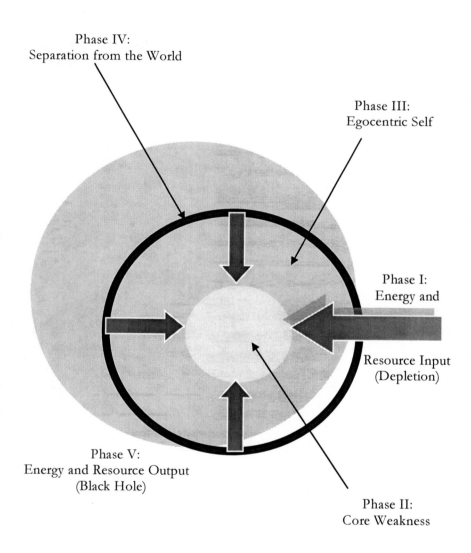

Phase IV:
Separation from the World

Phase III:
Egocentric Self

Phase I:
Energy and

Resource Input
(Depletion)

Phase V:
Energy and Resource Output
(Black Hole)

Phase II:
Core Weakness

Personal Struggle in Conflict with the World

The Journey of Heroes

Joseph Campell described the *hero's journey* as an archetypal quest for spiritual ascendancy and power in *The Power of Myth* (1988). To illuminate our journey, even today, he offers the primary counsel that we *follow our bliss*: that we discover and follow the primary track for which our lives are intended—pursuing the goals and dreams for which we have greatest passion—and through which we awaken spiritually to become aligned with the highest consciousness from which we were created. In dying to our former self, we become regenerated with heartfelt compassion for all living creatures and the universe we share—the key that differentiates us as human beings from the animal world. Accordingly, he asserts that each of us longs to find our bliss and thus become part of the human race through embodiment of our highest calling—our *Holy Grail*—and suggests the following:

> "The Grail represents the fulfillment of the highest spiritual potentialities of the human consciousness...love is perfect kindness...spiritual life is the bouquet of natural life, not a supernatural thing imposed upon it...the best we can do is lean toward the light!"

Anything short of this aspiration, frankly, turns us in another direction, one in which we remain absent of love, devoid of connection, and unhappily isolated amidst self-absorption. It is our capacity for unconditional love, therefore—both toward self and others—that elevates us beyond our primordial selves. A lack of such love arrests our development and creates an inner emptiness that cannot be filled, even through a lifetime of investing energies and resources inwardly. Instead, healthy self-love combined with humility attained through a subordinated ego permits extension of love to others. Such is the differentiation that makes us most human, and through which we can approximate our personal greatness in what Campbell describes as the *rapture* of living.

I also agree with Campbell that a key requirement for our journey toward *Healthy Power* is that we find and make daily use of our own *sacred place*.

> "It is an absolute necessity for anybody today...a place where you can simply experience and bring forth what you

are, and what you might be…this is the place of creative incubation."

It is here that we pursue the journey, engage in the struggle, and come forth transformed through regular meditation, prayer, reading, and otherwise listening in stillness to the deeper inclinations of our heart and soul.

Building Core Strength: *The Butterfly in Its Cocoon*

If you ask, "How should I struggle, and what is the key to my transformation?" then please consider the following metaphoric story as a guide in your journey.

A young girl participated with excitement along with her classmates and teacher in her science class field trip to a nearby forest. When the teacher stopped along the wooded path to gather the group's attention, she became particularly interested. A cocoon had been neatly woven into a fork between the small limbs of a sapling tree, white and wispy, having the appearance of a little cotton pouch. The teacher then invited each student to observe how the cocoon was gently pulsating, to which the inquiring minds awaited their leader's reply. "A caterpillar created this cocoon so that it could change itself into a butterfly; but, as you can see, it's still struggling to break free before it can fly away." For the rest of their outdoor excursion, the girl pondered the plight of this butterfly, unable yet to hatch from its cocoon. After school, she returned to the spot in the forest where the cocoon had been found that morning, longing to lend assistance to the struggle. She carefully cut the cocoon from the fork with scissors and then trimmed its edges to release the quivering creature inside. However, much to her shock and dismay, when she opened the cocoon, she discovered only an unrecognizable thing—neither caterpillar nor butterfly—and it had just died!

In science class the next day, she shared her disturbing story with the teacher in pursuit of an explanation (and hoping to find relief from her guilt). Understanding her intention, the teacher explained to her and the class, "The caterpillar was going through stages of development inside the cocoon in gradual steps. When we saw it yesterday, its tiny wings were not yet fully grown. It was pressing against the inner walls as a way to strengthen its wings—the pressure and resistance causing them to grow. The struggle and growth it creates would enable the transformation to be complete, so eventually the butterfly would emerge with mature wings to fly away. You certainly meant well, even though you didn't understand this process and how important it was for the struggle to continue so the butterfly could become complete. Like that butterfly, we, too, must struggle successfully and complete each necessary step to become full-grown, mature, and free!"

In parallel fashion, such is the process through which we grow and mature in our development of power. The key to our transformation is the struggle, including all the necessary and gradual steps involved in the process toward becoming full grown. And, like the caterpillar holding the potential for metamorphosis into a majestic butterfly, we must struggle successfully through stages of childhood, adolescence, and the seasons of adulthood. If for any reason we fail in the struggle, then we do not grow. Instead, we remain developmentally backward, underdeveloped, and primitive. We are then arrested in our forward progress and retain the most basic aspects of our animalistic nature, rather than progressing toward higher consciousness and more uniquely human qualities.

Failure in the struggle can result from numerous factors. Early abuse and/or deprivation and trauma usually have a negative impact upon the developing child's ability to develop the core strength required for successful struggle during key milestones of living. Another factor results from caregivers who are overly protective and/or indulgent toward a child. While perhaps well-meaning in such parenting, much like the girl who attempted to free the struggling butterfly, the resistance required for healthy struggle is absent, and the child fails to grow, accordingly. Whether resulting from early environmental experience that stifles growth by making the struggle too difficult or too easy, the adverse impact is the same: forward progress is interrupted and developmental immaturity is the consequence. Given that our quest for power is a universal birthright and natural instinct, the person who remains developmentally immature and underdeveloped will lean toward forks in the road where *Unhealthy Power* is found. Conversely, as we struggle successfully and mature accordingly, our leanings take a different turn in seeking power. We are then able to mobilize the core strength required for the development of *Healthy Power*, and this has the circular effect of further contributing to our reservoir of core strength.

But why even struggle at all? Making transformation is highly difficult, and the risk of failure or disappointment is ever present—even with metamorphosis completed—since life holds no guarantees for either success or happiness. Clearly, it is easier simply to seek comfort and to allow inertia to hold us in place without strain or exertion. And it certainly feels right to settle in this manner, permitting us to feel more solid and stable, after all. As we've heard, "A bird in hand is worth two in the bush," right? Thus we face a dilemma: caterpillar or butterfly? Both are options. Do we take the path of least resistance—along which we will find more than ample company—or the path leading to growth and change, even change we might not be able to anticipate or perhaps ever attain?

In the end, this is a matter of personal choice, of course, for which each of us has the power to choose and is appropriately responsible. My writing about these issues and challenges is not intended to dictate the path you take. Even if you passively followed the signposts toward *Healthy Power* I've laid out here, you would not be fully committed to the journey, nor would you uncover the adventure that would otherwise lie ahead if the paths you follow were wholly by your own choice. Therefore, my driving intention throughout this book has been to empower you with information that you could consider in charting your own course, and to do so from an informed stance, more fully appreciating the risks versus the rewards. I sincerely hope that the information provided here empowers you so!

Synthesis: *The Eight-Part Symphony of Effective Leadership*

Healthy Power in leadership comes from the eight root psychological principles working together in harmonious balance so that the whole they create is greater than the sum of its parts. They then combine and resonate like the finely tuned instruments of an orchestra to produce a powerful and beautiful symphony. Accordingly, as the conductors leading any such concerted effort, we manifest those principles most effectively by:

1) Taking complete *Personal Responsibility* for every choice, decision, and action that we undertake, and then holding others accountable fairly in like fashion.

195

...The voice of *Personal Responsibility*

"I take complete responsibility for my choices and the consequences of my actions, neither making excuses nor blaming others. Therefore, I am accountable to myself and others. I become more powerful each time I take responsibility, thus I hold others accountable appropriately with the acknowledgment that my doing so can serve to empower them also."

2) Developing and expressing our *Optimistic Expectations* with unwavering confidence and faith that we and our families or other teams will ultimately prevail.

...The voice of *Optimistic Expectations*

"I build and maintain positive expectations for the future while bringing a positive spirit and outlook to the present moment in all that I do. I do these things knowing that I am likely to fulfill my own expectations, and because I understand how positive energy and faith tend to be contagiously helpful and uplifting, both for me and those around me."

3) Building *Win-Win Relationships* with everyone as much as possible in an atmosphere of abundance and good spirited competition, comparing ourselves primarily with ourselves using internally identified and defined benchmarks.

...The voice of *Win-Win Relationships*

"I am neither greater than nor less than any other human being, and we are interdependent with each other and our planet. Therefore, I always strive to develop *Win-Win Relationships* knowing that any great relationship is mutually empowering and that life is enhanced and made more rewarding through healthy personal/social connections."

4) Creating a lifestyle of *Energizing Joy* in which we, our loved ones, and colleagues experience intrinsic motivation, an internal locus of control, and freedom from self-serving distractions with any related over-dependency—staying off the *hedonic treadmill.*

   …The voice of *Energizing Joy*

   "I seek joy and fulfillment in all that I do, knowing that it comes from the heart and stems from unconditional love. While I enjoy healthy pleasures, I do so in moderation in order to avoid over-dependency and addiction. When I become energized in joyful pursuits, I am enlivened through feelings of gratitude, contentment, and peace."

5) Making only *Reality-Based Choices* with careful and thorough information gathering, fact-based analyses, and team planning so that decisions foster confident action and minimize the need for any rework or damage control later.

   …The voice of *Reality-Based Choices*

   "I acknowledge truth as the foundation of *Healthy Power,* thus I strive to use facts, accurate data, and other credible input to form my opinions and make key decisions. To the greatest extent possible, I speak the truth and strive to empower others with reliable information. I have biases, so I confer with others when necessary to validate my thinking."

6) Initiating and mobilizing intensively *Focused Action* through effective management of all 3 facets—*Selection, Concentration,* and *Perspective*—in order to maximize alignment of prioritized effort and to create sufficient impact toward breakthrough successes as an individual or group.

   …The voice of *Focused Action*

   "I make constructive use of focus in all three facets: *Selection*— the object of my attention, *Concentration*—how I maintain attention, and *Perspective*—the lens through which I view things. Knowing that my focus tends to expand, I use focus constructively for my inner world, thoughts and emotions, and my outer world, the universe in which I live."

7) Demonstrating *Unrelenting Courage* by taking decisive, effective action, even amidst fears, doubts, or other discomfort, and then expecting and supporting the same in others.

...The voice of *Unrelenting Courage*

"I acknowledge my need to take effective action, even in the presence of fear, discomfort, and other negative feelings, so I can maximize my life experiences and reach my greatest potential. While always exercising good judgment before taking risk, I welcome challenges and adventures with a courageous spirit of confidence and commitment in order to live and die with no regret."

8) Envisioning a *Lifelong Purpose* for ourselves and for any organization serving others with which we become affiliated through our passionate, inspired, and altruistic behavior, trusting that both the journey and the outcomes will be tangibly rewarding and emotionally fulfilling for everyone touched by our leadership legacy.

...The voice of *Lifelong Purpose*

"I acknowledge my most important developmental milestone: making the shift from myself toward others to find a purpose greater than myself. I can then accept my mortality in a manner that makes life a joyful pursuit. I strive to be altruistic, to leave a positive legacy, and to die with grace and dignity—at peace for having attained my personal greatness."

The combined effect of the *Healthy Power* described above fosters a seemingly effortless ability to create positive, values-driven results through people within our sphere of influence. Such results flow from loyal, committed, and enthusiastically engaged supporters—people providing the followership that empowers our leadership in a healthy *quid pro quo* paradigm. As a key part of such, the most effective leaders nimbly play alternating roles: at times the teacher, at other times the student; at times the speaker, at other times the listener; at times the service-oriented leader, at other times the appropriately enabling follower.

Especially in the workplace, we do well to commit ourselves to gaining the confident, undying trust of others by being both professionally competent and of fine character, for both are necessary but insufficient conditions for gaining trust. And when people trust us unflinchingly as the result of experiencing both our competence and character, they will then entrust us with their most precious assets, tangibly and intangibly, thereby empowering us to influence even greater and more positive changes in their lives.

A Call for Change from Richie Havens

I have had the very good fortune to attend live, intimate concerts with Richie Havens twice over a 40-year period. The first was one he gave at Youngstown State University in the mid 1970s while I was attending undergraduate school at Grove City College nearby. He played *Here Comes the Sun* with such passion and enthusiasm (much as he had done singing *Motherless Child/Freedom* so memorably at Woodstock in 1969) that he broke his guitar string and simply kept on playing—undaunted and undeterred—much to my exuberance, along with that of the throng huddled together in that auditorium. Then I saw him again during May of 2007 when he performed in Wilkes-Barre, PA. He was generous to speak with me as I eagerly waited for him to autograph his recently released CD, *Grace of the Sun*. I felt again much as I had back in college, standing so close to a cultural icon and music legend. When we spoke briefly about his lengthy and inspiring career, he shared some life lessons with me, especially about maintaining our youthful spirit and vigor (he then being 66). In addition to his wise counsel that we not over-indulge in life's pleasures, he emphasized the importance of being committed to making a positive difference in this world, much in the manner of a popular expression of the 1970s that we *think globally and act locally.*

His sentiments and call to action are beautifully expressed in the lyrics to his song, *Pulling Up the Stone* (*Grace of the Sun*, produced by Richie Havens, Stormy Forest Productions, Inc. 2004):

> *To pull the stone up*
> *It takes believing*
> *To change directions*
> *Signals deceiving*
> *To tell the truth is what they fear*
> *All of us here*
> *Can change tomorrow*
>
> *To have a vision*
> *We all must stand still*
> *Simple decision*
> *To kill the lie, to kill the lie*
> *To stop the clock is what they fear*
> *All of us here*
> *Can change today*
>
> *Be who you are*
> *Be who you are*
> *Be who you are*
> *Say what you're feeling*
> *Say what you're feeling*
>
> *To let the stone down*
> *Means we are failing*
> *To let the truth be*
> *Ever revealing*
> *To stop the slavery we all feel*
> *All of us here*
> *Can change right now*

Spoken in the Voice of *Healthy Power*

...Mahatma Gandhi

"Nonviolence is the greatest force at the disposal of mankind. It is mightier than the mightiest weapon of destruction devised by the ingenuity of man...Strength does not come from physical capacity. It comes from an indomitable will... Where there is love, there is life; hatred leads to destruction... Love is the strongest force the world possesses, and yet it is the humblest imaginable."

...Joan Z. Borysenko

"Margaret Meade believed that cultural change would come less from legislation and big social programs than it would from small groups of people meeting in living rooms. I agree. If we are to create a new future, the power to do so is magnified exponentially wherever two or more of us gather for a good purpose. Remember the basics: breathe, take time for a walk, take care of yourself, be a good listener, practice gratitude, forgive, search for meaning, learn to manage your mind, keep things simple, and practice a few random acts of kindness."

...William C. Menninger, MD—Signs of Emotional Security:

1) Ability to deal constructively with reality
2) Capacity to adapt to change
3) Few symptoms of tension and anxiety
4) Ability to find more satisfaction in giving than receiving
5) Capacity to consistently relate to others with mutual satisfaction and helpfulness
6) Ability to direct hostile energy into constructive outlets
7) Capacity to love

...John Izzo, Ph.D.—*The Five Secrets You Must Discover Before You Die* (2008):

1) Be true to yourself
2) Live so that you leave no regrets
3) Become love
4) Live in the present moment
5) Give more than you receive

...The Dalai Lama

"Take into account that great love and great achievements involve great risk. When you lose, don't lose the lesson. Follow the three Rs: Respect for self, respect for others, and responsibility for all your actions. Remember that not getting what you want is sometimes a wonderful stroke of luck. Learn the rules so that you know how to break them properly. Don't let a little dispute injure a great friendship. When you realize you've made a mistake, take immediate steps to correct it. Spend some time alone every day. Open your arms to change, but don't let go of your values. Remember that silence is sometimes the best answer. Live a good, honorable life—then when you get older and think back, you'll be able to enjoy it a second time. A loving atmosphere in your home is the foundation for your life. In disagreements with loved ones, deal only with the current situation—don't bring up the past. Share your knowledge—it's a way to achieve immortality. Be gentle with the earth. Once a year, go someplace you've never been before. Remember that the best relationship is one in which your love for each other exceeds your need for each other. Judge your success by what you had to give up in order to get it. Approach love and cooking with reckless abandon!"

Some Final Thoughts

If we experience worldwide crises even greater in magnitude than those we are witnessing today—economically, politically, ecologically, and socio-culturally—what forms of power will emerge globally to protect and preserve life on Earth? Going forward as a global community—one in which each part becomes more intricately linked to form the whole—will *Healthy* or *Unhealthy Power* predominate? Will the prevailing powers rule through force and oppression, like George Orwell's *Big Brother*, with another Nazi regime, or in the movie *Mad Max: Beyond Thunderdome*—a post-apocalyptic era of violent chaos in which *survival of the fittest, dog-eat-dog, might makes right*, and *the end justifies the means* become the predominant rules of engagement? Or, instead, will sufficient numbers of people acting in unison muster the courage and leadership to counter-balance and offset such insidious threats? Will organized bodies composed of citizen soldiers banded by common values of strengths-based, benevolent service become mobilized to the greater good—even in the face of personal hardship and peril—thereby enabling our planet to survive, even thrive, because of the positive ripple effect of power they embody and spread?

Recognizing the far-reaching impact of the *butterfly effect* and the type of power each of us holds the potential to wield on any given day, let us make positive differences where we live today to influence and shape a better tomorrow, leading ourselves and others into our best possible future, setting the stage unselfishly and lovingly for those still to come.

The End

ABOUT THE AUTHOR

Struggle & Success Through Tempering Fires

I was born and raised in Pittsburgh, PA in a middle class, suburban neighborhood with nice neighbors and good schools. I was four years old when my family moved from the city to the North Hills to live in the house built by my father—a master carpenter—in order to give us "a better life" than the one he and my mother endured as children. Both were raised in impoverished environments during the Great Depression and had suffered tremendous family losses, abuses, and heartaches.

My three sisters and I were brought up in strict accordance with "Old Country" values—father's parents being from Austria, and mother's grandparents from Germany and England/Wales—thus, "children were to be seen and not heard." Both parents had been deeply wounded in their youth, leaving them largely self-absorbed, emotionally unavailable and insensitive, and much more interested in working for things than being close to us as children. All four of us learned from an early age to *walk on eggshells*, sensing we were primarily a burden and source of misery, trying hard not to provoke their frustration, anger, and punishment. By doing exactly what was expected, we avoided the verbal and physical abuse that loomed darkly like a shadow threatening our day-to-day existence. I became hyper-vigilant to anticipate my parents' negative moods, trying to stay one step ahead, often trying to read their mind in order to avoid the pitfalls of failure. But each of us invariably took turns coming up short and paid the price. If we behaved as if we had "a mind of our own" or otherwise failed to meet either parent's sternly rigid expectations, then the torture resumed with redoubled effort to bring us into alignment. "Spare the rod and spoil the child" became the regular, terrifying mantra that would precede the beatings I received with merciless cruelty, usually in front of my sisters, deepening my suffering through humiliation and public shame. Sadly, I have almost no memory of ever of being touched by either parent in a way that did not bring physical and/or emotional pain. The emotional wounds still disturbed me well into my adult years, long after the physical injuries had healed.

On the surface, we lived in a clean, well-constructed house. But family life was a disempowering and depressing existence. I ran away frequently into my imagination, seeking adventures while hiking in the woods, bicycling for hours to explore new worlds, and immersing myself in activities that would bring at least temporary relief from my misery. Each pursuit provided a much needed break from my unbearable feelings, otherwise, especially upon re-entering the house at night.

Father was raised in dire hardship with his alcoholic, abusive, and neglectful father—a "hunky" coalminer—and his alcoholic mother, both of whom he was greatly ashamed and toward whom he remained angry until death. When he was sober, he embodied many truly admirable traits and qualities, thus I'm indebted to him for many of my strengths and abilities. But when drinking heavily, he often became critical/judgmental, impatient, paranoid, verbally and physically abusive, demeaning, and embarrassing. He had been fighting against the world he perceived as having mistreated him for his entire life, thus he was still having episodic fist fights in bars into his late forties.

Mother possessed many admirable qualities, including keen intelligence, exceptionally high standards, and well intended aspirations for our family. It was from her that I came to appreciate the importance of education as the key to self-empowerment. Having been a fine student herself, she instilled in me a commitment to my studies, and she spent time with me in the early years to ensure that I, too, would excel academically, in spite of my short attention span and hyperactivity. She was determined to exceed the culture and quality of life she ascribed to her family of origin—people for whom she had lifelong disdain and minimal emotional ties.

In her zeal for self advancement and perfection, however, the strengths that usually served us well were often overdone and led to our suffering. For example, she placed an extremely high value upon cleanliness and organization, always insisting that the house and children be free of dirt and clutter. At the same time, she lacked empathy for us, and placed her own emotional needs in front of our own. Her intolerance for what amounted to the normal inconveniences created by children—dirt, dishes, and disarray—overwhelmed and enraged her. Hard as it still is to admit, I have vivid memories as a young child being bathed by my mother in scalding hot water into which she had poured laundry detergent with bleach in order to ensure my cleanliness—asserting with self satisfaction that "cleanliness is next to godliness"—especially after my coming home in the soiled clothing she also resented having to wash. In her agitation, she ignored my tear-laden screams, making pleas for her to stop—my skin reddening as she poured steaming water over my head to rinse my hair, the laundry soap with bleach burning my eyes. Instead of showing me any compassion, or simply a merciful respite from the unbearable torture, I received an even more vigorous burning rinse while being cracked on the head with a large stainless steel pot she always borrowed from the kitchen. My feelings, good or bad, never seemed to matter because she could only relate to the world, including her children, through the lens of self-absorption that characterized her personality until she died. Since her death at age 80 in 2008, I have forgiven her, but I will never forget a lifetime of disappointment at her failure to nurture me emotionally or to love me in the most fundamental ways mothers normally love their offspring.

I always struggled in school—too emotionally backward, anxious, and traumatized to achieve up to my true potential. Recognizing early that I was a promising student who was struggling to sit still, my father offered me $5.00 for any report card with all As and Bs, and $10.00 for all As—a relative fortune for our family and, thus, a wonderful expression of the value that both of my parents placed upon education. From that point forward starting in elementary school, I almost never missed a cash reward through high school, not because I wanted the money, but to get my parents' positive attention and approval, which, sadly, almost never came otherwise.

I was an enthusiastic athlete from early childhood, which became a driving passion—offsetting feelings of worthlessness and despair—especially my passion for baseball. I elevated my self-image by believing I had the potential to become an exceptional baseball player, but my parents wouldn't allow me to join Little League, not wanting to pay the fees or take me to practice/games. It depressed me to witness my neighborhood buddies going to their games, dressed up in their colorfully numbered uniforms, being part of the real thing it seemed, and learning to develop fundamental skills for which I thought I had the raw potential as a young and talented natural.

Organized athletics started for me in 7th grade where I excelled in track and received tremendous social affirmation and praise, briefly filling the emptiness within me. At a fork in the road upon entering 10th grade—needing to choose between track and baseball for my spring sport—I chose track, being too afraid to risk failure at my true passion, baseball, while clinging to ongoing success in my secondary one. I simply couldn't afford to fail back then.

This was one of my great regrets in life because I wanted so much to emulate Roberto Clemente, my childhood hero—the toll I paid for my *Unsettling Fear*. I had made the wrong turn at that fork in the road during my sophomore year of high school—I had settled for good instead of reaching courageously for what could have been great!

In Chapter 7, I shared the story of how I changed my undergraduate major to Psychology, a major milestone in my development that required courage because it was the first time I willfully acted on my own behalf as an adult without parental permission. In fact, I dreaded telling my parents of my action even more than I had feared approaching my academic advisor—he had never berated nor abused me, although I had been primed to expect he would. Upon nervously telling my parents of my decision to change my major that weekend, my father insisted that I learn to burn metal with an acetylene torch and to weld with equipment he maintained in our backyard so I could at least earn a living somehow, expecting my career path toward becoming a psychologist would eventually fizzle. To say the least, I did not have their blessing, although their commitment to my education and long-term success, in general, never wavered.

Finally feeling free to chart my own course and strongly motivated to prove my parents wrong, I took every Psychology course offered at Grove City College. Unfortunately, only my mother would be present at my college graduation.

I worked as a boilermaker along with my father to construct a water tower in Columbus, Ohio during Christmas break during my junior year in college in order to help pay my tuition expenses—highly paid but very dangerous work, even on good days. The job foreman decided we would put in the day and work on New Year's Eve, December 31, 1974, despite freezing rain and cutting winds.

Upon hearing the news, my father admonished me to be extra cautious, foretelling that "someone's going to get hurt today" because of the treacherous working conditions in which every step was like walking on an ice skating rink. Numerous safety violations existed on the job, including failure to affix the safety cage that surrounded the vertical ladder welded to the tower's central pillar, making traversing that ladder especially dangerous with a veneer of ice glazed upon each and every rung, now to a height of 120 feet.

Shortly after lunch, while working on a scaffold at 110 feet, I was interrupted when one of the guys yelled "Pete fell!" Believing that he had fallen from the scaffold above me, 12 stories high, I assumed that he was dead when I looked down to see him lying motionless on his back on a steel platform, appearing from that enormous height like a mere speck. Panic-stricken and traumatized, I made my way down 11 stories of that same treacherous ladder, knowing full well that I, too, could fall to my likely death if I did not proceed with extreme caution, but also knowing that my father awaited me below. I was overwhelmed with anguish, restraint, and helplessness amid the rush of adrenaline that I could not express nor move fast enough, and it was agonizing. Making the perilous trip slowly down that slippery ladder seemed like an eternity!

My father had actually fallen 35 feet, landing on his back after colliding with a steel cable on the way down. He suffered broken vertebrae in his neck—the hardhat he had been wearing absorbed much of the impact force—and he shattered his kneecap. Although he was expected to live through these serious but not life-threatening injuries, he died of internal injuries secondary to medical malpractice four days later on January 4, 1975. That was not only the most traumatic day of my life, but also a key turning point in my growth.

My mother fell apart emotionally, as did my sisters, and I was called upon to become the "man of the house," which I did to the best of abilities, even though I, too, was traumatized and ill-prepared for such huge responsibilities at age twenty. I returned to college, resolving to excel in my career as my father had instructed me with my "head," not simply with my "hands." However, I continued to work at least one more summer break from school on another water tower to pay for college, in spite of having developed a paralyzing fear of heights from the earlier trauma. My father's previous insistence that I learn to burn and weld paid high dividends in helping me pay my way through college, thus he was prophetic by teaching me those timely and valuable skills.

His tragic death was simultaneously horrific and liberating—horrific because he had been my hero, but liberating because he was no longer controlling and mistreating me. Amidst my mixed emotions, I suffered for six months of unrelenting nightmares. Each nightmare was the same. He was alive again, initially spawning tears of joy upon his miraculous return to life. Then quickly each dream would transform into agony since he was back in my life, beating me once again both physically and emotionally, recreating my feelings of worthlessness and powerlessness. Instead of being happy for his renewed life, it was as if my life was being sacrificed at Auschwitz concentration camp, to my despair and rage.

After six months of torment, I accepted that he had always cruelly dominated each of us—the side of him that I couldn't recognize consciously while memorializing him. I had been clinging to an idealized image that I wished, in reality, he had been. The seemingly miraculous end to the nightmares taught me a powerful psychological lesson: recognition and acceptance of any truth, no matter how disturbing, is both liberating and empowering.

After graduating college, I entered the University of Pittsburgh for five years of graduate studies in Educational Psychology where I earned both MA and Ph.D. degrees. I worked both as a Teaching Assistant and Teaching Fellow, and I continued to strive as a student to become my very best.

In 1979, two years before graduating from Pitt, I began to work full-time at my first non-blue collar job as a mental health clinician at a community mental health center children's outpatient department in Pittsburgh. While working there for almost five years, I concurrently earned both my Ph.D. and Psychologist license, and I attended a weekly seminar for Family Systems Therapy training. Subsequently, my career spanned numerous professional roles with recurring growth opportunities and challenges until December 30, 2008, the day I registered my new enterprise, Piso and Associates, LLC. I finally became my own boss—completely free to stretch and grow unfettered.

During the past four years, I have spent the majority of my professional time working as a consultant for health care, business, and educational clients across the country. My activities have also included research, book and journal publications, and presentations at varied professional conferences. My personal and career successes have evolved in direct proportion to my development of *Healthy Power* in a journey spanning many years, providing both the catalyst and content for writing this book.

My journey at every key fork in the road has included painful struggle, frustrating setbacks (including many failures), recurring sacrifice, and continued learning with fervent passion. I have striven to assimilate all of these experiences—especially the most difficult ones—and then transform them into personal assets and strengths. Like crafting a sword, the forging process has involved repeated beating of the metals and gradual tempering in hot fires before the final polishing would produce an effective tool. I have come from a place of suffering, powerlessness, humiliation, depression, anxiety, loneliness, and a fragile sense of self-esteem; but I have attempted to grow and to embody *Healthy Power* as much as possible. My journey has opened doors to joy, confident strength, humility, graciousness, social connectedness, and a life of passionate service with fulfillment. I thank God for my rich blessings, including the trials and turbulence that continue to work together for my refinement and tempering.

Biographical Sketch...

Craig N. Piso, Ph.D. is president of Piso and Associates, LLC, an organizational development consulting firm based in northeastern Pennsylvania. A licensed Psychologist with training/experience over 33 years, he has played roles in family systems clinical practice, corporate managed behavioral health, and health care/business/educational consulting. Specializations include: Leadership Development; Vision-Mission-Values Development; Team-Building; Cultural Transformation & Organizational Health/Effectiveness; Health Coaching; Board Functionality & Partner Conflict Resolution; Physician Interpersonal Behavior; and Strategic Planning. Raised in Pittsburgh, PA, Craig graduated Summa Cum Laude in Psychology from Grove City College, and he earned MA and Ph.D. degrees in Educational Psychology at the University of Pittsburgh. He and his wife, Theresa, reside in Wilkes-Barre, PA.

APPENDICES

APPENDIX A: *THE 10 LAWS FOR LIVING WELL*

Let us live so that when we come to die even the undertaker will be sorry.

Mark Twain

1) **Humility:** Accept and embrace the truth of all your strengths and weaknesses humbly and honestly. Such truths will then empower your fact-based decisions, actions, and more successful outcomes.

2) **Responsibility:** Take complete responsibility for your choices and actions to gain *Healthy Power.* Remember the functional law that *power* and *responsibility* always move in direct proportion to each other in any healthy person or system.

3) **Serenity:** Practice the *Serenity Prayer* each day to experience peace of mind. That is, accept what you cannot change, muster the courage to change those things which you can (especially yourself), and seek the wisdom to know the difference.

4) **Focus:** Create and refine a positive outlook and expectations. Recognize that your focus on people and things tends to expand, either positively or negatively, thereby influencing how you interact with them.

5) **Hope:** Dream of life with visions of thriving and then taking courageous action toward their present and future realization.

Confident faith in your meaningful dreams generates hope, and hope provides you with energy for living and striving.

6) *Joy:* Seek joy through inner transformation, relaxed self-mastery, and autonomous freedom. Minimize cravings for external pleasures and any accompanying self-deception, over-dependency, and addiction.

7) *Balance:* Achieve balance and harmony among your body, mind, and spirit to develop strength, resilience, and freedom from all forms of distress. Become the responsible, effective steward of your personal well-being.

8) *Purpose:* Find and fulfill the special purpose and meaning of your life. Develop your unique means of expressing your gifts through faithful adherence to your higher order value system, mindfulness, and spiritual growth.

9) *Appreciation:* Appreciate your blessings to find joy and contentment, comparing yourself and your life situation with no one else. Failure to appreciate your blessings is the root of bitterness, jealousy, and regret.

10) *Interdependence:* Recognize and nurture the interdependence between yourself and your family/friends and community. Serve others with generous and unconditional goodwill while creating a legacy of living well yourself.

APPENDIX B: THE 10 LAWS FOR LEADING WELL

Leadership is much more of an art, a belief, a condition of the heart, than a set of things to do. The visible signs of artful leadership are expressed, ultimately, in its practice.

Max DePree

1) ***Control yourself masterfully*** to influence positive change in others. Lead with full accountability for your decisions and actions, therein through your finest example, to inspire loyal *followership* among your team.

2) ***Demonstrate strong integrity***–the transparent link connecting your healthy values and external behavior. Your consistent genuineness, authenticity, and competence build *trust* among those following you.

3) ***Become a Servant Leader***, embracing your power with a mature sense of responsible stewardship while honoring your position of authority. Choose your language carefully, and always *let your word be your bond*.

4) ***Earn respect from others*** through your strong, decisive action, courageous and skillful risk-taking, and humble acceptance of your mistakes. Your strength melded with benevolent intentions is the ideal means of influencing others to follow your lead with commitment and good *spirit*.

5) ***Delegate appropriately to others*** as investments in their development, knowing that your patience, guidance, and positive expectations for their eventual mastery in their performance are gifts that reap lasting rewards.

6) ***Catch your people in the act of doing well*** more often than doing poorly, recognizing that *what we focus upon tends to expand*.

They will then appreciate and amplify your positive focus upon them going forward.

7) ***Expect the very best from your people*** and they will more than likely prove you to be right, affirming the power of *self-fulfilling prophecy*. Accordingly, if you expect the worst from them, then they will also prove you to be right, to your mutual loss.

8) ***Model what you wish to see in your people*** since they will imitate you. Inspirational words produce meaningful change only when they are matched with your good actions. Therefore, always *walk the talk*.

9) ***Empower your people to do their best***, potentially for their next employer, even to surpass you in their performance. It's their loyal support that then empowers you in return to succeed at your mission.

10) ***Focus upon the greater vision, mission, and values*** of your enterprise, undeterred by distractions, so that everyone shares your passion for purposeful dreams becoming fulfilled. Maintain such focus when making key decisions regarding your priorities, goals, and strategies.

Appendix C: The 10 Laws for Feeling Well

All you can take with you is that which you've given away.

Peter Bailey, *It's a Wonderful Life*

1) ***Understand and accept the truth***—facts, reality—since truth is the basis of *enlightenment*...that which is seen and understood in the light. Such acceptance then liberates energy that otherwise is wasted in denying or avoiding the truth.

2) ***Practice being non-defensive*** with others by developing realistic self-confidence and self-acceptance. Act as your own final judge, holding yourself wholly accountable for your choices with authenticity and public transparency.

3) ***Become mindfully present*** as much as possible, focusing upon and appreciating every aspect of each moment. A past and/or future orientation detracts from your experiential engagement and otherwise limits your being present to others.

4) ***Dare to dream of life*** with zest for living, a sense of adventure, and excitement about embracing appropriate risks. Confident faith in your meaningful dreams generates hope, and hope provides you with energy for living and striving.

5) ***Walk to the beat of your own drum***—thinking, feeling, and acting as the driver of your life. Be your own person, honoring yourself as author and creator of your life by doing what is right for you and knowingly paying the toll when sometimes being unpopular with others.

6) ***Look internally for joy*** since it always comes from deep within, while pleasure always comes from the outside. Joy brings true freedom and fulfillment, while even healthy pleasures when overdone diminish our sense of well-being.

7) *Strengthen your social connections*—meaningful ties to others—because healthy interdependence between yourself and your family/friends and community is important for living with a sense of wholeness, safety, and purposeful fulfillment.

8) *Be optimistic* by adopting a positive attitude, perspective, and expected future outlook. Whenever you fail, make mistakes, or have a setback, bounce back with self-forgiveness and renewed faith that you will succeed eventually through your perseverance.

9) *Count your blessings* with daily appreciation and a joyful focus, comparing yourself and your life situation with no one else. Failure to appreciate your blessings is the root of discontent, a sense of want, and painful envy.

10) *Find a purpose greater than yourself* and a mission for serving that purpose in order to avoid becoming self-absorbed or preoccupied with personal issues. Happiness and fulfillment naturally flow from such unselfish, outwardly directed service and responsible giving.

MORAL CODE FOR YOUTH
(recreated from Collier's, *The National Weekly*, 1925)

IN GOD WE TRUST
If I Want To Be a Happy, Useful Citizen I Must Have:

COURAGE AND HOPE

I must be brave—This means I must be brave enough and strong enough to control what I think, and what I say and what I do, and I must always be hopeful because hope is power for improvement.

WISDOM

I must act wisely—In school, at home, playing, working, reading or talking, I must learn how to choose the good, and how to avoid the bad.

INDUSTRY AND GOOD HABITS

I must make my character strong—My character is what I am, if not in the eyes of others, then in the eyes of my own conscience. Good thoughts in my mind will keep out bad thoughts. When I am busy doing good I shall have no time to do evil. I can build my character by training myself in good habits.

KNOWLEDGE AND USEFULNESS

I must make my mind strong—The better I know myself, my fellows and the world about me, the happier and more useful I shall be. I must always welcome useful knowledge in school, at home, everywhere.

TRUTH AND HONESTY

I must be truthful and honest—I must know what is true in order to do what is right. I must tell the truth without fear. I must be honest in all my dealings and in all my thoughts. Unless I am honest I cannot have self-respect.

HEALTHFULNESS AND CLEANLINESS

I must make my body strong—My eyes, my teeth, my heart, my whole body must be healthful so that my mind can work properly. I must keep physically and morally clean.

HELPFULNESS AND UNSELFISHNESS

I must use my strength to help others who need help—If I am strong I can help others, I can be kind, I can forgive those who hurt me and I can help and protect the weak, the suffering, the young and the old, and dumb animals.

CHARITY

I must love—I must love God, who created not only this earth but also all men of all races, nations and creeds, who are my brothers. I must love my parents, my home, my neighbors, my country and be loyal to all these.

HUMILITY AND REVERENCE

I must know that there are always more things to learn—What I may know is small compared to what can be known. I must respect all who have more wisdom than I, and have reverence for all that is good. And I must know how and whom to obey.

FAITH AND RESPONSIBILITY

I must do all these things because I am accountable to God and humanity for how I live and how I can help my fellows, and for the extent to which my fellows may trust and depend upon me.

SORROW   or   *JOY*

Reaching Down to Stand Tall
(elementary school lessons about *Healthy Power*)

We dug good soil from fields nearby…
wagon teaming I pulled through grass.
Milk carton seeds at window sill…
watered and waiting while in class.

Teacher told us, "Watch carefully"…
tending our crops—nothing showing.
Then one day tiny shoots appeared…
fresh new buds were gently growing!

Magic seedlings became beanstalks…
sunlit green, growing oh so fast!
Then weekend draught wilted our crop…
little farmer hearts sad alas.

Teacher helped us to nurse them back,
with loving care and water cans.
Hope renewed, *Healthy Power* shown,
lifting them with firm little hands.

Teacher taught us to transplant them…
outgrowing the homes we had made.
We pulled them too hard from their beds…
tiny root hairs thus became frayed.

Replanted they went into *shock*...
next day became yellow drooping...
teaching that growth and change require
firm yet benevolent rooting.

More deeply in soil reached the roots,
thus taller the plants they did grow.
Reach downward...stand taller...bear fruits:
Healthy Power through living so!

Finding I Am

I feel my breath at the tip of my nose,
relaxing into the chair.
Gravity holds me in soft embrace,
while noises fill the air.

Deeper I go into breath and dark,
while opening heart and mind.
Calming the press of busy life,
a tranquil space I find.

Alert, yet relaxed, I scan my thoughts
with tenderness and compassion.
Drifting about, then startled anew—
control being my passion.

I hold myself in tender care
while letting down my guard.
Strange but now familiar state—
this once was not so hard.

Rooting down into the earth,
settling firm and strong,
I now grow up toward heaven,
windswept with branches long.

My roots cling to the mountain
for deeper calm and peace.
My branches flow together,
like chevron flight of geese.

A lake beside the mountain,
still and limpid clear,
reflects my mountain fortress—
so little left to fear.

"Be still and know that I am God"
resounds within my soul.
Open, fearless heart of mine—
come back to sacred shoal.

Find your seat at other times,
whole-hearted and at peace.
Live each moment presently—
control found in release!

Appendix G: Dream of Life...Live Your Dream!

Dream of Life...Live Your Dream!

Begin with a dream that stirs your heart,
and press on until you hear it
beating a path that is clear from the start,
and thrilling unto your spirit!

Your dream offers hope and energy, too.
It lifts you then to succeed.
Awaken from sleep, focused anew...
you *work* to nurture the seed.

It begins as a whim, a half-baked notion...
cloudy and clearly unclear.
But remember that deep within our ocean
are shells we're waiting to hear.

Without dreams and hope we waste away...
our emptiness fills with despair.
Depression turns our world into gray,
and we lack psychological air.

Create for yourself a positive view.
Capture your life a new way.
Take steps to become the possible you,
and do it starting today.

See a new day with dreams untold…
the new you living with ease.
Write a new script, make it unfold:
mind, body and spirit at peace.

Commit yourself now, seize control…
plot the course your life will take.
Dream of life that's balanced and whole,
then *live* that life *wide awake*!

Appendix H: Becoming the Bright Light of a Darkened Room

Becoming the Bright Light of a Darkened Room

Dwelling within a darkened room,
I confused shadows for light.
Stricken blind and frightened there…
struggling through deadened night.

Asleep in blissful ignorance,
I snored and bored through life.
If I should die before I wake…
light dawn upon my strife!

Thinking: *I think therefore I am*
helped me through the drama.
Finding *I am* when thinking stopped
unveiled to me my karma.

I saw the darkened room anew,
not framed merely as cinema.
Inner rays beamed pure and bright
to reveal my life enigma.

My inner light did then break through,
this beacon from peaceful shoal.
Now I move toward the radiance
that emanates from my soul.

My world is filled with paradox.
New light gives life its meaning.
I yearn for stillness, clear and true...
from darkness I am weaning.

Stay open, my glad heart shine forth.
Illuminate *all* the room.
Liberated—afire—aglow...
freed as light from darkened tomb!

APPENDIX I: *SOAP HAPPINESS WORKSHEET*

SOAP Happiness Worksheet

(based on *The Science of Happiness: A Positive Psychology Report*
by Bill O'Hanlon, 2009)

Report Summary

Research within the area of *Positive Psychology* has shown in recent years that happier people tend to live better, longer lives with a higher degree of health, both physically and emotionally. There are four primary factors ("SOAP") that determine the extent to which people become and remain happy: 1) *Social Connection*; 2) *Optimism*; 3) *Appreciation*; and 4) *Purpose Greater Than Oneself.*

Social Connection—This is the depth of closeness in our relationships and the volume of such people with whom we connect throughout our lifetime. Overall health, happiness, and quality of life are closely linked with the experience of making and maintaining meaningful connections with others at home, at work, and in our communities.

"S" Assessment: *How well connected am I with others within my home, at work, and within my community?*

_____

_____

_____

_____

_____

_____

"S" Plan for Increased Happiness: *What will I do to increase both the depth (closeness) and breadth (volume) of my relationships within my home/work/ community?*

_____

_____

_____

_____

_____

Optimism—This is a positive attitude and perspective that we apply to our life experiences, especially regarding our expectations and future outlook, characterized by confidence and hopefulness. It is like a positive filter or lens through which we see the world, ourselves, and others so that we have better experiences, even when our life situations are actually negative.

"O" Assessment: *How positive and hopeful am I generally about my life situations and the future?*

_____

_____

_____

_____

_____

"O" Plan for Increased Happiness: *What will I do to develop more confident faith, improve my perspective, and develop and show a more positive attitude?*

_____

_____

_____

_____

Appreciation—This is the practice of *counting our blessings* with a sense of gratitude, especially by focusing upon the part of *glass that is half full* rather than focusing upon what is missing or lacking. Such an *abundance mentality* enables us to feel more contented and full, thus more satisfied, while a *scarcity mentality* produces feelings of envy, greed, compulsion, and dissatisfaction.

"A" Assessment: *How often and how well do I experience and express gratitude for my blessings and otherwise notice and pay attention to the good things in my life?*

_____

_____

_____

_____

_____

_____

"A" Plan for Increased Happiness: *What will I do to become more grateful and appreciative for all that I have, rather than bemoaning or being bitter about what I lack and/or desire?*

_____

_____

_____

_____

_____

_____

Purpose Greater Than Oneself—This is a commitment to serving others or a cause with a sense of purpose that moves us away from being self-absorbed or overly concerned with personal issues. Ironically, this focus upon others can only be done well when we have developed our own strength and stability in life, thereby enabling us to enjoy the happiness and fulfillment that naturally flow from altruistic behavior (i.e., unselfish giving or sharing with no expectation of any external reward in return).

"P" Assessment: *How often and how well do I meet the needs of others unselfishly as part of my devotion to a purpose or cause in life that is greater than myself?*

_____

_____

_____

_____

_____

_____

"P" Plan for Increased Happiness: *What will I do to become more strong and stable so that I can shift my focus to serving others with fulfillment and a sense of devotion to a purpose or cause in life that is greater than myself?*

_____

_____

_____

_____

_____

_____

APPENDIX J: CORE STRENGTHS WORKSHEET

Core Strengths Worksheet

Instructions: Please rate yourself regarding the following four areas of core strength by circling the number that best represents your daily experience during both work and non-work activities.

Presence—experiencing a sense of *presence* means feeling centered and at peace, here and now. It's about living mindfully in each present moment without distraction from thoughts about the past or future...*living in the moment*...feeling relaxed, confident, and self-assured.

Rating: *Most of the time, I feel present...*

1......2......3......4......5......6......7......8......9......10
Not at all   *Completely*

Self-Control—having enough *Healthy Power* to control one's self and to be free, rather than acting with compulsion, impulsivity, or any form of over-dependency. It involves good emotion management skills and the ability to think rationally, even under pressure (i.e., being logical and proactive, letting your *cooler head prevail*).

Rating: *Most of the time, I feel self-control...*

1......2......3......4......5......6......7......8......9......10
Not at all   *Completely*

Focus—as a core strength, *focus* is having the ability to maintain sustained attention to a particular thought and/or effort with freedom from distraction or boredom. It involves working and playing intently with clear vision and purpose, rather than being scattered or disorganized.

Rating: *Most of the time, I am able to focus...*

> 1......2......3......4......5......6......7......8......9......10
> *Not at all*   *Completely*

Energy—having a full reservoir of emotional *energy* enables us to feel strong and to cope well with stress, rather than becoming depressed and fatigued, or experiencing some form of negative mood. Therefore, it's being able to work and to play with drive, enthusiasm, and a positive attitude.

Rating: *Most of the time, I feel energized...*

> 1......2......3......4......5......6......7......8......9......10
> *Not at all*   *Completely*

Hedgehog Focus Worksheet
(based on *Good to Great* by Jim Collins, 2001)

*For a hedgehog, anything that does not somehow
relate to the hedgehog idea holds no relevance.*

Jim Collins

The Hedgehog Concept

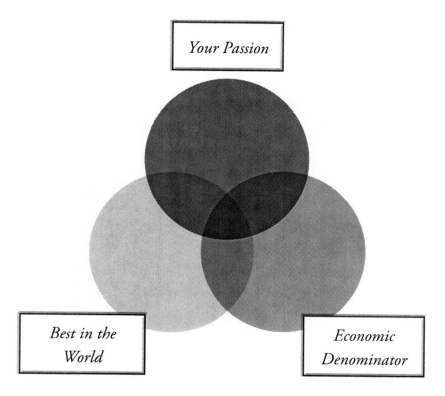

Instructions: Please answer the following questions to assist you in identifying your *Hedgehog Focus*—the intersection of the three circles that will lead you toward your greatest success in your work/personal life—*Your Passion, Best in the World, and Economic Denominator:*

1) *What is my greatest Passion? That is, what types of activities enliven me, make me feel enthusiastic, and awaken strong feelings of motivation and fulfillment within me?*

_____

_____

_____

_____

_____

_____

2) *What am I built to be the Best in the World at doing? That is, what are my particular strengths and skills that make up my gifts and special abilities—the things that just come naturally to me or otherwise seem to be what I'm best suited to be doing?*

_____

_____

_____

_____

_____

_____

3) *What are the keys to creating an effective Economic Denominator? That is, how can I create value in my work (e.g., earning power with satisfaction) and otherwise in the quality of my personal life (e.g., loving relationships; good health)?*

_____

_____

_____

_____

_____

_____

4) Key overarching questions: *How will I pursue the intersection of the three circles above in order to be fulfilled, happy, and successful in my life/work—engaged in activities about which I feel passion and which draw upon my unique gifts, talents, and abilities? What is the first step I can take immediately within this focus?*

_____

_____

_____

_____

_____

References

Becker, E. 1973. *The Denial of Death.* New York: The Free Press.

Boldt, L. G. 2010. *Zen and the art of making a living: A practical guide to creative career design.* New York: Penguin Books.

Borysenko, J. Z. 2001. *Inner peace for busy people.* Carlsbad, CA: Hay House.

Buscaglia, L. F. 1972. *Love.* New York: Ballantine Books.

Campbell, J. 1988. *The power of myth.* New York: Broadway Books.

Carnegie, D. 1981. *How to win friends & influence people,* revised edition. New York: Simon & Schuster.

Chödrön, P. 2002. *Comfortable with uncertainty.* Boston, MA: Shambhala Publications, Inc.

Chödrön, P. 1998. *Noble heart: A self-guided retreat on befriending your obstacles.* (audiocassette). Sounds True, Inc.

Chopra, D. 1994. *The seven spiritual laws of success: A practical guide to the fulfillment of your dreams.* San Rafael, CA: New World Library and Amber-Allen Publishing.

Collins, J. 2001. *Good to great: Why some companies make the leap and others don't.* New York: Harper Business.

Collins, J. 2005. *Good to great and the social sectors: A monograph to accompany Good to Great.* New York: Harper Collins.

Collins, J. 2009. *How the mighty fall: And why some companies never give in.* New York: Harper Collins.

Collins, J. and Porras, J. 1994. *Built to last: Successful habits of visionary companies.* New York: Harper Collins.

239

Covey, S. 2004. *The 8th habit: From effectiveness to greatness.* New York: Free Press.

Covey, S. 1991. *Principle-centered leadership.* New York: Fireside Press.

Covey, S. 1989. *The 7 habits of highly effective people: Powerful lessons in personal change.* New York: Free Press.

Covey, S., Merrill, A. R., and Merrill, R. R. 1994. *First things first.* New York: Free Press.

Csikszentmihalyi, M. 1990. *Flow: The psychology of optimal experience.* New York: Harper and Row.

De Pree, M. 2004. *Leadership is an art.* New York: Doubleday.

Disney, W. Disney Institute Business Programs. http://disneyinstitute.com/.

Dyer, W. 2010. *The shift: Taking your life from ambition to meaning.* Australia: Hay House, Inc.

Dyer, W. 2009. *Excuses begone! How to change lifelong, self-defeating thinking habits.* Australia: Hay House, Inc.

Dyer, W. 2006. *The secrets of an inspirational (in-spirit) life.* (audio 6-CD set) Australia: Hay House, Inc.

Erikson, E. H. 1963. *Childhood and society.* New York: W. W. Norton and Company, Inc.

Frankl, V. E. 1959. *Man's search for meaning.* Boston: Beacon Press.

Fromm, E. 1964. *The heart of man: Its genius for good and evil.* New York: Harper-Collins.

Gallwey, W. T. 1997. *The inner game of tennis: The classic guide to the mental side of peak performance,* revised edition. New York: Random House, Inc.

Golas, T. 1972. *The lazy man's guide to enlightenment.* Self published.

Goleman, D. 2005. *Emotional intelligence: 10th anniversary edition; Why it can matter more than IQ.* New York: Bantam Dell.

Hill, N. 1987. *Think and grow rich,* reissue edition. New York: Ballantine Books.

Izzo, J. 2008. *The five secrets you must discover before you die.* San Francisco, CA: Berrett-Koehler Publishers, Inc.

Kahneman, D. 2011. *Thinking, fast and slow.* New York: Farrar, Straus & Giroux.

Kubler-Ross, E. 1969. *On death and dying.* New York: Touchstone.

Lindbergh, A. M. 2003. *Gift from the sea.* New York: Pantheon Books.

Lundin, S. C., Paul, H., Christensen, J., and Blanchard, K. 2000. *Fish: A proven way to boost morale and improve results.* New York: Hyperion.

Maxwell, J. C. 2000. *Failing forward: Turning mistakes into stepping stones for success.* Nashville, TN: Thomas Nelson.

Miller, W. R., and Rollnick, S. 2013. *Motivational interviewing: Helping people change,* 3rd edition. New York: The Guilford Press.

Moore, T. 2010. *Care of the soul in medicine: Healing guidance for patients, families, and the people who care for them.* U.S.: Hay House, Inc.

Murray, A. 1982. *Humility: The beauty of holiness.* New Kensington, PA: Whitaker House.

Naar, R. 2009. *Rachamim...From darkness into light.* Self-published: iUniverse.

Nhat Hanh, T. 1998. *Transforming suffering into peace, joy, and liberation.* Berkeley, CA: Parallax Press.

Nhat Hanh, T. 1997. *Living Buddha, living Christ.* New York: Riverhead Books.

Nhat Hanh, T. 1991. *Peace is every step: The path of mindfulness in everyday life.* New York: Bantam Books.

O'Hanlon, B. 2007. *A lazy man's guide to success.* Self-published: Create Space Independent Publishing Platform.

O'Hanlon, B. 1999. *Do one thing different: Ten simple ways to change your life.* New York: Harper Collins.

O'Hanlon, B. 2009. *The science of happiness: A positive psychology update* (e-book). Mansfield Center, CT: NICABM.

Olendzki, A. 2010. *Unlimiting mind: The radically experiential psychology of Buddhism*. Somerville, MA: Wisdom Publications.

Peck, M. S. 1983. *People of the lie: The hope for healing human evil*. New York: Touchstone.

Peck, M. S. 1978. *The road less traveled: A new psychology of love, traditional values, and spiritual growth*. New York: Touchstone.

Pink, D. H. 2009. *Drive: The surprising truth about what motivates us*. New York: Riverhead Books.

Prochaska, J. O., Norcross, J., and DiClemente, C. 1994. *Changing for good: A revolutionary six-stage program for overcoming bad habits and moving your life forward*. New York: Avon Books, Inc.

Siegel, B. 1986. *Love, medicine and miracles: Lessons learned about self-healing from a surgeon's experience with exceptional patients*. New York: Harper and Row.

Siegel, R. D., Germer, C. K., and Olendzki, A. 2008. "Mindfulness: What is it? Where does it come from?" In *Clinical handbook of mindfulness*. New York: Springer.

Stevenson, R. L. 1886. *Strange case of Dr. Jekyll and Mr. Hyde*. New York: W. W. Norton and Company, Inc.

Suzuki, S. 1970. *Zen mind, beginner's mind: Informal talks on Zen meditation and practice*. Boston: Shambhala Publications, Inc.

Tolkien, J. R. R. 1954. *The lord of the rings*. New York: Mariner Books; 50th anniversary edition (2012).

Tolle, E. 2005. *A new Earth: Awakening to your life's purpose*. New York: Plume.

Tolle, E. 2001. *The power of now: A guide to spiritual enlightenment*. Novato, CA: New World Library.

Warren, R. 2007. *The purpose driven life: What on Earth am I here for?* Grand Rapids, MI: Zondervan Publishing House.

INDEX

Symbols

12 Angry Men 91

A

A Beautiful Mind 84
aberrant 7, 8, 97, 98, 100
abolitionist 95
Abraham Lincoln xv
abundance 46, 175, 196, 231
abuse xv, 16, 17, 36, 37, 50, 55, 56,
    70, 74, 80, 95, 98, 100, 103,
    176, 194, 205
acceptance 41, 56, 57, 60–62, 86, 92,
    102, 103, 105–107, 137, 174,
    185, 210, 215, 217
accountability 1, 10–12, 14–16, 19,
    63, 126, 215
action 6, 7, 11, 12, 13, 14, 18, 19,
    21–24, 26, 28, 42, 52, 84, 85,
    90–92, 96, 97, 102, 107, 110,
    112, 117–122, 123, 127, 131,
    133–136, 139–141, 146, 149,
    150, 153, 157, 175, 178, 180,
    195–198, 200, 202, 208, 213,
    215, 216
addiction 7, 68, 70–75, 71, 80, 84, 86,
    92, 102, 103, 122, 126, 171,
    174, 176, 197, 214
adjustment 2, 3, 7, 15, 16, 99, 163
adolescence 194
Adolf Hitler 99, 134
adulthood 7, 100, 142, 143, 167, 194
African American 96
aggression 53, 54, 56
alcohol 7, 36, 37, 50, 70, 74, 83, 95,
    102, 125, 126

Alcoholics Anonymous 102, 103
alignment 127, 197, 205
Allied forces 134
altruism xxii, 179
American Indian 94
Andrew Murray 101
Andrew Olendzki 72, 104, 110, 133
anger 17, 58, 62, 98, 101, 104,
    108–110, 111, 112, 114, 152,
    177, 205
animal 76, 84, 110, 149, 165, 183,
    184, 186, 192, 220
Annie Hall 87
anxiety 32, 62, 109, 139, 140, 144,
    145, 147, 167, 201, 211
appreciation 48, 86, 87, 154, 175, 176,
    188, 214, 218, 229, 231
authentic 62, 69, 78, 104, 167
autonomy 48, 78, 119, 175
Axis power 142

B

bedside manner 32
belief 29, 49, 74, 94, 95, 99, 101, 114,
    215
benevolence 94, 97, 108, 135, 162
Bernie Siegel 32
bias 90–93, 124, 197
Bill O'Hanlon xxii, 21, 40, 67, 114,
    129, 229
birth xix
birthright xix, 1, 194
black hole 74, 190
blessing xix, 86, 112, 154, 208, 211,
    214, 218, 231
Blind Spots 98, 101, 123, 124
bliss 101, 170, 192

243

thought xv, 28, 31, 32, 35, 37, 39, 42, 47, 59–62, 65, 73, 80, 82, 84, 91, 92, 97, 99, 102, 106, 112, 117, 119, 124, 130, 132, 133, 141, 156, 170, 198, 203, 208, 219, 220, 223, 233

thriving 5, 162, 168, 213

toll 2, 55, 82, 100, 146, 208, 217

torture xv, 15, 17, 51, 82, 205, 207

toxicity 4

transformation xvii, 1, 73, 86, 193–195, 211, 214

transition 2, 157, 158, 176, 179

trap 16, 75, 77, 112, 133, 182

trauma 11, 16, 36, 80, 176, 194, 210

treatment 16, 38, 102, 176

tree 5, 75, 76, 79, 92, 93, 124, 167, 193

True North Principle 15, 128

trust 1, 3, 4, 8, 14, 40, 58, 64, 65, 90, 97, 98, 104, 114, 150, 168, 199, 215, 219, 220

truth 2, 13, 15, 59, 64–66, 74, 77, 78, 82, 92, 94, 97–102, 104, 105, 107, 108, 125, 131, 140, 146, 168–171, 173, 174, 177, 178, 185, 197, 200, 210, 213, 217, 220, 242

U

understanding xvi, xvii, 2, 3, 5, 6, 8, 11, 29, 60, 64, 81, 90–92, 102, 113, 115, 128, 140, 157, 158, 169, 184, 193

Unhealthy Power xiii, xvii, xviii, xxi, 3, 4, 6, 14–17, 28, 29, 31, 32, 34, 35, 49–53, 68, 70, 73, 90, 94, 96, 97, 100, 101, 119, 120, 134, 135, 144, 147, 162, 167, 168, 186, 190, 194, 203

Unrelenting Courage 6, 92, 139, 144, 146–148, 150, 157, 158, 166, 198

Unsettling Fear 6, 92, 139, 140, 144, 146, 147, 170, 208

V

value xiii, xvii, xxii, 2, 3, 9, 15, 42, 46, 48, 52, 59, 61–63, 67, 72, 73, 79, 108, 152, 161, 164, 178–180, 198, 202, 203, 205–207, 211, 214–216, 236, 242

victim xv, 1, 12, 18, 37, 51, 55, 71, 74, 97, 173

Viktor Frankl xvi, xviii, 11, 13, 14, 33, 162

violence xv, 16, 48, 51, 53, 54, 56, 58, 65, 68, 95, 108, 147, 185

virtue 23, 67, 81, 88, 108, 113

vision 21, 28, 39, 74, 89, 114, 122, 123, 125, 128, 132, 137, 161, 180, 200, 211, 213, 216, 234

voluntary suspension of disbelief 127

W

Wayne Dyer i, xxi, 67, 80, 127, 178

well-being 5, 15, 23, 25, 26, 32, 50, 82, 100, 104, 107, 145, 163, 172, 175, 214, 217

wellness xvi, 26, 82, 101

what we resist persists 106, 185

wholeness 115, 180, 190, 218

Wind and the Weather Vane 18

Win-Lose Relationships 6, 45, 49, 51, 53, 135, 147

winner 20, 46, 50, 63, 64, 126, 169

Win-Win Relationships xviii, 6, 45, 47, 48, 51, 54, 57, 63, 107, 151, 196

wisdom xiii, xvii, xix, xxii, 103, 104, 108, 110, 115, 118, 152, 182, 213, 219, 220, 242

World War II xv, 27, 134, 142, 144, 162

W. Timothy Gallwey 79, 131

Y

You Can't Take It with You 180

CPSIA information can be obtained at www.ICGtesting.com
Printed in the USA
BVOW04s2008240314

348613BV00002B/4/P

9 781452 563824